I0223073

Staging Citizenship

DANCE AND PERFORMANCE STUDIES

General Editors:

Helena Wulff, *Stockholm University and* **Jonathan Skinner,** *University of Roehampton*

Advisory Board:

Alexandra Carter, Marion Kant, Tim Scholl

In all cultures, and across time, people have danced. For performers and spectators, the expressive nature of dance opens up spaces where social and political circumstances are creatively negotiated. Grounded in ethnography, this series explores dance, music and bodily movement in cultural contexts at the juncture of history, ritual and performance in an interconnected world.

Staging Citizenship

Roma, Performance and Belonging in EU Romania

Ioana Szeman

berghahn
NEW YORK · OXFORD
www.berghahnbooks.com

First published in 2018 by
Berghahn Books
www.berghahnbooks.com

© 2018, 2020 Ioana Szeman
First paperback edition published in 2020

All rights reserved. Except for the quotation of short passages
for the purposes of criticism and review, no part of this book
may be reproduced in any form or by any means, electronic or
mechanical, including photocopying, recording, or any information
storage and retrieval system now known or to be invented,
without written permission of the publisher.

Library of Congress Cataloging-in-Publication Data
A C.I.P. cataloging record is available from the Library of Congress

British Library Cataloguing in Publication Data
A catalogue record for this book is available from the British Library

ISBN: 978-1-78533-730-7 Hardback
ISBN: 978-1-78920-797-2 Paperback
E-ISBN: 978-1-78533-731-4 Ebook

Contents

Illustrations

Acknowledgments

I would like to thank all the Roma friends who have given their time and support to my research. I have learned so much from your creativity, resilience and generosity.

The beginnings of this book go back to my graduate school years at Northwestern University and I would like to thank Margaret Thompson Drewal, whose work has been a constant model and inspiration, Micaela di Leonardo, who planted many seeds of feminist critical thinking, and Tracy C. Davis, who inspired my historical research and kindly provided feedback on early sections of the manuscript. Dwight Conquergood's vision, unwavering support, and enthusiasm for ethnography and performance studies have shaped this book in fundamental ways. He is truly missed.

The formative stages of this book developed with intellectual and collegial support from my dissertation writing group at Northwestern: Leslie Buxbaum-Danzig, Amy Partridge, Karima Robinson, Rebecca Rossen, Emily Roxworthy and Jason Winslade. The spirit of those generous scholarly exchanges continues to inspire me.

At Berghahn, I am grateful to Chris Chappell, for believing in this project, and to Amanda Horn, Caroline Kuhtz and the whole production team, for their invaluable assistance. Many thanks to the anonymous reviewers for their helpful and detailed feedback. While I have followed many of their suggestions, the final manuscript reflects my own point of view.

For research leave that has allowed me to conduct fieldwork and to revise the manuscript, I am grateful to the University of Roehampton. Josh Abrams, Lis Austin, Simon Bayly, Ernst Fischer, Laure Fernandez, Sarah Gorman, Susanne Greenhalgh, Adrian Heathfield, Joe Kelleher, Johanna Linsley, Glenn Odom, Emily Orley, Susan Painter, Jen Parker-Starbuck, Maggie Pittard, Eleanor Roberts, PA Skantze, Graham White, Lee White, Fiona Wilkie and the late Peter Majer provided collegiality and encouragement throughout the research and writing of this book. Many thanks to Stephanie Laryea and Judith Stevens for being wonderful colleagues and exquisite administrators.

For their generosity and for intellectual inspiration I thank Margaret Beissinger, Grégory Busquet, Ana Croegaert, Amber Day, Adriana Diaconu,

Matthew Engelke, Suk-Young Kim, Robert Kulpa, Jacob Juntunen, Christine Matzke, Rebecca Nash, Lisa Peschel, Carol Silverman, and Maurya Wickstrom. Over the years I have benefitted from inspiring conversations with and the collegiality of Christopher Balme, Robin Bernstein, Bianca Botea, Esra Cizmeci, Karen Fricker, Helen Gilbert, Milija Gluhovic, Silvija Jestrovic, Margarita Kompelmakher, Branislava Kuburovic, Dominika Laster, Bryce Lease, Marin Marian-Bălaşa, Meida McNeal, Yana Meerzon, Lisa Merrill, Stefka Mihaylova, Sophie Nield, Louise Owen, Coya Paz, Suvenderini Perera, Oyku Potuoglu-Cook, Sheila Preston, Janelle Reinelt, Clémence Scalbert-Yürcel, Berenika Szimansky-Düll, Amanda Stuart-Fisher, Aniko Szucs, and Jennifer Tyburczy.

For their scholarly brilliance, which is a continuous source of inspiration, and for their solidarity, I am indebted to former and current members of the Feminist Review Collective: Nadje Al-Ali, Joan Anim-Ado, Avtar Brah, Rutvica Andrijasevic, Irene Gedalof, Aisha Gill, Carrie Hamilton, Gina Heathcote, Clare Hemmings, Yasmin Gunaratnam, Laleh Khalili, Joanna Pares Hoare, Suzanne Scafe, Sadie Wearing and Kyoung Kim.

I am deeply grateful to Carol Silverman and Maurya Wickstrom for reading full early drafts of the manuscript, and for their rigorous, detailed and generous comments that have improved this book in many significant ways. Heartfelt thanks to Jen Parker-Starbuck for guidance and support in key moments and to Susanne Greenhalgh, Branislava Kuburovic and Emily Orley for engaging in many intellectual conversations about the book and reading sections of the manuscript. Ana Croegaert has been a constant intellectual interlocutor and dear friend from the beginnings of this project through to the final writing stages; her astute feedback on different aspects of the manuscript and her moral support have been invaluable. My profound gratitude goes to Rutvica Andrijasevic, and Irene Gedalof for reading sections and the entire manuscript at crucial points and for providing insightful comments and generous advice.

For their friendship, generosity and assistance during fieldwork and beyond, I am grateful to Ioana Ghibănescu, Olimpia Mălai, Mihaela Stoienescu, Ligia Stoienescu, Mariana Soporan, Cristina Marian, Iulia Marian, Daniel Mezö, Dorin Raţiu, Mirela Borza, Caro d'Offay, Laura Gilmore, Tricia Rumbolz, Toufique Khan, Sean O'Neill, Snezana Zabic, the late Rodica Nebert, Oana Stăncioiu, Anca Rozor, Audrey Albert and Beatriz Fernandes. Thank you to Teodora Szeman for helping in so many essential ways that have made the writing of this book possible and to Ishti for all the joy that he has brought into my life.

Introduction

Roma are always the last to count, but we won first prize. We would not settle for
second or third place.

—Maria, Roma dancer, interview with the author, 2009

I've worked hard. When you look at me, you can see that I've succeeded through my
voice, not my looks.

—Viorica, Roma singer, Romanian reality TV show *Clejanii*, December 2012

Moderator: Why is there tension between Roma and Romanians?
Roma activist: First of all, you should not use these terms; you should speak of Roma
and non-Roma, as all Roma [in Romania] are Romanian citizens.

—Talk show on Romanian national TV channel Realitatea, December 2007

According to Maria, dance was the only avenue of success available to her
as a Romni.[1] High rents and unemployment had driven Maria and her
family to Pod,[2] a settlement where people squatted in improvised lodgings and
collected recyclables from a nearby refuse site. Living in difficult conditions,
without infrastructure or medical facilities and far away from schools, Roma in
Pod could be mistaken for refugees in a camp, even though they were citizens
of Romania. Local media looked down on Roma from Pod and often described
them as poor, dirty and lazy. A far cry from such stereotypes, thirty-five-year-old

Maria – always impeccably dressed in modern clothing – lived with her family in a wooden house, one of several wooden and brick houses that some residents had managed to build in Pod with the money they made from scavenging on the refuse site. She had been a member of a Roma dance group that was formed and active during the first post-socialist decade; she showed me her dance costumes, which included long, colourful skirts, scarves decorated with coins, and high-heeled shoes. Sitting in her spotlessly clean living room, Maria, dressed in jeans and a T-shirt, proudly reminisced about her dance group's success in competitions: 'When they heard that we were coming, they were surprised, and the last ones to come ended up winning first prize. Roma are always the last to count, but we won first prize. We would not settle for second or third place.' She told me that even though sometimes they were looked at with suspicion because they were Roma, their performances always earned them praise.

At the opposite end of the social spectrum, Viorica, a famous Roma singer from the band Taraful din Clejani, explains that her successful musical career is the result of hard work, not looks. With her musician partner and two children, Viorica featured on *Clejanii*, a reality show on Romanian television portraying their daily life. The quotation in the epigraph is from the third episode, in which she and her daughter Margherita pay a visit to a designer. When the designer offers Margherita a modelling job (a way for the designer to gain publicity through the reality show) and asks her to lose a little weight for the purpose, Viorica – blonde, slightly overweight and in her late thirties – tells her daughter: 'Yes, make sure you do not end up like me. Once you've gained weight, it's hard to lose it.' Then she turns to the camera: 'Thank God I did not make my living that way. I succeeded through hard work, through my voice.' Viorica expresses her relief at being successful because of her musical abilities when most female artists in Romania are evaluated for their image and appeal as sex objects. She is one of very few female Roma musicians to have enjoyed success in a field where Roma men reign. And yet, despite their success and prosperity, famous Roma musicians such as Viorica are not considered part of the nation in Romania; indeed the reality show trod a fine line between admiration and mockery of Viorica and her family.

The final quotation in the epigraph is from a discussion between a non-Roma moderator and a Roma activist during a 2007 talk show on Romanian national television. The moderator refused to refer to Roma as Romanian citizens, even though most Roma in Romania have Romanian citizenship. Two Roma activists – a man and a woman – were the only Roma on this talk show, which focused on the question 'why is there tension between Roma and Romanians?' and featured five other guests. The moderator, a non-Roma woman, did not seem to understand why the activists were insisting that Roma were Romanian citizens, and she proceeded to call them 'Ţigani' even after the activists had told her that the term was not acceptable and she should use 'Roma' instead.

These three examples illustrate what this book defines as the citizenship gap for Roma: the distance between legal citizenship, which most Roma hold, and actual citizenship,[3] which the majority of them cannot access fully. Actual citizenship is the ability to take advantage of the citizenship rights that have been gained through legal citizenship but which, if 'understood as private "liberties" or "choices", are meaningless, especially for the poorest and most disenfranchised, without enabling conditions through which they can be realized' (Yuval-Davis 1997b, 18). Actual citizenship encompasses both cultural citizenship, 'the right to belong while being different' (Rosaldo 1994, 402) – with material and symbolic consequences – and basic citizenship rights such as the right to medical facilities, running water and so on.[4] In this book I argue that all Roma experience a citizenship gap to different degrees, depending on class, gender, occupation, age, geographical location and so on, despite the visibility of Roma post-1989 as performers or as victims of poverty and discrimination, in Romania and beyond. Even though they were recognized as an ethnic minority in 1991, Roma in Romania continue to be seen as foreigners, while most Roma see themselves as both Roma and Romanian. Viorica and the Roma activists discussed above experienced the citizenship gap in terms of cultural citizenship and belonging; in addition to the deficit in cultural citizenship, Maria and numerous other Roma, in Pod and elsewhere in Romania, who live in poverty and face eviction and discrimination on a daily basis, also lack basic citizenship rights, despite new measures officially designed to improve their situation. I argue that all Roma face a cultural citizenship gap in post-socialist Romania, and many Roma also experience a complete citizenship gap with regard to both cultural belonging and basic citizenship rights.

Indeed, this book shows that Roma are denied cultural citizenship not only in Romania, but also in most other European countries; and, at the same time, many of them suffer discrimination and abuses of their basic rights. I argue that policies and social programmes for Roma need to be linked to interventions in the official and symbolic definitions of citizenship, which are not captured by a focus on legal citizenship or poverty alone. This book intervenes in current debates on Roma and citizenship in Europe (see Sigona and Trehan 2009; van Baar 2011; Sigona 2015; Hepworth 2015) by introducing (the lack of) cultural citizenship as a key concept for understanding the lack of access to citizenship for Roma.

Numerous reports by international NGOs have brought to global attention the discrimination and abuses Roma suffer across East Central Europe. From Albania to the former Yugoslavia and Ukraine, many Roma lack access to public services, experience violence and are denied basic human rights.[5] Even though minority rights for Roma were high on the agenda of Eastern European countries' EU accession negotiations, which have seen thirteen additional states join the EU over the last ten years, the situation of many Roma in these countries has not changed significantly. Furthermore, police violence against Roma in Western Europe, including the fingerprinting of Roma in Italy in 2008 and the expulsions of Romanian and Bulgarian Roma from France from 2010 onwards,[6] have brought to light the struggles of Roma across Europe. Both the forced eviction of numerous Roma to places like Pod, inside Romania, and the expulsions and police violence targeting Roma in France, Italy and elsewhere in Europe, can be regarded as state-sponsored attacks on Roma, who are not treated as equal citizens by their governments. Hepworth (2015) discusses Romanian Roma living in camps in Italy who were deported to Romania, despite their legal status, as 'abject citizens' in the EU. Sigona (2015) coins the phrase 'campzenship' for the status of refugee and migrant Roma in Italy, while van Baar (2017) proposes the concept of evictability to underline the internal biopolitical border within Europe. At the same time that Romanian Roma, who were EU citizens, were being expelled from Western Europe, impoverished Roma in Pod were literally and metaphorically being pushed to the margins of Romanian society through evictions, poverty and joblessness. I show how the precarious status of migrant Roma in the EU is predicated on the citizenship gap they experience in their countries. In Romania these expulsions failed to cause widespread outrage, as most non-Roma did not identify with those who were being expelled; media coverage condemned the migrants rather than the expulsions, reinforcing the citizenship gap for Roma. Furthermore, the Romanian government collaborated with its French counterpart in the repatriation process. There was widespread frustration in Romania at perceived anti-Romanian sentiments in France in the aftermath of the expulsions, and members of Romanian parliament proposed to replace the name of the ethnicity 'Roma' with 'Ţigani', supposedly to avoid further conflation between Roma and Romanians – as if Romanian Roma were not Romanian citizens. Such instances reveal the lived reality of the citizenship gap for Roma on the one hand, and the symbolic and actual reinforcement of this gap by many non-Roma, including politicians and state employees, on the other.

Staging Citizenship shows that the citizenship gap for Roma has persisted because official recognition has not granted Roma the same status as other, 'legitimate' minorities in Romania. I argue that the Romanian state has not changed its hegemonic definitions – which equate citizenship with ethnic Romanians and draw on ethnicity-based paradigms of citizenship, national culture and history – and has thus maintained the citizenship gap for Roma. In this book I use performance paradigms and examine how different Roma have negotiated and resisted the citizenship gap and claimed citizenship and belonging through music, dance, activism and everyday encounters. Drawing on more than a decade (2001–2012) of ethnographic research among Roma living in or touring cities in Romania and Western Europe, this study is the first to address at length the perspective of the urban and rural impoverished Roma who are part of the mass exodus to the margins of society, in places like Pod.[7] This book discusses ethnoculture in relation to political economy, gender and history. It engages with disenfranchised urban Roma – most of them with part-time careers as amateur dancers or musicians – in the squat settlement of Pod, Transylvania, and with Roma artists, intellectuals and activists; it also discusses concerts, fairs, cultural performances and activist training sessions. *Staging Citizenship* explores the proliferation of a wide range of Roma performances and representations, from live music to TV soaps and reality shows, and the rise of Roma activism in the post-socialist period, examining the citizenship gap that all these different Roma experience to different degrees.

Market expansion to the east, in the context of EU enlargement, and the corresponding import of civil society and democracy, including a focus on the Roma minority, have led to the recent ubiquity of Roma music and dance performances, both in the West and in Romania. The figure of the passionate Gypsy has become one of the latest sources of exoticism in the West. Marketed as timeless and exotic, Roma bands from Romania and other Balkan countries feature in international festivals; DJs play 'Gypsy music'; Gypsy dress parties have spread, from London and Paris to New York and Houston. In Romania, Roma dance and music groups have proliferated, while new TV soaps about Roma (acted by non-Roma) and reality shows featuring famous Roma musicians (such as *Clejanii*, featuring Viorica) have become increasingly popular. However, the visibility of Roma music and dance performance has not translated into Roma being recognized as citizens, despite the fact that Roma express cultural citizenship through these media.

This book uses performance to theorize the racialization of Roma, which leads to their misrecognition in everyday life, onstage and in media representations. At the same time, I show how Roma claim a form of cultural citizenship through these media, which goes unrecognized in official and mainstream understandings of citizenship. The book traces how divergent or parallel definitions of 'culture' – from the Romanian state's definition of national culture in exclusively ethnic terms, to the authenticity criteria promulgated in EU definitions of Roma culture, to the commodified versions of culture promoted in commercial media – constitute the grounds upon which Roma continue to be denied full citizenship, cultural and otherwise. The absence of Roma from Romanian theatre is one illustration of how Roma have been excluded from the institutionalized, state-supported version of national culture. If national theatre is a reflection of the nation as imagined by its cultural producers, playwrights and so on, Roma – who have been made invisible in theatre – have instead populated other performance spaces, especially music spaces, and have become symbols of the nation while being denied their own culture. Taking its cue from performance studies scholarship on citizenship (Joseph 1999; Shimakawa 2002; Nield 2006; Roxworthy 2008; Kim 2014), on Travellers (Wickstrom 2012), and on performance ethnography (Conquergood 2002; Madison 2005, 2011;

Johnson 2003) and work in Romani studies, anthropology, ethnomusicology and media studies (Lemon 2000; Beissinger 2007; Silverman 2007 2012; Imre 2009, Seeman forthcoming), this book uses performance to analyse Roma cultural production across the genres where Roma have become most visible: in music, dance and television in relation to the citizenship gap. I also analyse the representations of Roma in these media – which are usually commercial and controlled by non-Roma – in relation to the performative aspects of the racialization of Roma in everyday life.[8] I situate these performances, in the wider structural constraints, both socio-economic and discursive/policy-related, and show how they confirm or challenge the citizenship gap. Performance, understood as "making, not faking",[9] in its multiplicity of occurrences—from everyday life to the stage and screen—represents a privileged lens into exploring the citizenship gap for Roma as a process, and it also brings into focus the limitations and radical potential of the new visibility of Roma artists and artefacts.

Through this book I argue that Roma in Romania are jettisoned as 'not us', a gesture that maintains the citizenship gap at the social and discursive levels for Roma, and the privilege of the majority through monoethnic paradigms of nation and citizenship. This jettisoning is also evident in the cultural representations and racialized hierarchies that assign low- and popular-culture roles to Roma artists and performers while maintaining their status as Other. I analyse the representations of Roma promoted through official state recognition and commercial media in relation to Romania's dominant racial, gendered and cultural hierarchies framed by monoethnic nationalism.[10] I present a diversity of Roma voices and performances, some of which have become more prominent, such as those of Roma activists, politicians and artists, while others have been overlooked, including the voices and performances of impoverished Roma, which I see as alternative performances of citizenship that resist dominant racial hierarchies and the citizenship gap for Roma.

In the rest of this introduction I provide a detailed description of the main threads of the book's argument, followed by a brief overview of the history of the Roma in Romania and wider region, a discussion of the book's methodology, and a chapter outline.

Performance and the Citizenship Gap

In this book I focus on performances by and about Roma – in the media, onstage, in schools and at international and local festivals – in relation to the citizenship gap and to symbolic and tacit understandings of who is included in the nation and the collective 'we'. I show how these representations influence the perception and racialization of Roma among non-Roma, including in everyday encounters, cultural events, and social programmes organized by state institutions and NGOs. I examine the citizenship gap in the everyday lives of Pod residents, and the ways they resist that citizenship gap through dance and performance, which

I analyse as expressions of cultural citizenship. I draw out the tensions between the state's definitions and recognition of the Roma on the one hand, and Roma activists and NGOs who resist or inadvertently accept the citizenship gap on the other. I analyse: the newly successful Romanian television soaps *Gypsy Heart* (*Inimă de Ţigan*), *The Queen* (*Regina*) and *State of Romania* (*State de România*), in which non-Roma actors play Roma characters; reality shows on Romanian television, such as *Clejanii*, which features famous Roma musicians; and music and dance performances, including *manele*, a controversial and extremely popular music genre played almost exclusively by Roma musicians in Romania. I also discuss internationally acclaimed Roma artists and young amateur performers in Pod, the very few television programmes by Roma in Romania (such as the weekly programme *Roma Caravan – Caravana Romilor*) and the presence of Roma activists on mainstream Romanian talk shows and television programmes.

This book analyses performances as expressions of belonging and cultural citizenship for Roma, transmitted across generations through what Diana Taylor (2003) calls the 'repertoire', and absent from institutionalized forms of culture in Romania. At the same time, the association between Roma and performance, especially music performance, has been a staple of perceptions and stereotypes of Roma (Okely 1983; Stewart 1997; Lemon 2000a; Silverman 2012). For centuries, Roma musicians in Russia and the countries of East Central Europe were considered mere vehicles of the genius of those nations, and as lacking a culture of their own. Roma were excluded from national culture and folklore in Romania, and Roma musicians' contribution was seen to be merely the transmission of Romanian folklore. The visibility of Roma as the exotic Other onstage and in works of literature and art by non-Roma was accompanied by constant monitoring and repression by the police and authorities across centuries.

The current visibility of Roma onstage and in the media relies upon the recycling of lucrative old stereotypes about Roma (see Silverman 2012; Imre 2009; Imre and Tremlett 2011) and, at the same time, I argue, it creates a Roma counterpublic. Like Trehan (2009), I see the Roma counterpublic as subaltern, following Nancy Fraser (1992)[11]: the Roma counterpublic's existence is denied by the state's equation of citizenship to Romanian ethnicity. However, I focus here on the transformative potential of counterpublics, conveyed by Michael Warner's definition, as 'spaces of circulation in which it is hoped that the poesis of scene making will be transformative, not replicative merely' (Warner 2002, 88). Viewed in this way, Roma counterpublics, which resist the citizenship gap and challenge the hegemony of ethnic nationalism,[12] have the potential to include non-Roma and Roma alike. Through performances analysed in this book, Roma articulate belonging to Romania, imagining Romania as a pluralistic, diverse nation and proposing alternative views of citizenship that do not equate the nation with an ethnic group. While I identify these counterpublics as Roma, non-Roma may share the same views, just as the hegemonic public can be both non-Roma and Roma. For example, in the reality show *Clejanii*, Viorica identifies herself as a hard-working woman who does not conform to commercially promoted standards of feminine beauty that objectify women. She appeals to a counterpublic who understand and appreciate the labour behind her successful musical performances as a Roma artist.

Another example of performance of citizenship addressing a Roma counterpublic is the August 2010 edition of the television programme *Roma Caravan*, dedicated to the expulsions of Roma from France. In this programme, Daniel Vasile, vice-president of the Roma Party for Europe, and George Răducanu, Roma activist, accused both French and Romanian governments of racism and criticized the treatment of Roma Romanian citizens as second-class citizens. They spoke to a Roma counterpublic and pointed out that the forceful expulsions and evictions of Roma in France and Romania, respectively, reflected the French and Romanian governments' similar attitudes towards Roma. This was one of the rare instances where unequivocal criticism of the expulsions was broadcast on Romanian television and media in general.

The Citizenship Gap in Pod: Basic Citizenship Rights and Cultural Citizenship

Pod, the settlement near the refuse site where I conducted ethnographic research with poor Roma, represents the materialization of the gap between legal and actual citizenship: the space, erased from official maps, where Roma with legal Romanian citizenship are de facto non-citizens and experience a complete failure of their citizenship rights. I see the spatial reality of the citizenship gap as a variation of Giorgio Agamben's (1998) camp. The camp, according to Agamben, is where refugees live as non-citizens, a place for *zoe* or 'bare life.' From the state's point of view, Pod has been reduced to a gap; however, my ethnographic research brings into focus the subjectivities of Pod's inhabitants – not unlike Sigona (2015), who uses the term 'campenization' to discuss the status of Roma living in camps in Italy (see also Sigona and Trehan 2009; Hepworth 2015).

This book shows how neoliberal economic policies – including large cuts in social security, the disappearance of low-skilled jobs and work opportunities for Roma, and evictions from formerly nationalized properties that were returned to their owners after 1989 – have disproportionately affected Roma. I discuss everyday experiences of the citizenship gap for Roma from Pod, such as the enrolment of Roma children in a school for children with learning disabilities, and mistreatment by the police; I also discuss how Roma in Pod have resisted the citizenship gap through dance performances and their own claims to belong in Romania. Pod and other similar places, contrary to media representations, are connected to Romanian society through a series of informal networks of relatives, acquaintances and new arrivals. Pod residents express these affective ties to Romania when they speak of 'our country, Romania', 'our politicians' and 'our language', the latter sometimes being Romani and sometimes Romanian. Their views on belonging echo those expressed by prominent Roma activists, whose strategies in the media and cultural events aim to raise public awareness about Roma history and Roma contributions to culture and society.

Using ethnographic evidence from Pod and elsewhere, I show that Roma continue to be racialized on the basis of external markers, a process that perpetuates the citizenship gap for Roma.[13] Throughout this book, I treat Roma as an ethnicity, as no immutable signs mark one as Țigan/Țigancă or Roma, despite widespread misconceptions that all Roma are dark skinned, for example.[14] I also focus on racialization processes: while 'race' as a classificatory term is a social construction which masquerades as truth and uses biology to do so, it is an important term that captures the reality of racism, which Roma continue to experience. Through performative processes of gendered and classed racialization and misrecognition, Roma fail to access actual citizenship, either materially or symbolically. Roma who are unmarked may pass as the majority, their Roma ethnicity erased, while Roma values are appropriated by the ethnic nation;[15] others fail to pass – for example, Roma in Pod are classified as abject Țigani, while Roma musicians and performers are seen as exotic Țigani. Paraphrasing Stuart Hall (1980), I argue that poor Roma in Romania experience their class as race and are racialized into Țigani.[16] Some Roma are able to escape the racialization of poverty in some contexts but not in others (see Emigh and Szelényi 2000; Stewart 2002; Ladányi and Szelényi 2006).[17] I show the limits of the relative fluidity in the racialization of Roma; and I argue that the markers of class can include an association with a specific location, such as Pod, in addition to external markers of low socioeconomic status, such as clothing and overall appearance or darker skin tone.

'Roma Culture' Clashes: The State, the EU and Roma NGOs

The Romanian government's ten-year National Strategy for Improving the Situation of Roma (NSISR), 2001–2010, funded in large part by the EU,[18] failed to acknowledge that Roma were first and foremost Romanian citizens.[19] The NSISR was a public policy document focused on several guiding principles, including decentralization, consensus, equality and identity differentiation. It prioritized ten development directions: community development and public administration, housing, social security, healthcare, justice and public order, child protection, education, culture and religion, communication, and civic participation.[20] The official recognition of the Roma minority did not lead to legislative power for Roma, unlike for other ethnonational minorities in Romania. In 2010 there was one Roma politician from the Roma Party for Europe in the Romanian parliament, representing up to two million Roma[21] in Romania, while a similarly sized Hungarian minority had twenty-two members of parliament in the Hungarians' Democratic Union Party.[22]

This citizenship gap has been maintained through the historical appropriation and erasure of Roma culture, which in Romania has resulted in the perception of the Roma as cultureless (a situation exacerbated by the former socialist regime's complete denial of Roma as an ethnocultural minority). Despite official recognition of Roma culture, in post-socialist Romania Roma are seen as both uncultured – individually and collectively – and lacking folklore (a proper tradition) or high culture.[23] On the one hand, the Romanian state recognizes Roma ethnoculture, but on the other it does not provide Roma with the kinds of ethnocultural institutions that support ethnic minorities of a similar size. For example, national minorities such as Hungarian and German Romanians enjoy state-sponsored ethnocultural institutions, including schools and theatres. There are no state-sponsored ethnocultural institutions for Roma in Romania, with the exception of the National Agency for Roma (the most recent iteration of the only government institution explicitly charged with coordinating public policies for Roma, which was founded in 2004) and the recently opened Museum of Roma Culture, an important and long-overdue institution.[24]

I define Romania's state-sponsored multiculturalism as normative monoethnic performativity, which includes the cohabitation of separate, non-intersecting ethnocultures, as illustrated by the Hungarian minority's successful lobbying for an autonomous education system (see Vincze 2011). The dominant essentialist understandings of identity create a system of non-intersecting cultures and parallel worldviews modelled on monoethnic nationalism and favouring ethnocultures that are also nationalities, such as Hungarian or German; this system continues to appropriate and erase Roma culture, failing to treat Roma culture as equal to other ethnocultures. One becomes Romanian or Hungarian by attending monoethnically denominated Romanian or Hungarian schools and dance ensembles, whereas Roma children from Pod, for example, continue to be stigmatized, and many attend special schools for students with learning disabilities.

During post-socialism Roma culture has resurfaced as a paradigm for Roma ethnicity, but not through public cultural policies. Instead, Roma culture has become visible in commercial and NGO representations, and neoliberal approaches to culture have converged with nationalism and xenophobia in the commodification of identifiable Roma cultural aspects that do not challenge nationalist paradigms.[25] The official recognition of Roma culture has thus become a mechanism of exclusion based on authenticity criteria that pigeonhole Roma into stereotypical images.

Current policies for Roma have promoted narrow definitions of culture that exclude the most impoverished. Cultural and social programmes for and about Roma focus on what makes Roma stand out from the majority: traditional occupations such a tin making, spoon making and playing music. For example, the 2002 Roma Fair held outside the Museum of the Romanian Peasant, in Bucharest, featured Roma demonstrating a range of traditional occupations, few of which are practised today. Such exotic images of Roma tradition and ahistorical cultural paradigms directly influence who is recognized as Roma under EU-guided neoliberal social policies. Official definitions of Roma communities, such as those used in EU programmes for social change among Roma, conceive of Roma in these terms, failing to take into account the current lives of most Roma, including the poorest. Poor Roma in Pod, for example, express and take pride in Roma culture, despite not fitting into officially sanctioned definitions of authentic Roma crafts, occupations or attire.

Social programmes sponsored by the EU and NGOs function as spaces of misrecognition for many poor Roma, and recycle Ţigani stereotypes: Roma are recognized by the state as activists if they possess the high culture Roma are supposed to lack, and if they can fashion themselves into self-sustaining individuals showing self-reliance.[26] Paradoxically, even as they recycle underclass stereotypes, social programmes for Roma are training activists in 'civility'.[27] The process of NGO training has turned activists into neoliberal subjects and cast some Roma, like those in Pod, as inauthentic. Obliged to operate within paradigms that equate Roma culture with tradition and authenticity, Roma activists are called upon by the state to demonstrate their own modernity by casting 'authentic' Roma as timeless and traditional and distinguishing them from the undeserving poor. In this way, poor Roma have been constructed as the abject Other, while exotic Roma have gained a new popularity that sits easily next to existing stereotypes.

In order to close the citizenship gap for Roma, monoethnic national paradigms, cultural policies and the official writing of national history need to be changed to include them. While I show that NGOs often contribute to maintaining the status quo of monoethnic performativity, the mushrooming of Roma NGOs – which Trehan defines as the 'NGO-ization of Roma rights' (2009, 56) – allows possibilities, albeit limited ones, for a critique and redefinition of citizenship. I use the term 'NGO historiography' for the alternative historical narratives that have foregrounded Roma, challenged ethnic-based definitions of Romanian citizenship and have been produced or disseminated through NGO events, institutions and initiatives. NGO historiography has to compete with the hegemony of the monoethnic nationalism promoted and supported by state institutions. It produces narratives that function as minor histories[28] (Stoler 2009) that challenge and cut across simplistic, victimized versions of the nation; national histories in the region have emphasized the negative effects of powerful empires and the annexation of national territories. I analyse the work of Roma activists under the constraints of neoliberalism and nationalism, and document their attempts to change hegemonic national paradigms to include Roma, regardless of class, gender or occupation, in definitions of citizenship and national history.

Roma in Romanian and European History: Stereotypes and Erasures

A nation-state since 1918, Romania has been home to numerous ethnic minorities. The appropriation and erasure of Roma culture has historical roots in definitions of the Romanian nation and in larger geopolitical realities; in the same way, today, the situation of the Roma in Romania can only be understood in relation to the wider EU context. While the Romanian nation has always been marginal in relation to the West, Roma within Romania, as a non-territorial, disenfranchised ethnic minority, have symbolically threatened national identities through abjection.[29] Romanian nationalism was modelled on Western Europe, and 'the West' continues to be an integral component of every discussion and definition of Romanian national identity. The Othering of Țigani – reflected in ongoing racism and the racialization of poverty in Romania – echoes Romania's subaltern position in relation to Western Europe: the Romanian nation is 'not quite European' and is in danger of contagion, of becoming like its abject Other, the Țigani. At work here are nesting relationships of marginality, with the Romanian nation being marginal in relation to the West, and the Roma threatening national identity through abjection.[30]

Today, non-Roma mainly learn about Roma through media representations, TV soaps and music, and all of these are for the most part controlled by non-Roma. Ian Hancock (1987), a prominent Roma scholar, points out that when other nations are portrayed as stereotypes, the school curriculum provides the necessary information to help students distinguish between fact and fiction. However, there is widespread amnesia about the past with regard to Roma, and very little information about Roma on mainstream school curricula, either in Romania or beyond. Artworks and fictional representations by non-Roma have for a long time been the only sources of information about Roma available to the public at large. Non-Roma works featuring stereotypical representations have created a whole field of signifiers similar to Orientalism, defined as stereotypical representations of Asia and the Middle East in the West (Said [1978] 1994; see Lemon 2000). These stereotypes continue to be quoted, recycled and perpetuated, to the extent that Roma use and quote them themselves.

Literary critic Katie Trumpener (1992) has eloquently argued that in Western literature, Gypsies function as triggers of memory and nostalgia, as a people without history, and as memory keepers for other nations. Other scholars have shown that 'literary Gypsies throughout Europe figure nationalist nostalgia – they are envisioned as a kind of time capsule for storing national forms (music, folklore, traditions) and a simpler past' (Lemon 2000a, 41). Trumpener argues that the mythologization of Gypsies as timeless preservers of the past is ambiguous, as it veils their marginalization in forgetfulness: 'The function of nostalgia is to restore innocence, by covering up other memories, harsher realities of tension and hostility and fear' (Trumpener 1992, 853). Gypsies have played this role in literary works from Mérimée's novella *Carmen* to Virginia Woolf's novel *Three Guineas*. Given how little known Roma are as a people with a history beyond the stereotypes, in this section I provide an overview of Roma history in relation to Roma representations in the arts.

It is not widely known in Romania or elsewhere that Roma – the self-ascription of most individuals using the Romani language, and of other groups identifying as Țigani, Rudara, Sinti and so on across Europe – share a common ancestry with the tribes that migrated from India in the twelfth century. Their language, Romani, which derives from Sanskrit and shares characteristics with today's South Asian languages, is the strongest evidence of this migration (Hancock 1987). Even though Roma were mentioned in official documents from the territories of today's Romania as long ago as 1385, many non-Roma in Romania see Roma as foreigners. Roma are probably the most heterogeneous among the different populations in Romania's territories, mainly because no state-sponsored Roma nation-building process has institutionalized Roma ethnocultural identities, as has been the case with Romanian, Hungarian and more recently Jewish ethnocultural identities.[31]

Most scholars divide Roma in Romania into several groups, based on traditional occupations, structures of social organization, family configuration and religion. The majority of Roma in Romania are Vlach (Vlax), one of several Roma denominations, which encompasses several smaller groups (*natsija* or *vitse*) including Vatrash ('assimilated' Roma, employed in agriculture), Lăutari (musicians), Kelderara (coppersmiths), Argintari (silversmiths), Boldeni (flower sellers), Lovara (horse traders), Ursara (bear handlers), Ciurara (knife makers), Pieptanara (comb makers), Fierari (smiths), Rudara (goldsmiths, later wood-carvers) and Karamidarja (brick makers). In Transylvania, a large number of Roma are Romungre (musicians), influenced by Hungarian culture and not Vlach. However, as anthropologist Alaina Lemon argues:

> No single, organic, segmentary Romani social structure exists; thus there can be no single way to name social relationships or categories. This does not mean that there are no Romani social orders or structures. It does mean that Romani rifts and affiliations have multiple historical causes – they are not the result of a single, internal principle (such as pollution or 'tribal law') that generated an ordered fission. (Lemon 2000a, 90)

These differences are determined by a variety of factors, including geographical location, gender and descent. Several dialects of Romani can be found across Europe and beyond, and the literary, standardized Romani, based on the Kelderari dialect, is familiar to most Roma.

Contemporary Romania's territory covers several historical provinces (Moldavia, Wallachia, Transylvania, Dobrudja, Bucovina and so on), and the history of the Roma across these regions varies accordingly. For example, in Moldavia and Wallachia Roma were slaves until 1856; while in Transylvania a very small number of Roma were slaves, mostly in areas previously part of Moldavia and Wallachia (Achim 1998, 44). For Roma, ethnicity overlapped with low socioeconomic status during slavery, when the terms 'Țigan' and 'slave' were synonymous. 'Țigan' meant 'slave' in Moldavia and Wallachia until 1856, and the two terms were used interchangeably until the second half of the nineteenth century, when slavery was abolished. In Transylvania 'Romanian' signified one of the ethnicities in the Austro-Hungarian Empire, while in the principalities it meant the majority ethnicity of various social classes, including serfs. The term 'Țigan' has preserved its connotations of lower social status into the present. The origins of Roma slavery represent a point of contention in Romanian historiography, and by extension in Romanian politics, as I show in Chapter 1.

In nineteenth-century Romanian literature, the Țigani – as Roma were known at the time – played similar roles to Gypsies in Western literature. Ion Budai Deleanu's *Țiganiada* is a comic epic that parodies the fate of the Romanian people under the mask of Țigani; written between 1800 and 1812, it was first published in 1875. Both Țigani and Romanians were minorities in the Austro-Hungarian Empire, to which Transylvania belonged, and Budai Deleanu used Țigani to reflect the oppression of subaltern Romanians. However, Budai Deleanu's background included Roma ancestry, and this work is often cited as an example of early literature by Roma. Vasile Alecsandri, an aristocrat, abolitionist, author and revolutionary from Moldavia, draws on autobiographical details to portray a Țigan slave from a slave owner's point of view in his short story *Vasile Porojan*, published in 1880. The tragic fate of a female Roma slave, Zamfira, is also a subplot in his other work, *Story of a Golden Coin* (1844). Alecsandri's short stories represent the best-known literary representations of Roma slaves.

The literary and visual portrayal of Roma in the arts in the Romanian territories fit in the larger European mythology of the noble savage. Exceptions include Gheorghe Asachi's 1847 play *Țiganii*, which describes the emancipation of privately owned slaves and imagines Roma and Romanians becoming one nation (Szeman 2017, forthcoming). In the early twentieth century most representations of Roma recycled old stereotypes; while during socialism the state denied the existence of an ethnocultural Roma identity, and as a result Roma were absent from the arts. Roma artists and intellectuals were assimilated into the nation, and their ethnic background was never mentioned officially.

Persecution and Erasures in the Twentieth Century

Between the two world wars, the unification of several territories into Greater Romania was marked by the Romanian state's increased attempts to assimilate other ethnicities (Livezeanu 1995). Roma activists and intellectuals in organizations such as the General Association of Țigani in Romania and the General

Union of Roma worked to establish a public Roma presence and to craft a modern identity – one based on integrating Roma through an emphasis on their Christian values (Potra, 1939). Despite the fact that Roma were recognized as an ethnicity, they were not included in the constitution, and the majority of Roma were impoverished and uneducated.

Perhaps the darkest period for Roma across Europe was the Roma Holocaust during World War II. Alongside Jews and homosexuals, Roma were the target of Nazi and fascist extermination campaigns. In Romania, Marshal Ion Antonescu sent around 25,000 Roma to concentration camps in the territories of today's Ukraine.

While slavery and the Holocaust were extreme examples of the marginalization of Roma, their state-sanctioned marginalization has operated as a veiled or explicit policy across different historical periods. For five decades during socialism in Romania, the Roma were treated as a social problem, their culture was not recognized or even mentioned in official documents and they were the target of assimilation campaigns. Through assimilation policies Roma and their contribution were appropriated by the nation and erased, while the stereotypes of the abject Ţigani persisted and were unofficially used to refer to Roma who failed to assimilate. From 1965 to 1989 Romania was ruled by Nicolae Ceauşescu, whose regime started with a few years of relative freedom before turning into a dictatorship that aggressively controlled the population. In this period ethnic nationalism flourished in Romania (Verdery 1991), and most Roma failed to assimilate. The socialist regime recognized 'cohabitating nationalities' (excluding Roma), and officially fostered a multinationalism in which majority and minority institutions coexisted but did not intersect – a system that continues today, and which in this book I term the normative monoethnic performativity of ethnocultural identities. Stereotypes about Ţigani as thieves, criminals and outcasts proliferated, despite the Communist government's official suppression of Roma identity. Roma became scapegoats for the majority, because of the alleged benefits that socialist propaganda claimed they received. Another effect of the Communist assimilation policies was the proletarianization of a large number of Roma through their employment in low-skilled jobs in factories or collective farms and their access to public housing. During socialism, the term 'Ţigan' was emptied of any positive or romantic connotations and became a synonym for the underclass. The stereotype of the poor Ţigani, however, presupposed the existence of the extremely rich traditional Ţigani. Despite their lack of success, Communist assimilation policies had lasting effects at the cultural, political, social and economic levels, all still visible in the context of post-socialist Romania.

The effects of various socialist cultural policies regarding the Roma in countries of the former Eastern bloc are also visible today in the preponderance of distinct stereotypes about Roma in each country, against a common background of marginalization and discrimination. Romania did not produce any films or cultural products identified as Roma or Țigani in the five decades of socialism. In contrast, in nearby Hungary, despite similar policies, the resurgence of a Roma cultural movement and the presence of self-identified Roma musicians onstage allowed the Roma to be considered cultural agents (Kovalcsik 2010; Stewart 1997), something that Roma in Romania were denied. In socialist Yugoslavia, to mention another example, Roma were recognized as having a culture, even if not on a par with other nationalities, and they were represented, albeit stereotypically, in many films, including Aleksandar Petrović's *I Even Met Happy Gypsies* (1967) and Emir Kusturica's *The Time of the Gypsies* (1987). Kusturica's films and Goran Bregović's music were popular in Romania, but they did not change the general perception of local Roma – not even in the sense of producing romantic stereotypes.

The economic-political changes of the transition to neoliberalism affected most Roma profoundly, especially those working on collective farms, which were dismantled, or in low-skilled jobs in plants and factories that were closed down. Social security was also significantly reduced. Roma found themselves with a recognized ethnicity, but holding fewer economic rights and placed outside national and European citizenship. However, some of these changes benefited the nomadic or semi-nomadic Roma, most of whom had been unemployed during socialism and who recovered some of their goods and valuables confiscated by the socialist state.

Despite the change in paradigm in relation to Roma, from a social problem during socialism to an ethnoculture during post-socialism, the majority of Roma continue to experience marginalization, and their economic condition has worsened. However, while the majority of Roma are poor, there is a burgeoning middle class of Roma activists, intellectuals and successful entrepreneurs. Affluent Roma spark resentment and are associated with and blamed for the negative effects of the transition to a market economy. Because of long-standing suspicion against Roma, Roma success, whether in the entertainment industry or in business, is often resented by the majority and perceived as illicit.

Methodology

This is a multisited ethnography that brings together different sites, people and performances in productive tension. I spent a total of seventeen months conducting fieldwork in Romania between 1999 and 2007, and I made a few more visits there between 2008 and 2012. The main vantage point for this ethnography is that of Pod. Pod's story is not unique, and similar Roma settlements can be found across Romania. Roma's reliance on recycling practices and their dispersion within Romania have been widespread phenomena over the last two decades (Zoon 2001). These settlements expanded within Romania after 1989, as many Roma lost their unskilled or low-skilled jobs and sought informal work, recycling from and living next to waste sites on the outskirts of urban areas.

Over the eleven years I visited Pod, its landscape changed considerably. Some of the improvised huts I saw in 2001, piled with rubbish, some out of sight of passers-by, had been replaced by 2008 with fully built houses proudly set on the main road. These constructions testified to the lucrative side of the informal collection of recyclables, and to some Pod residents' efficient management skills. Most of the intra-community economy circulated through informal arrangements, which often involved a main collector for whom others collected recyclables in exchange for goods or credit. Living conditions did improve during the 2000s for some Roma in Pod; but some things did not change. In 2001, there was no running water or electricity, and virtually no medical facilities. Residents collected water from a broken pipe, and powered electrical equipment with batteries. They had no access to healthcare, and many children either did not go to school or else attended special schools for children with disabilities. This situation had not improved much by 2012. For example, despite the existence of a medical facility built with European funds, no medical staff were available and it was closed down.

As a 'co-performative witness' (Conquergood 2001; Madison 2011, 25) in Pod, I got to know the complexity of people's lives, and not only the hardships and struggles. As Madison aptly puts it: 'Performative witnessing is also to emphasize the political act (responsibility) of witnessing over the neutrality (voyeurism) of observation.' (2011, 25) Inside their homes, which I visited often, residents built a safer world of 'normalcy.' My co-performative witnessing sometimes involved performing together at dances and celebrations, events that were both frequent and necessary: they made life worth living. At celebrations, guests were not allowed to pay, and were expected to be served. Tables full of food and drinks greeted visitors at these special times, even when the goods were being paid for with credit from the better-off Roma.

As a co-performative witness in Pod and elsewhere, I accompanied my Roma friends and acquaintances to state institutions, on doctor's and social services appointments, and I went on field trips with Roma school mediator Armando to visit Roma students who were struggling academically. I engaged and built connections with many different people in Pod: I got to know adults and children, young Roma who were studying in schools for the disabled because of their ethnicity, and undocumented adults. Elsewhere I met Roma and non-Roma activists and artists, young people and school staff. I conducted formal and informal interviews, and I attended school performances, concerts and festivals, fairs and exhibitions, in different parts of Romania and abroad in London and Paris. In many of these instances I could gauge how Pod residents' everyday experiences of citizenship differed from or resembled my own. I experienced, for example, how Roma performances abroad were often received by non-Roma audiences as expressions of national folklore that excluded Roma even as the latter were performing onstage.

Throughout my fieldwork in Romania I consumed and engaged with different types of media, from television and radio to newspapers, with an eye to how Roma were represented. This was a frustrating experience, given the racism and sexism of mainstream media, the misrepresentation of Roma and the lack of Roma voices. Roma in Pod engaged with different media, mainly television, and they reappropriated some of the cultural products for which they felt an affinity. When watching daytime North American and Latin American soaps, literate residents read subtitles aloud to small groups of (mostly) women gathered around small black-and-white television sets. More recently, television sets in Pod often played music by both Roma and non-Roma from the *manele*-focused music channel Taraf, identified as a 'Ţigani' channel. Roma in Pod appreciated 'Gypsy soaps', even though these represented *gadge's*[32] exoticized projections of Gypsiness.

Aside from my own analysis, when I discuss media representations of Roma, including in the television soaps, I will present Pod residents' views of these productions. In the early years I watched North American soaps with Pod residents, and in the later years I discussed Gypsy soaps with several Roma from Pod in both formal and informal interviews, which changed my own perception of the soaps. In mapping the reception of the soaps and music performances, I also use audience comments from soap websites and YouTube. My media ethnography is situated between a fully embedded reception analysis (Abu-Lughod 2005) and one focused on audience members who participate in or comment on programmes through social media (di Leonardo 2012; Imre and Tremlett 2011). While Roma have rarely been analysed as consumers of media, including television (see Tremlett 2013), I engage with both the majority's consumption and the readings of a Roma counterpublic that identified with or challenged the images of Roma presented in these cultural productions.

I am a *gadgi* (non-Roma) and Romanian citizen of mixed Romanian-Hungarian descent, with a Ph.D. gained in the United States and currently working in the United Kingdom. Some of my non-Roma Romanian friends and acquaintances rolled their eyes upon hearing about my research topic, and worried that I would reiterate or add to many Westerners' mistaking of Romanians for Roma; some asked me 'please don't make us all look like Ţigani.' My Western location at the time of my fieldwork in Romania, being the United States and, after 2005, London, bestowed upon me a certain cachet among some of my informants: one of the Romnja in Pod decided I was Spanish, a nation to which she felt connected; one Romni from the village of Clejani called me a 'foreign *gadgi*', as opposed to a local, Romanian *gadgi*. At times the perception of my identity shifted – for example, when a lawyer asked me whether I was a Romni friend's daughter, even though we were both in our thirties. This instance, when I was taken for a Romni by a non-Roma, was a shocking (for me but not, as it turned out, for my Romni friend) reminder of the widespread gendered stereotypes about Romnja as young, over-fertile mothers with dozens of children. Several times, when I accompanied friends and witnessed similar situations, the casualness of such incidents and the everydayness of racism really struck me. My shock reflected my privileged position: for my Roma friends and acquaintances these incidents were not surprising. As I show in Chapter 2, there was no short-age of such incidents: encounters in hospitals, schools, shops and police stations, and often with state employees, demonstrated this everyday racism.

In many instances my ethnographic journey involved making the familiar strange and the strange familiar. Performance and theatre scholar Baz Kershaw discusses radical theatre, which has the power to change the ideological inclina-tion and worldviews of audiences: 'theatre which mounts a radical attack on the status quo may prove deceptive. The slow burning fuse of efficacy may be invisible' (1992, 28). I see the slow burning fuse metaphor as an apt descrip-tion of the change in subjectivity that I experienced when making the strange familiar and vice versa. The slow burning fuse was started for me most likely at a Christmas celebration in Pod, when I visited with non-Roma friends. In these moments, when I was allowed into people's lives, the expected power balance was temporarily redressed; instead of only witnessing suffering and injustice, I spent enjoyable moments with Pod friends. These became turning points in the co-witnessing process of ethnography, when the initial impulse, of seeing Pod as a problem that needed a solution, receded to some extent. I started listening to people more carefully, to their music, their dances and their actions. My sense of outrage at their situation never disappeared, but it became equally important for me to document their other stories – in addition to stories about injustice and discrimination – from the way they saw Gypsy soaps to their perspectives on belonging in Romania.

From Pod, this study moves to other places within Romania, including Bucharest, and then abroad to the West, following the trajectory of 'Gypsy music'. In addition to Pod, I conducted fieldwork in Bucharest and in Clejani, the village in southern Romania from where the famous (in the West) Roma band Taraf de Haïdouks originate. In London I experienced first hand the considerable international success of 'Gypsy music': from traditional music to the ubiquitous *manele*,[33] everything had become prime material for mixing into dance music in venues such as the Barbican and clubs such as Koko and Cargo. I attended concerts at these venues, as well as other cultural events. I attended many perfor-mances of the dance group Together, composed of both young Roma and *gadge*, which initially started at a local school near Pod. My travels across Romania took me to different parts of the country, where I interacted with different Roma: Romungre, Gabors (traders and welders), Kelderara, Karamidarja and Vatrash, Lăutari, Ursara, Kelderara and Rudara, as well as activists and intellectuals.

The ethnographic material in this book focuses mainly on Roma from Transylvania and Wallachia, regions within Romania's national borders. The distinct histories and social status of different Roma, including musicians, in Transylvania and Wallachia influence current perceptions of these musicians and the different stereotypes associated with them. Roma known as Romungre were historically Hungarian speaking, and had musical occupations during the Austro-Hungarian Empire. I met some Romungre in Pod, most of whom only spoke Romanian. Roma musicians in Wallachia were known as Lăutari; I met some Lăutari in Clejani. The repertoire and audiences of Romungre and Lăutari musicians diverged with the music and histories of Austro-Hungary and Romania respectively, until 1918, when Transylvania became part of Greater Romania. Transylvanian music and Romungre musicians were 'rediscovered' by the Tanchaz movement as Hungarian folk music in the 1970s. From socialism to post-socialism, Transylvania remained the repository of folk music for Hungarian musicologists and nationalists alike. Muzica lăutărească – the music of the Lăutari in Wallachia – had strong Turkish influences, evident today in *manele*, the most popular genre, played predominantly by Roma musicians in Wallachia. Today *manele* production is most powerful in Bucharest, and the concentration of media production and political power in the city has made certain groups of Roma, especially those in and around Bucharest, more visible in the national arena. The media brought to Pod the sounds and sights of *manele* from Bucharest, and Roma in Pod enjoyed, consumed and performed *manele* and a traditional Roma dance known locally as *csingeralas*, a type of *verbunk*, part of the Tanchaz music. However, 'manelists' are most numerous in the south of Romania, and *manele* are equally popular in Transylvania.

Despite the diversity that characterizes both Roma and their musical production, and despite their significant musical success, this book shows that Roma have not gained a legitimate place as a culture in the national imaginary, and they continue to be denied cultural citizenship, even when their music is praised. While Roma musicians' performances may continue lucrative stereotypes about Roma that have existed for centuries, from the perspective of a Roma counterpublic, these performances can be read as performances of citizenship. As the advent of neoliberalism under monoethnic nationalism has maintained the citizenship gap for Roma, paying attention to the subjectivities of Roma and including them as equal partners in social and cultural programmes could be a first step for state institutions to take in bridging this gap.

Chapter Outline

Part I: Poor Roma, Roma Activists and the Romanian State

Chapters 1 and 2 focus on the lived structural constraints within which everyday performances of citizenship are enacted, while Chapter 3 addresses the discursive constraints of policy framings on the performances of citizenship for Roma.

1. 'We Will Build a Beautiful Future Together': NGO Historiography, Roma Culture and Monoethnic Nationalism
Focusing on Roma activists' work at a 2002 Roma fair and cultural festival in Bucharest, the chapter shows that cultural events' outreach was limited by the Romanian state's hegemonic constructions of the nation and of citizenship, and as a result these events became venues for the consumption of ethnic artefacts.

2. Living in the Citizenship Gap: Roma and the Permanent State of Emergency in Pod
Chapter 2 is an ethnography of the impoverished urban Roma community of Pod, and focuses on the complete citizenship gap that Roma in Pod experienced. The chapter uses a performance lens to discuss the collective and individual experiences of the citizenship gap in Pod, including discrimination and abuse, and everyday experiences of racism. The chapter demonstrates how the diversity of Pod residents' cultural practices belie Romanian media's images of sameness among the Roma and stereotypes that poor Roma, or Țigani, lacked culture.

3. 'Too Poor to Have Culture': The Post-Socialist Politics of Authenticity in Roma NGO Training
Through an ethnographic account and performative analysis of a training work-shop for Roma activists, this chapter shows that programmes promoting Roma development in Romania inadvertently reproduce the stereotypical Țigani and the citizenship gap for Roma. EU-sponsored social programmes for Roma exclude the most impoverished, while claiming to aim to improve the situation of Roma.

Part II: Roma Performance and the Citizenship Gap: From Exoticism to Creative Resistance
Chapters 4 through 6 bring material, structural and discursive constraints directly into conversation with a range of settings and practices, from media to the stage, in which performances of citizenship take place.

4. Performing Bollywood: Young Roma Dance Cultural Citizenship
Chapter 4 focuses on a student dance group, Together, comprised of young Roma from Pod and non-Roma, who perform at festivals and schools in Transylvania and abroad. Many Roma students continue to be discriminated against in schools that boast multicultural policies and for the young Roma in this group, dance was one of their few avenues of success.

5. Consuming Exoticism/Reimagining Citizenship: Romanian Nationalism and Roma Counterpublics on Romanian Television
Chapter 5 combines media analysis and ethnographic research, discussing the representations of Roma by non-Roma in the hugely successful television soaps

Gypsy Heart, The Queen and *State of Romania*, and in talk shows and debates on current affairs programmes. It analyses Roma performances of citizenship in the media and their reception among different Roma.

6. The Ambivalence of Success: Roma Musicians and the Citizenship Gap
Focusing on musical performances as performances of citizenship, Chapter 6 discusses Roma musicians and their success in relation to the citizenship gap for Roma. The chapter discusses *manele* singer Florin Salam's unsuccessful attempt to represent Romania at the Eurovision Song Contest in 2010, and Viorica and Ioniță's performances on the reality show *Clejanii*, in relation to both the citizenship gap and Roma counterpublics.

Conclusion: Unlearning the Forgetting
The conclusion discusses Hungarian Roma artist Tibor Balogh's performance installation 'Rain of Tears' as a metaphor for the work that states and individuals alike need to undertake in order to close the citizenship gap for Roma.

Notes

1. All translations from the Romanian are mine, unless otherwise noted. I use the terms Rom (masculine singular), Roma (masculine plural), Romni (feminine singular) and Romnja (feminine plural) to describe individuals from this ethnic minority, and I also employ Roma as an adjective. I use Gypsy when discussing stereotypes in and from the West; Gypsy is also the term with which Roma in the United Kingdom identify, and does not necessarily denote a stereotype (Okely 1983). I use the nouns Țigan (masculine singular), Țiganca (feminine singular), Țigani (masculine plural), Țigănci (feminine plural) and the adjectival form Țigan to describe local stereotypes and the way some Roma in Romania identify.
2. 'Pod' is a fictitious name I use to protect the anonymity of this community. 'Pod' means bridge in Romanian. In addition to using pseudonyms for people, in several instances I have created composite identities.
3. See Delanty (1997) for one of the first articulations of the difference between legal and actual citizenship.
4. While a large number of Roma live in poverty, all Roma experience the citizenship gap at the level of cultural citizenship, and this has real, material consequences in their everyday lives.
5. Discrimination against Roma children in schools is still common across East Central Europe (ERRC 2004). The European Court of Human Rights ruled that there was discrimination against Roma children in the Czech Republic. In 2007, a year after an initial referral to the Grand Chamber of that court, the court found that 'the practice of racial segregation in education violated Article 14 of the European Convention on Human Rights, which prohibits discrimination, taken together with Article 2 of Protocol 1, which secures the right to education'. The court noted that 'the Czech Republic is not alone in this practice and that discriminatory barriers to education for Roma children are present in a number of European countries' (ERRC 2007).

6. In the summer of 2010 the French government initiated a virulent expulsion campaign that targeted over 300 settlements on the outskirts of cities, with thousands of Roma migrants forced to return to Romania or Bulgaria.

7. See Enikő Magyari-Vincze, 2007, who engages with Roma in similar situations.

8. Performance studies scholarship that has paved the way for a critical investigation of citizenship through a performance lens includes: May Joseph (1999) on the performative links between legal and cultural citizenship; Karen Shimakawa (2002) on Asian–American identity; Sophie Nield on performances of citizenship at the border (2006); Emily Roxworthy (2008) on the performative logic of citizenship in the United States;, and Suk-Young Kim (2014) on the affective aspects of citizenship in the DMZ between North and South Korea.

9. This phrase was coined by anthropologist Victor Turner (1982, 93); Richard Schechner defines performance as 'restored behavior' or 'twice-behaved behavior' (2013), while Dwight Conquergood discusses performance as kinesis (making) in relation to minority cultures and subjugated knowledge (2002).

10. The terms used for the majority ethnicity (Romanian) and for citizenship are identical in Romania. Ethnic minorities use separate terms to refer to their citizenship and their ethnicity. Ethnic nationalism differs in principle from civic nationalism, where membership is not based on ethnic belonging; however, both types of nationalism engender racism (see Kymlicka 2000; Brubaker 1999). For example, notwithstanding claims to civic nationalism, the legal protection of racial divisions in the United States lasted for centuries; as Aiwha Ong (2003, 6) writes, 'racial logic has always lain like a serpent in the sacred ideal of American citizenship'.

11. Nancy Fraser sees subaltern counterpublics as: 'parallel discursive arenas where members of subordinated social groups invent and circulate counterdiscourses to formulate oppositional interpretations of their identities, interests and needs' (1992, 123).

12. Warner's (2002) focus on the transformative possibilities of counterpublics signals their radical potential.

13. Judith Butler (1990) discusses the performative constructions of gender identities, while Fredrik Barth (1969) and Michael Omi and Howard Winant (2014) show that ethnic and racial identities are performatively deployed in the crucible of economic and political tensions and contingent upon changing relations of power.

14. See debates on the cross-cultural use of 'race' in Bourdieu and Wacquant (1999), Shohat and Stam (1994) and Hanchard (2003).

15. Étienne Balibar (2004, 8) defines 'demos' as the collective subject of representation, decision making and rights, and 'ethnos' as the historical communities based on ethnic belonging. When Roma pass as citizens, unrecognized as Roma, their contribution is appropriated by the ethnos, the ethnic nation.

16. Stuart Hall (1980) argues that Blacks in Britain experienced racial discrimination through class.

17. Scheper-Hughes and Hoffman (1998) made similar observations about the relationship between race and class in Brazil.

18. The European Commission for Culture uses the terms 'diversity' and 'interculturalism', a version of multiculturalism that focuses on the individual rather than the recognition of groups and is closer to integration and assimilation (see http://www.coe.int/t/dg4/default_en.asp, accessed 1 December 2011). The term 'multiculturalism' mobilizes several meanings, from the coexistence of multiple cultures and ethnicities within a ter-

ritory, to a political ideology. Romania and its different territories have always been multicultural in the first sense. The EU does not espouse multicultural policies, even though legal, rights-based non-discrimination is intrinsic to EU legislation in an increasingly multicultural (in the first sense) EU. The few EU member states that had explicit multicultural legislation in the past, such as the United Kingdom and the Netherlands, have replaced multiculturalism as a political strategy with measures to integrate migrants, especially Muslims.

19. The new long-term strategy, approved in December 2011, recognizes this fact in its name: 'The Strategy for the Inclusion of Romanian Citizens from the Roma Minority'.

20. Strategia Nationala de Imbunatatire a Situatiei Romilor, Capitolul VII, 2001 (see http://www.anr.gov.ro/html/Biblioteca.html, last accessed 22 March 2010). An official report on the strategy is available at www.publicinfo.gov.ro/library/10_raport_tipar_p_ro.pdf. Romania endorsed several other related public policies, without necessarily initiating them, including: the Decade of Roma Inclusion 2005–2015, organized by the World Bank and the Open Society Institute, which involved eight East Central European states; the Common Implementation Strategy for Social Inclusion, 2005–2010, a shared policy between the EU and Romania following the Lisbon Treaty; and the National Plan for Inclusion and Eradication of Poverty, 2002–2012, one chapter of which was devoted to Roma (Preoteasa et al., eds. 2009, 34–38).

21. The number of Roma in Romania varies, depending on the source, from half a million to two million.

22. Figures from the Romanian Parliament website (http://www.cdep.ro/pls/parlam/structura.gp?leg=2008&cam=2&idg=&poz=0&idl=1, accessed 12 September 2010).

23. Wendy Brown (2006) discusses how culture can be used to undermine the very identities it is supposed to highlight, which are seen as 'being culture'.

24. The existence of state-sponsored cultural institutions for Roma does not necessarily guarantee equal citizenship and inclusion in the nation: compare the ghettoization of Roma museums and theatres in the Czech Republic and Russia respectively. The current National Strategy for Roma (2012–2020) in Romania stipulates the creation of a Roma State Theatre and a Museum of Roma Culture and Civilization. So far only the latter has materialized, yet it is potentially marred by spatial marginalization as it is situated on the outskirts of Bucharest.

25. As Paul Gilroy (2000) argues, culture as a trope of neoliberalism 'compounds rather than resolves the problems associating "race" with embodied or somatic variation'.

26. Arlene Dávila (2001) defines the 'politics of suspicion' in relation to Latinos/as in the United States, where a market-dictated construction of the Latino/a identity became the norm against which people's authenticity was judged.

27. Aiwha Ong's (2006) critique of the middle-class aspect of cultural diversity and the Comaroffs' (2009) argument that class becomes erased in the neoliberal promotion of ethnic identities are relevant here.

28. Here I borrow Ann Stoler's (2009) reworking of Deleuze and Guattari's 'minor literature' (1986). For Deleuze and Guattari minor literature is the work of minority writers who reinvent the dominant language; for Stoler minor history is made for 'cutting' across dominant historical narratives (9).

29. Julia Kristeva (1982) defines the abject Other as that which is expelled from the self in order to define the self.

30. See Susan Gal (1991) on nesting East–West dichotomies in Hungary.
31. Other ethnic minorities in the region, including Romanians, Hungarians, Germans and more recently Jews, relate their ethnocultural identities transnationally to other nation-states that support their diasporas (see Verdery, 1994).
32. A term meaning 'non-Roma' (plural) in the Romani language: *gadgi* (fem.; sg.) and *gadgo* (masc.; sg.).
33. Music similar to the very popular *manele* in Romania, bearing influences from an Ottoman form called *mana*, and which today extends into fusion styles, can be found across the Balkans in other ethnopop incarnations such as turbo folk and *chalga*.

Chapter 1

'We Will Build a Beautiful Future Together'
NGO Historiography, Roma Culture and Monoethnic Nationalism

We must tell our children that, six decades ago, children just like them
were sent by the Romanian state to die of starvation and cold. We must tell
mothers in Romania that the Romanian state killed Roma mothers through
subjugation and misery. We must also mention that Roma men fighting for
the homeland were taken out of the army and sent between Denester and
Bug. Education in Romania has the duty to inform and teach the new generations about the Holocaust, just as it has a duty to talk about the period of
Roma slavery or about the crimes of Communism.

—Patrasconiu, 'Exterminarea Țiganilor'

So went former Romanian President Traian Băsescu's address for Holocaust
Memorial day on 22 October 2007, when he decorated three Holocaust
survivors with the National Order of Faithful Service. Denester and Bug, mentioned in his speech, are the two rivers (in present-day Ukraine) that mark the
territory where an estimated 25,000 Roma were deported by the Romanian
state during World War II and approximately 11,000 lost their lives. Those who
returned, including the three survivors decorated at the event, had never before
been considered Holocaust victims, as Romania had failed to acknowledge its
contribution to the Holocaust until recent EU negotiations and pressure from
Israel. The President's speech included a few sentences in Romani, and a plea to
the EU: 'We need a European policy for Roma. ... There is, of course, a need for
financial resources, because, for the time being, since the revolution, the funds

allocated for the social inclusion of Roma have been insignificant' (Patrasconiu 2009, no page number). Băsescu ended his remarks with an apology and a promise for the future: 'Forgive us, brothers and sisters, and we will build a beautiful future together'.

In this chapter I focus on the 2002 Roma Fair held at the Museum of the Romanian Peasant in Bucharest – one of the first events on a national scale representing Roma culture post-1989 – and on political debates before and after EU accession about Roma slavery and the Roma Holocaust. I show how Romanian institutions and officials moulded Roma identity through spatial marginalization and commodification, demonstrated at the Roma Fair in the tension between the museum itself and the marginal spaces assigned to the Roma activists and participants.

I also argue that the framing of Roma culture and Roma history has become increasingly commodified in the celebration of a consumable version of culture and a selective and perfunctory engagement with the past. The Roma Fair offered Roma cultural artefacts for consumption through the commodification of Roma identities in the context of a general expansion of the market and consumer culture in Romania. Indeed, during the autumn following the Roma Fair, the first Romanian branch of the multinational company Pier 1 Imports opened in Bucharest, offering well-off Romanians 'authentic' Developing World artefacts and ethnic chic, filtered through Western taste and endorsement, and available at Western prices. Such commodification has maintained the citizenship gap for Roma by harmonizing neoliberalism and monoethnic nationalism.

The state has imposed a form of what Rey Chow defines as 'coercive mimeticism': an identitarian, existential, cultural or textual process whereby those defined as 'ethnics' are expected to 'resemble and replicate the very banal preconceptions that have been appended to them, a process in which they are expected to objectify themselves in accordance with the already seen and thus to authenticate the familiar imaginings of them as ethnics' (2002, 107). The Roma Fair illustrates the tension between the state's imposition of monoethnic paradigms and the Roma activists' attempt to bridge the citizenship gap from within those paradigms. I will show how activists at the fair turned a critical eye on the cultural politics of Roma representations across the centuries, and through NGO historiography assessed the construction of national history in Romania. The fair put forward the perspective of minor history and challenged monoethnic national history by including Roma as subjects of national history. It made visible subaltern Roma identities and addressed an emergent Roma counterpublic.[1]

Lastly, I consider the appropriation and erasure of Roma culture and its survival through oral transmission across generations, using a minor historical and transnational approach to discuss the institution of the Museum of the Romanian Peasant in relation to the construction of Romanian folklore and Romanian nationalism. Focusing on the narratives told by archival evidence,

pictures and books at the exhibition, and by the performances, voices and negotiations taking place outside, I point to the cracks that the fair opened up in the
grand narrative of monoethnic nationalism told by the museum and countless
other institutions in Romania.

Outside the Archive/the Outside Archive: Consuming Roma Culture in the Marketplace

The 2002 Roma Fair, entitled 'Mahala și Țigănie' ('Slums and Gypsydom')
included a wide range of participants, both Roma and *gadge*: Roma activists,
artists, students, Roma craftspeople from across the country, prominent and
lesser-known musicians, magicians, Roma businesspeople and leaders and so
on. Jointly organized by the Resource Centre for Roma Communities, and
the Mircea Dinescu Poetry Foundation under the auspices of the European
Commission and the Romanian Ministry of Culture, it was not an exclusively Roma event, and the prominent Romanian poet and intellectual Mircea
Dinescu was one of its organizers.

Inside the museum, the fair occupied the foyer, where launch events for
academic and literary books were held, including the memoirs of the magician Maria, Queen of White Magic. The book exhibition featured works by
Roma scholars, such as: *Roma Slavery in the Romanian Territories*, an important
work of NGO historiography edited by Vasile Ionescu, one of the organizers
from the Roma association Aven Amentza; volumes of poetry by Roma poet
Luminița Cioabă, who was present at the fair; and the Bible in Romani. In the
room designated 'Laolaltă' ('Together'), which hosted temporary exhibitions on
minorities, the exhibition 'Între o Del și o Beng' ('Between God and the Devil')
provided a historical timeline of the Roma presence in arts and culture. There
was a Roma NGO forum in one of the larger auditoria, and a Roma student
ball playfully entitled 'O Soarea la Mahala' ('An Evening in the Mahala'). The
museum courtyard hosted an exhibition of traditional Roma crafts and several
open-air concerts, with bands from across the country performing under the
banner 'Muzică Lăutărească Veche' ('Old Lăutari Music').

As one stepped into the museum courtyard, where Roma of different
denominations were selling objects, ranging from costumes to household items,
among the transplanted peasant houses that constitute the museum's permanent fixtures, there was a sense of a return of the repressed in the very heart of
Romanian nationalism. Two Kelderara women with ribbon-woven plaits and
colourful outfits proudly stood in front of a table displaying similar garments
(see Figure 1.1). They were selling long pleated skirts and matching blouses
made of a patchwork of multicoloured fabrics – red, green, blue, yellow and
purple. Each skirt had two layers: one, wrapped around the waist, covered the
body, and the other, apron-like, lay on top. The blouses were also very colourful,
short and very loose, almost like skirts for the upper body. Browsing the stall

Figure 1.1. Kelderara Roma selling outfits and copper pots at the Roma Fair, Romanian Peasant Museum, Bucharest, October 2002 (photo by Ioana Szeman).

Figure 1.2. Kelderar Rom on the left and Rudara selling wooden household objects (right); in the background the stand of the Kelderara, and a television reporter. Roma Fair, Romanian Peasant Museum, October 2002 (photo by Ioana Szeman).

alongside many other visitors, I was shocked to find that the asking prices for single garments ranged from €50 to €100 euros: the average monthly wage in Romania at the time was roughly €100. The women were evidently targeting Western tourists, or newly rich Romanians who had acquired Western habits and Western pockets. At the next stall, two long-bearded, long-moustached silversmiths in wide-brimmed black hats were demonstrating the art of jewellery making. Further along, a few young women in urban clothes were offering their services in white magic, described in the fair brochure as divination and palm reading. On the left-hand side of the yard, Kelderara men dressed in urban clothes were displaying huge copper containers of various shapes, popular in Romania and used for the home brewing of alcohol. These Roma wore modern attire and were visibly well off, with Kelderara men and women alike wearing gold chains, big gold rings, and large gold earrings for the women.

On the right-hand side, placed more marginally and with fewer visitors, several women dressed in subdued colours and dark scarves were selling garments that looked nothing like the Kelderara outfits and seemed identical to the peasant garb exhibited within the museum: white shirts, long white gowns with coloured embroidery, dark scarves and so on. The asking prices for these items did not exceed €20 each. Across from these women, woodcarvers wearing dark trousers and coats and black hats were selling wooden spoons, bowls and pots (see Figure 1.2). Unlike the Kelderara, these participants did not conform to popular depictions of Roma. I identified them from the official brochure as possibly Rudara.

The live demonstrations at the fair were part of the Programme of Revaluing Traditional Roma Crafts, which brought 'traditional' crafts and craftspeople to the Museum of the Romanian Peasant. The fair brochure identified the live demonstrations as a first stage in a larger programme designed to adapt traditional Roma crafts to the demands of the market economy and 'improve tools, working techniques and product development' (Roma Fair Guide 2002, 1) – a possible survival strategy, and an avenue for the development of the larger Roma community: 'Furthermore, the utilitarian character of these crafts could undergo a shift, in the sense of acquiring an artistic character endowed with an ethnic marker, and thus become a form of reassessment of Roma cultural heritage and an affirmation of Roma identity' (Roma Fair Guide, 2002, 2). The brochure listed the following occupations, with illustrations: blacksmiths, coppersmiths (Kelderara), silver- and goldsmiths, welders, woodcarvers (Rudara), brick makers, tanners, comb makers, brush makers, bear handlers, horse traders (Lovara), fiddlers and magicians. The fair itself featured coppersmiths, silversmiths, woodcarvers, magicians and fiddlers.

I asked one of the woodcarvers about his occupation and showed him the brochure. He told me that he was not really a Rom, but welcomed the opportunity to sell his work at the fair. I asked one of the women selling the peasant-style costumes about the shirts, skirts and gowns on display in front of her. She said that she was a Rudari, not a Romni or Ţiganca, and that she had inherited the clothes, but she was not sad about putting them up for sale as long as she made good money from them. She said that if she told people she was a Rudari, few would understand who she was; and rather than risk being taken for a Ţigancă, she preferred to be mistaken for a Romanian peasant.

Economic differences among the participants were reflected not only in their attitudes towards Roma identification, but also in their self-confidence and market knowledge. The common denominator 'Roma' covered multiple groups that engaged in the so-called traditional occupations listed in the brochure. The presentation of the live demonstrations as part of a fair with merchandise for sale favoured some occupations and Roma groups over others. The simple garments of the Rudara failed to live up to expectations of authenticity and attracted less visitor attention. Kelderara showed the most distinctive features that 'branded best' in relation to the commodification of ethnicity in neoliberal capitalism (Comaroff and Comaroff 2009). Indeed, Kelderara metonymically replace the common denominator 'Roma' in popular perceptions: their costumes and artefacts are the most recognizable and most cited in other instances of identity commodification, from Gypsy soaps to music and ethnic chic. At the fair the Kelderara clothing underwent the shift mentioned in the brochure, from utilitarian objects to artworks, and sold successfully – not simply as ethnic 'Roma' markers, but as ethnicity itself.

The Kelderara artefacts and products that enjoyed the most success at the fair became ethnocapital, a means of both self-construction and sustenance (Comaroff and Comaroff 2009). Whereas visitors inside the museum had to wait to reach the museum shop to purchase merchandise, at the fair they could buy directly from the stalls. This process, which combined recognition as a minority with consumption in the marketplace, reflected identity formation processes during post-socialism. Heritage represents culture named and projected into the past, and simultaneously the past congealed into culture (Kirshenblatt-Gimblett 1998, 149). This understanding of culture equally pervaded social programmes that sought to revive the utilitarian character of traditional occupations along with training for other types of income-generating activities, as I show in Chapter 3.

The Roma themselves are absent from official histories in Romania, and for them the past is veiled by their construction as living in a continuous present, without care or concern for the past. Recognizable, lucrative stereotypes facilitate the continued forgetting of Roma history. As the Comaroffs show, 'identity, from this vantage, resides in recognition from significant others, but the type of recognition, specifically, expressed in consumer desire' (Comaroff and Comaroff 2009, 10). The incorporation of Roma culture as ethnocapital through its most recognizable and distinctive aspects has not only responded to market demand, but has also become compatible with ethnic nationalism in Romania through commodification.

Offered temporary shelter inside and outside the museum, which told the story of the ethnic nation and its folklore, the fair exceeded national paradigms. Both indoor and outdoor events at the fair were temporarily hosted by the 'archive', represented by the museum itself – from which the Roma had been excluded, even while elements of Roma culture had been appropriated. The place of the museum was anchored in hegemonic narratives supported by the state, whereas the fair was a temporary space.[2] For those who cared to listen and pay attention to the contradictions in the ostensibly seamless narrative of the museum, the fair wrote minor history by combining the archive and the repertoire, using archival evidence of Roma history while foregrounding the living cultures of diverse Roma.

The Rudara objects and costumes were less successful in the marketplace than the Kelderara because the Rudara artefacts looked similar to the Romanian peasant outfits displayed inside the museum. While the museum's hosting of the fair emphasized the distinction between what was inside (the Romanian peasants and their traditions) and what was outside (the Roma and their occupations and costumes), the Rudara disrupted this clear separation dictated by normative monoethnic performativity, and made apparent the arbitrariness of official definitions of the Romanian folk versus Roma culture. The display of almost identical items inside the museum and outside at the fair, under different denominations and prices, was thus a strong statement about the similarities between some Roma (such as Rudara) and Romanian peasants, and about the processes of cohabitation and mutual influence over centuries. Rather than inserting a rupture between Romanian peasants and Roma craftspeople in the guise of Self and Other, the Rudara and their costumes suggested a continuum along which different ethnic identities could be placed and contextually self-identified, always in relation to one another.

The Museum of the Romanian Peasant as an institution has excluded any other ethnicity and established a monocultural history of the Romanian nation. A minor history approach reveals precisely how multiplicity and multivocality – lived experience in a multicultural context – have been translated into a univocal narrative of the nation at the museum.

Minor Histories: From Slavery to the Holocaust

The speech cited at the opening of this chapter is illustrative of a more widespread attitude among the Romanian political class towards the Roma minority: the formal embrace of European policies on Roma on the one hand, and the absence of their practical application on the other. More specifically, the speech reflects the treatment of Roma history, where the acknowledgment and discussion of little-known aspects such as the Holocaust or Roma slavery do not lead to a change in national paradigms based on ethnicity. Similarly, legislative changes to end discrimination against Roma have not altered national institutions and their discriminatory practices. The President's plea for EU money at the end of his speech indicates an expectation that, as far as he was concerned, the Roma in Romania were the EU's responsibility.

President Băsescu's speeches over the years reflect the evolution of some sections of the political class's attitude in Romania. The post-socialist diversity discourse, a result of Romania's EU negotiations, slowly gained traction in political rhetoric and reflected a change in direction for some politicians, from inflammatory rhetoric regarding Roma to a more 'politically correct' attitude. Many journalists viewed Băsescu's 2007 Roma Holocaust speech with suspicion as a pre-election campaign manoeuvre, with the photo shoot featuring the President flanked by the three survivors, politicians from the Roma Party, and Roma King Florin Cioabă, a Kelderara leader from the Sibiu region. Journalists reminded the public that only a few months previously the President had called a female journalist a 'stinking Țigancă' because she had insisted on getting an answer from him in an unsolicited interview. Faced with international pressure, the President apologized for using an inappropriate phrase in public, but made no mention of the racial slur or sexist remark. Roma NGOs considered the apology inappropriate.[3] A few years before this incident, when Băsescu was Mayor of Bucharest, he called for Roma to be placed in ghettoes outside cities.[4] These examples show that politicians' convenient adoption of a progressive rhetoric has entailed little in the way of treating Roma as equal citizens.

In 2010 the Romanian Senate debated a proposal by Roma activist and scholar Vasile Ionescu and the Roma Party to mark the end of Roma slavery with an annual commemoration day and to include Roma slavery as a topic on the general school curriculum. The senators – all of them non-Roma – rejected the proposal. (In fact, Senator Paul Hasoti proposed 'Țigan' as an ethnonym to be used instead of 'Roma'. He claimed it was not a pejorative term, as it meant 'alien' and could equally be found in other languages.[5])The Romanian Senate's initial rejection of the emancipation commemoration day is a reflection of the privilege of the majority and the refusal to grant Roma the right to define themselves. Eventually the proposal was accepted and passed into law in March 2011, and 20 February became Emancipation Day. Roma activists annually celebrate Emancipation Day with commemorations and public events. Like the Roma Fair, these events tell a story that is uncomfortable and incompatible with the logic of monoethnic nationalism. However, these public events address and engender growing counterpublics that do not share the nationalist paradigm. As long as they take place in public spaces tolerated and sanctioned by the state, these events' radical potential can be either heeded or ignored, depending on the participants' perspectives. As Floya Anthias (1998) has argued in a British context, the true test of multiculturalism is not adding 'cultures' devoid of historical and social context, but renouncing hegemonic symbols and paradigms. For non-Roma in Romania, the true test of inclusivity is the confrontation with the self beyond binary definitions of Self and Other, and the willingness to listen to counternarratives that might be uncomfortable or seem inflammatory at first.

Despite the President's urging (cited at the opening of this chapter) that schools should teach about the Roma Holocaust and slavery, only Roma students learn about them. In general, the curriculum teaches optional courses on Roma language and culture to Roma students only. Unlike in Hungarian and German schools, where the whole curriculum is taught in the respective language, Roma students are taught mainly in Romanian. Despite recent publications and the reappraisal of Antonescu's role in Romanian history, the curriculum does not teach the fact that the Romanian state was responsible for the deportations of Roma and Jews from Romanian territories. For example, during an International Roma Day celebration I attended in 2008, the exhibition outside the performance hall displayed documents about the Holocaust and explained that the German state had sent Roma to concentration camps; the Romanian state was not mentioned. Furthermore, only Roma students attended the celebration. Discussions of Roma slavery are equally controversial as those of the Holocaust, if not even more so, because in the case of slavery it is difficult to shift the blame onto other nations: the owners of Roma slaves were Romanians – royals, monasteries and nobles. Collective accountability is absent from national history narratives, where the victimization and resistance of the nation are the main motif.

A focus on Roma history as minor history entails undoing victimized images of the monoethnic nation and breaking open the binaries inherent in its construction. There is no centralized place, in the sense of an institutionalized location (de Certeau 1984), for writing Roma history, even within one country; but the many Roma communities' diverse perspectives are often seen as arising from their own lack of unity and coherence, rather than from a lack of centralized institutions. For example, the presence of different words in Romani for the Holocaust, such as 'Porrajmos' ('the Devouring') (Hancock 2006), also spelled by some Roma as 'Pharrajimos' (Bársony and Daróczi 2008) or 'Samudaripen' ('Murder of All') (Cioabă 2006), point to the many perspectives from which Roma history is written, and reinforce the importance of considering national and transnational perspectives simultaneously when discussing these events.

Roma activists, artists and intellectuals have published oral histories and archival research and created documentaries and artworks that break the silence on Roma history, challenging national histories that present the Romanian nation as a victim of the Nazis, Communists or earlier empires while excluding Roma and Jews. Oral histories and testimonies have revealed the marginalization and neglect of survivors upon their return home from concentration camps and other places of deportation after World War II. Prominent Roma poet and activist Luminiţa Cioabă (2006), in an oral history project with Roma

Holocaust survivors, has shown that many survivors did not have the know-how to successfully apply for the compensation to which they were entitled.

Despite the fact that the complex history of and around World War II has been reappraised and rewritten many times, including after 1989, the Roma Holocaust is little known, and not only in East Central Europe. Across Europe, the Roma Holocaust – a result of 'racial science' and an attempt to completely annihilate the Roma during Nazism – was the most extreme moment in a long history of Roma marginalization. The 1935 Nuremberg racial laws involved 'mixed' Gypsies' incarceration and sterilization on the one hand, and 'pure' Gypsies' group resettlement and 'species preservation' in special camps on the other. Prisoners in the separate Gypsy camp at Auschwitz were assigned the most debilitating labour (Trumpener 1992, 855). In Romania, one of Germany's allies during World War II, authorities implemented similar anti-Roma policies, including the deportation of 25,000 Roma to Transnistrian labour camps after confiscation of their belongings. The deported included all nomads and the majority of sedentary Roma. Those who survived the harsh camp conditions returned to Romania after the war (Achim 1998).

In East Central Europe, national narratives reproduce binaries of Self versus Other, binaries exacerbated by fascist and Communist ideologies. In Romania, Communist-era World War II historiography focused on the anti-Nazi victory; since the fall of Communism, history has been rewritten with a strong anti-Communist ethos. The reshuffling of hero/villain roles between Communists and Nazis after World War II conveniently displaced any blame from the 'nation' while portraying it as the victim of either of the two extremist ideologies. The new heroes of the nation after 1989 were anti-Communists or local fascists who may have fought against Communism, such as Marshal Antonescu, who ordered the deportation of Roma and Jews in Romania. Pressure from Jewish communities has put an end to what was becoming a national admiration of Antonescu, who sent tens of thousands of Jews and Roma to their deaths.

The pictorial display inside the museum at the 2002 Roma Fair, 'Între o Del și o Beng', was an exercise in NGO historiography. It aimed to offer 'an image-based excursion through the material and spiritual aspects of Roma culture in its happy or miserable interaction with Romanian culture, from social fracture to resolidarization and intercultural dialogue' (Jurnalul Național, 2002, 1). The display included exoticized representations of Roma by non-Roma. Such bohemian representations of Gypsies need to be approached cautiously, and to be treated as artistic conventions rather than as historical referents. In the nineteenth century, Gypsies became a favourite topic for Western artists, who projected onto them their own condition as outsiders in an increasingly mercantile society (Brown 1985). Romanian artists joined this trend, portraying exotic and beautiful Țigănci who were often presented as lustful and oversexualized; some of these portraits featured in the exhibition. The oversexualized and idealized images of Roma women on display were also similar to current representations in Gypsy soaps on television.

Through an invocation of the past, this display at the fair offered a critical analysis of such representations by juxtaposing them with historical documents about slavery and the Roma Holocaust. From a minor history perspective, the juxtaposition of Roma representations by non-Roma with historical documents about slavery and the Holocaust cuts across the forgetting of Roma history and critiques the stereotypical representations of Roma. However, by exercising their hegemonic ignorance, visitors could still enjoy the consumption of Roma culture and images that complied with neoliberalism and globalization and that maintained the citizenship gap for Roma.

Minor Histories and Social Etymologies: 'Țigani' and Slaves

Through its name – 'Mahala și Țigănie' ('Slums and Gypsydom') – the Roma Fair signalled that it brought together low and high culture, by bringing the slums and Gypsydom to the centre, and thus implying a reversal in the ordering of centre and periphery within the city of Bucharest. 'Mahala și Țigănie' indexed the social etymology of two words, both of which are derogatory in Romanian today. 'Mahala', a Turkish word, initially meant a Turkish district or quarter, and later became a synonym for 'slum' with an Orientalist undertone. 'Țigăn/ie' is used negatively in the Romanian language to imply a place or a group characterized by disorder and chaos, irrespective of the ethnicity of its inhabitants.

The organizers of the fair were inviting the audience to rethink the meanings of these words within the precincts of a museum that had erased the histories they represented (Țigani, like all other ethnic minorities, had been absent from the museum; and both 'Țigani' and 'mahala' were associated with negative foreign cultural influences, from the Roma and the Middle East respectively). However, depending on the participants' perspectives, the hegemony of ethnonationalism in the museum and the commodification of Roma cultural elements under neoliberalism framed this project in ways that threatened to undermine its radical potential.

'Țigan' meant 'slave' in Moldavia and Wallachia until 1856, and the terms were used interchangeably until slavery was abolished in the second half of the nineteenth century. The territories of Moldavia and Wallachia, part of today's Romania, were the only European region – at least from the fifteenth century onwards – where Țigani were slaves.[6] These histories continue to be silenced or perfunctorily addressed, and for these reasons the derogatory meaning of the word is unleashed when non-Roma choose to call Roma 'Țigani', a term that has preserved its connotations of lower social status into the present day. Today the social etymology of the term is rarely discussed, yet it continues to be used by non-Roma, and even prescribed as an alternative to the ethnonym 'Roma', as mentioned above. In what follows I will trace the social etymology of the term and uncover the 'histories that have found quiet refuge' in it (Stoler 2009, 35).

Although the initial migration of Roma from India and the Middle East approximately 1,000 years ago is a more or less generally accepted hypothesis, their arrival in the Romanian territories from the Balkans and the origins of slavery represent points of contention in Romanian historiography, and by extension in Romanian politics. Different theories exist in Romania as to whether Roma were slaves before or became enslaved after their arrival in the Romanian territories. Non-Roma Romanian historian Viorel Achim (1998) argues that Roma were slaves in medieval Bulgaria and Serbia, before they entered Romanian territories. Non-Roma historian Nicolae Grigoraş, on the other hand, maintains that Roma who migrated to Wallachia and Moldavia became enslaved after their arrival. Some free Roma even sold themselves after crossing the border into Wallachia in order to pay their debts, or else became enslaved by marrying slaves (Grigoraş 2000, 79). Roma scholar Nicolae Gheorghe refutes the thesis that Roma had slave status prior to their arrival in the Romanian territories. He argues that this hypothesis attempts to shift the blame for the Roma's marginalization and to characterize it as an innate condition (Gheorghe 1983, 15).

Beyond these controversies about the origins of Roma slavery, it is undisputed that Roma were the individual property of the crown, the nobility (*boyars*) or the monasteries, and they appeared on property inventories alongside cattle and goods in Moldavia and Wallachia (Mircea 2000, 61). Whether their owner was the crown, a noble or a monastery, slaves were always at the mercy of their owners, and potentially subject to any kind of mistreatment except killing. Documents legalizing the donation or purchase of a slave were as official as any other property act of the time. For the dominant class under Romanian feudalism, slavery was a stable and solid institution strengthened by Church support. The princes and nobles who were slave owners endowed monasteries with large numbers of slaves and thus gained these religious institutions' endorsement of slavery. Monastery slaves were the most numerous and the most oppressed (Grigoraş 2000, 85).

The first documents to attest to the existence of Roma slavery date from the fourteenth century for Wallachia and the fifteenth century for Moldavia. Grigoraş argues that Roma slavery originated with the enslavement of captives during the wars against Tatars; although initially slaves were named 'Tatars' – a term gradually replaced with 'Ţigani' – Grigoraş contends that the slaves had always been Roma. A relatively small number of Roma came to the Romanian territories from east of the Denester River, where fights with the Tatars took place. Most Roma arrived in Wallachia and Moldavia in the fourteenth century by crossing the Danube to the north, because of wars in the territories of present-day Bulgaria and Serbia. When they entered Romanian lands they became slaves and property of the crown because of legislation regarding Țigani (Grigoraș 2000, 77).

Roma were considered foreigners, and their situation differed from that of local serfs, who were destitute and often tied to the land. During slavery, laws upheld strict distinctions between slaves and free people through the regulation of mixed marriages. Free people who married slaves became slaves, and the offspring of mixed marriages were born slaves (Grigoraș 2000). The categories 'slave' and 'serf' distinguished between slaves, serfs and free persons, and the policing of the boundaries between these categories ensured the maintenance of the institutions of slavery and serfdom.

Historian Viorel Achim (1998) lists five different Roma groups during slavery, groups that have maintained the same or similar denominations in the present. Goldsmiths, later known as Rudara, were the property of the prince, and over time had to give up working with gold, which was scarce, in favour of woodcarving. Lingurara, or spoon makers, also fabricated wooden objects, and were the property of either the prince or nobles. Ursara, or bear handlers, were nomads who belonged to the crown. Layesh, also known as Kalderash or Kelderara, were coppersmiths and the property of either nobles or monasteries (Achim 1998, 75). Most Kelderara were nomads, and were allowed to wander as long as they paid their dues to their overlord. In summer they travelled across the country selling various metal household items to villagers. In winter they withdrew near forests and lived in huts. Because Kelderara interacted frequently with the majority population, they were often perceived as the authentic Țigani. Vatrash, the most numerous group, were agricultural workers and the property of either nobles or monasteries. Many of them lost the nomadic aspects of Roma life and became sedentary, tied to the land. From among them came the musicians renowned for fiddle-playing (Achim 1998, 78). Significant status differences among these groups existed during slavery: the Layesh, including Kelderara, had more freedom as craftspeople and were better off than the Vatrash; among the latter, fiddle-playing was the most prestigious occupation; Roma chiefs, who negotiated between their groups and the Romanian masters, had a higher status than the average slave.

In the early 1830s, the first attempts to free the Roma slaves came from intellectuals who had studied in the West and who, under the influence of Western ideas, deemed slavery anachronistic for a small new nation aspiring to European status. In Moldavia and Wallachia, Romanian abolitionists Vasile Alecsandri and Mihail Kogălniceanu criticized slavery as an outdated practice. In his 1837 nonfiction text about Roma, written in French and intended for a Western audience, Kogălniceanu described the tenuous distinction between peasants and Țigani, specifically the Vatrash. Because the Vatrash were sedentary and had lost their language and customs, Kogălniceanu referred to their assimilation into the peasant population:

The Vatrash are today more civilized than the peasants and deserve that their masters should finally confer on them a freedom of which they are worthy. Boyars have the right to free them and many, those enlightened with the brilliance of civilized Europe, use this privilege in not few circumstances, re-establishing the rights that nature has bestowed on all humans. (Kogălniceanu 1837 [2000], 248)

Kogălniceanu decried Europeans' lack of concern with the slave problem and hoped to raise an interest which:

unfortunately, will certainly only be temporary, because that is how Europeans are! They form philanthropic societies to abolish slavery in America, while in the heart of their continent, in Europe, there are 400,000 Ţigani slaves and 200,000 more lost in the darkness of ignorance and barbarism! And no one cares to civilize this people. (Kogălniceanu 1837 [2000], 234)

The cause of emancipation intersected with that of nineteenth-century Romanian nationalism: intellectual nobles such as Alecsandri and Kogălniceanu militated for freedom for the Roma from their Romanian masters at the same time as they supported a Romanian nation independent of the empires – Russian and Ottoman – that had ruled it for centuries. The nationalist game began in the mid nineteenth century with competing claims over the territories of Transylvania, Bessarabia and Bucovina. Following the 1848 revolutions in Austria, Hungary and much of Western Europe, Wallachian and Moldavian revolutions occurred that same year. As social historian Daniel Chirot (1978, 111) shows, the goals of the 'national bourgeois' revolutions were to end foreign domination – specifically by the Ottomans and Russians – and to create a modern nation-state. This was one of the first attempts to consecrate the Romanian nation. The revolutionaries' emphasis was mostly nationalist and political, rather than social or economic. The peasantry they chose to represent the nation and demonstrate its traditions lived in extremely precarious conditions, while Roma were still enslaved. Joint Russian–Ottoman military action crushed the revolution, and Russia remained Wallachia and Moldavia's protector, while the Ottoman Empire continued to be the nominal overlord.

The abolition of slavery in the two principalities was a twenty-year process that ended in 1856. Initially the princes of Moldavia and Wallachia issued laws to free the slaves they owned, only later freeing those who were private property. Owners could receive an amount of cash in redemption for their freed slaves. The abolition of slavery had political but few economic consequences for Ţigani, according to Achim: even when they were given small plots of land, they found the taxes and responsibilities that came with them overwhelming, and allegedly preferred to revert to their situation as slaves. The assimilation of the Roma population increased after the abolition of slavery and became even stronger in the late nineteenth and twentieth centuries, especially for the Vatrash (Achim 1998, 56).

The synonymy between 'Ţigan' and 'slave' in the Romanian language left deep traces in the racialization of inferior social status in Romania, a process that continues today. In 2007 the Romanian government instituted a Committee for the Study of Slavery, modelled on similar committees for the study of the Holocaust and of Communism. However, the Romanian Senate's discussions of Roma slavery and the disputes within the Committee for the Study of Slavery revealed strong opposition to any critical assessment of the history of Roma slavery. Despite the historical evidence, some non-Roma senators strongly rejected the argument that Roma were not born enslaved outside the territories of today's Romania. This resistance to a critical appraisal of Roma slavery reflected a refusal to address the history of the Romanian territories through lenses other than the nationalist one, which celebrates heroes and decries the subjugation by successive empires of the small Romanian nation *avant la lettre*. The argument that the crown and other institutions in Moldavia and Wallachia had actively enslaved Roma, and that the institution of slavery was specific to those territories, contradicted the narrative of victimization of the Romanian nation.

As discussed earlier in this chapter, during the 2010 Senate debate about the declaration of Emancipation Day, politicians used the construction of Roma as foreign as a justification for proposing the ethnonym 'Ţigani' instead of 'Roma'. The insistence of non-Roma senators on defining Roma, and their attempts to legislate distinctions between Roma and non-Roma, maintained the racialized logic of Ţigani as Other. As I show in Chapter 5, non-Roma take the liberty of naming Roma 'Ţigani' on national television, even when the latter reject this ethnonym. The symbolic violence of this renaming is obscured and trivialized by claims that Roma use the term themselves. Non-Roma's use of this term to name Roma symbolically excludes Roma from the prerogatives of citizenship, and represents an imposition of racial privilege.

The Roma and Romanian Nationalism

The invention of a folk, the imposition of a standard language, the claim over a national territory, and the naturalization of 'imagined communities' were all part of the nationalist projects that swept throughout Europe and Latin America in the second half of the nineteenth century, as Benedict Anderson shows (1983). In this section I discuss the Romanian nationalist project in relation to Roma in two ways: first, by showing that Roma stand out from other ethnic groups and minorities across Europe, in that they did not go through this process in the nineteenth century; and second, by showing the changing role of the Roma in the development of Romanian nationalism.

Roma do not have a territory to claim as exclusively theirs, and their Indian origins have not engendered a 'return to the motherland' type of nationalism. The ethnic nationalisms hegemonic in the region do not help us to understand how Roma relate to their homelands. Similarly, the focus during post-socialism on 'distinct cultures' erases how Roma and other ethnicities have interacted across centuries. The 2002 Roma Fair made this process visible through the presence of Rudara, as I have demonstrated above.

The relationship between Roma and the development of Romanian nationalism has changed since the nineteenth century. While in the mid nineteenth century Romanian nationalism was a subaltern cause, just like the emancipation of Roma slaves, after Romanian independence the two causes were no longer congruent. Many nineteenth-century abolitionist-nationalists predicted a seamless transition of the Roma into the Romanian nation post-emancipation and post-independence and did not foresee that Roma would continue to be marginalized in the new nation. As Étienne Balibar (1991, 54) argues: 'racism is not an "expression" of nationalism, but *a supplement of nationalism* or more precisely *a supplement internal to nationalism*' (emphasis in original). While Balibar focuses on Jews as the inside Others and fails to mention Roma, Roma fulfilled the same role – albeit from a different place in the social order. As ethnic nationalism essentialized identities into Self and Other, the Ţigani served as the abject Other, despite the abolition of slavery, as Roma were the most impoverished in society.

In the early twentieth century, Roma were extremely heterogeneous. Some groups maintained a nomadic lifestyle, while others became more or less integrated in rural or urban settings. Several groups preserved their crafts, often considered Roma specialities, such as tinkering and woodcarving but with the advent of industrialization, Roma lost their monopoly over crafts and attempted to respecialize. Some received small land plots after the land reform of 1918–1920, a process that accelerated Roma assimilation and by the end of World War I traditional Roma crafts had almost completely disappeared. In urban areas, Roma used their skills in industry and construction, while in the countryside they worked as unskilled labourers on collective farms (Achim 1998, 156). The collection of recyclables and trading on the black market constituted alternative survival strategies for some Roma. It is therefore ironic, given the almost complete extinction of traditional crafts, that the focus of current EU policies for Roma is on the revival of these crafts, as testified by the Programme of Revaluing Traditional Crafts at the 2002 Roma Fair. This is problematic because it facilitates coercive mimeticism, in this case the association of authentic Roma with certain skills and occupations.

Nationalism remained a powerful ideology in Romania under socialism as the country metamorphosed 'from capitalist colony into socialist satellite' (Verdery 1991, 73). The situation of the Roma did not improve politically, and state propaganda denied their plight completely. As far as ethnic minorities were concerned, Communist ideology attempted to erase differences by drawing on the general claim that all people were equal. The phrase 'cohabitating nationalities' replaced the term 'minorities'; however, Roma were not recognized among them. Roma were not seen as an ethnic minority, but as a social condition to be overcome; assimilation policies regarding Roma aimed to change their lifestyle and turn them into 'good' Romanians, full citizens of the socialist state.[7] The rest of the population resented them for supposedly benefiting from what official propaganda claimed were social policies intended for Roma.

The socialist era was a period 'of increasing "proletarianisation" and in spite of continuing discrimination they [Roma] were able to benefit from regular wages to improve their social situation, by building new and better houses and sending their children to school' (Guy 2001, 10). Roma activists later emerged from among these children. Some Roma fared better during socialism than in its aftermath, because the centralized socialist economy needed their unskilled labour: working-class Vatrash and other settled Roma experienced a relative improvement in their situation during socialism. However, socialist policies affected Roma groups differently. The restructuring of the economic system post-1989 resulted in the closure of large state-owned plants and the privatization of collective farms, which left many Roma unemployed. Roma elites, on the other hand, whose fortunes had been confiscated by the state during socialism were able to reclaim their possessions after 1989.

The Museum of the Romanian Peasant reiterates the structures of nationalism that circulated throughout Europe from the nineteenth century onwards. While legislation had maintained the distinction between Țigani and free people during slavery, the nationalist project institutionalized the appropriation, iconization and erasure (Irvine and Gal 2000) of Roma culture at the same time as it constructed an idealized Romanian folk. In 1906, when the museum was constructed, the peasants were disenfranchised and at the mercy of landowners: a peasant uprising, known as the 1907 rebellion, ended in bloodshed. The search for an authentic folk, part of the building of ethnonations, was premised on an idea of the folk as distanced in time, remote from contemporary urban working classes and peasants alike. Cultural difference was constructed in the service of nationalism to distinguish popular and mass culture from folk and elite cultures (Bendix 1997, 48). The Romanian folk incorporated and appropriated numerous Roma elements, while Roma culture was erased. Peasants became icons of the nation, and the Roma its abject Other, as Țigani. However, as Chirot (1978, 120) argues, 'the very peasant class that was supposed to be the bearer of tradition was a nineteenth century creation, since before that time rural villagers were more pastoralist than agricultural'.

The Museum of the Romanian Peasant became the Museum of the Communist Party during socialism, when interest in folk authenticity waned.

Ethnology and folklore were relegated to the bottom of the pile, as a new socialist folklore, reflecting Communist realities and peasants' progress in the new collective agricultural institutions, became the focus of national representations. Dance groups and musicians had to follow this new trend, with national contests such as Cântarea României supposed to represent the best and most relevant socialist folklore. One of the lasting effects of assimilation policies during socialism was the erasure of Roma from the world of arts and culture, and the complete denial of Roma culture.

Post-1989 the museum was given a makeover and returned to its original function under the leadership of artist Horia Bernea. Overturning the culture-as-glass-case paradigm, Bernea created the museum's current postmodernist outlook, and maintained its focus on the Romanian peasant as emblem of the nation. This ideological direction has remained unchanged since the museum's inception, despite the different inflections and definitions of the Romanian peasant across the last century (Mesnil 2006). Inside the museum, peasant artefacts and garments are sold for exorbitant prices, targeting foreign tourists.

The displays inside and outside the museum at the 2002 Roma Fair revealed the shift from socialist folk ideologies to the post-socialist focus on authenticity. The Romanian folk costumes inside the museum – advertised as authentic and expensive when they were for sale in the museum shop – were proof of the changing face of the Romanian peasant as symbol of the nation, mobilized in institutions such as the Museum of the Romanian Peasant and backed by state support. Tellingly, as I walked around the courtyard at the 2002 Roma Fair, I noticed several museum workers selling, out of cardboard boxes, folk costumes that I was told had been used by folk dance groups during socialism. Discarded and devalued as lacking 'authenticity' because of their Communist mass-produced origin, these costumes sold for ten or twenty times less than items inside the museum.

Most of the audience at the fair focused on those who for many counted as the 'authentic' Roma: the colourfully clad Kelderara, the picturesque silversmiths, and the gold-clad magician. Nonetheless, the fair created a space for cultural exchange between Roma and non-Roma that blurred the boundaries set up within the museum and provided an opportunity to rethink the exclusions within the officially recognized national folklore. For example, the music and dance performances in the museum courtyard included belly dancing and the music of the band Mambo Siria, who came from a village where allegedly there were no Roma. This demonstrated the circulation and multiplicity of musical and dance genres beyond those considered authentic at the museum. Music and performance, the fields for which Roma were best known, have been appropriated, and Roma seen as mere 'carriers' of national folklores that are not theirs. Romanian musicological discourse has perpetuated this view of Roma musicians for a long time. Romanian musicologist Viorel Cosma (1996), in a work dedicated to the history of Roma musicians, acknowledges their musical talent and claims they have contributed to the spreading of Romanian national folklore. Cosma explains that Roma musicians' repertoire in the past would have been the result of borrowings between Roma and indentured peasants. Because both serfs and slaves suffered marginalization, similar songs circulated among them, 'songs of lamentation, pain, hatred for injustice, folk dances, ballads, haiduc songs' (Cosma 1996, 22). He posits that the majority of Wallachia and Moldavia's musicians were Roma who played the panpipe, fiddle, cimbalom and cobza, a small plucked lute (Garfias 1984, 87). The peasants, on the other hand, played the fluier, a flute blown at one end, and three other woodwind instruments of different sizes. According to Cosma, Roma borrowed these musical forms from the Romanian peasants, and made them known to the public at large through their specific interpretations and their mastery of precise techniques. Cosma sees Roma as instruments in the circulation of Romanian folk songs, with no contribution to musical content. His evidence suggests, however, that the borrowings could only have been reciprocal and, if nothing else, Roma improvisation and interpretation constituted an important proof of their contribution to the music. Speaking of one of the most famous Roma musicians, Barbu Lăutarul, Cosma (1996, 50) concludes: 'he created a taste for national art, he lifted it to the rank of authentic music, and offered it as a source of inspiration to composers of cultivated music'.[8] This view of the role of the Roma in the dissemination of 'national folklore' reflects the erasure and appropriation of Roma culture that continues today in the absence of designated institutions that might support it.

Conclusion

One television reporter at the 2002 Roma Fair, a young woman, tried on a full Kelderara outfit priced at around €200 and continued her reporting on the fair in this garb, which she found very exciting. Twenty, or even ten, years before it would have been unthinkable to sell these items in Romania at such prices. These objects' entry into the transnational flows of capital and their success with Westerners have raised 'authentic' Roma products to the level of exotic and fashionable objects for Romanians. The products have become part of the commodification and consumption of Otherness, an integral component of global capitalism. After all, only if they identified with a Western lifestyle could wealthy Romanians see Roma as exotic instead of abject Ţigani.

The fair and its television coverage were opportunities for non-Roma visitors to perform and consume exoticism. From this angle, the fair reconfirmed exoticism, focusing on Roma women and their garments as the favourite and most colourful illustration of these stereotypes. But it would be reductive to stop at the hegemonic interpretation of the outdoor displays at the Roma Fair that specularized exotic images and wealth. As I have shown in this chapter, the organizers exceeded this narrow focus with the multiple events of the fair, the event's ironic name, and the focus on NGO historiography. Cultural performances and displays run the risk of imposing standards of authenticity, but the fair exceeded such essentialist understandings through the diversity of its participants and their heterogeneous views. As a simultaneously transnational, national and local event, the fair was an opportunity for Roma activists to critique the operations of the museum and the erasure of Roma history; and, at the same time, the fair reflected the larger international structures that dictated the focus on 'culture', as Romania was negotiating EU membership and opening up to global capital flows and neoliberal democracy. While the fair displayed 'tradition' as the bedrock of Roma culture, in addition to books, films and music performances, it also deconstructed Romanian ethnogenesis and critiqued 'majority culture'. The diverse participants at the fair pointed to multiplicity and complex identities, as opposed to the coercive mimeticism encouraged by the Romanian state.

Thus, as a performative event, the fair could not be reduced to the hegemonic commodification and consumption of Roma culture. However, this did not mean that its overall effect was necessarily counterhegemonic. The physical proximity between Romanian folk objects at the museum and Roma artefacts at the fair allowed their similarities to stand out, and made apparent the institutionally enforced boundaries of nationalism that separated them; but the lack of a permanent site limited the impact of the counterhegemonic aspects of the fair, which remained provisional and tactical in de Certeau's (1984) sense.[9]

Moreover, the pressure from the EU and other international institutions to focus on culture as heritage and 'traditional' occupations was evident at this fair. There were no urban, working-class Roma, because they did not engage in the occupations the fair featured; and the class differences between the Rudara, who were trading in small household wooden objects, and the Kelderara, with their copper vessels and highly priced costumes, also showed that the revitalization of 'traditional' occupations would offer very different opportunities for these two groups, and for Rudara would not bring prosperity. Furthermore, Roma who no longer engaged in such occupations were excluded from the EU-inspired focus.

Funded by NGOs and EU institutions, the fair illustrated the market logic and coercive mimeticism that simultaneously underpin the recognition of Roma culture and maintain the citizenship gap for Roma. The government looked to the EU, NGOs and other donors to support Roma with money other than public funds in Romania. In this sense, Băsescu's plea for more funding for Roma from the EU reflected the outsourcing of minority identity-building in post-socialism at a time when the state had withdrawn most of its financial support for the disadvantaged, many of whom were Roma. The paradigm shift from social concerns about Roma to the recognition of Roma identities reflected the shift from socialism, when the denial of their ethnicity was coupled with aggressive assimilation policies. The withdrawal of state support and the rise of market demand for a distinct Roma culture, under the pressure of both neoliberal capitalism and Romanian nationalism, limited the countercultural work of the fair, where only distinctive and recognizable features of Roma culture received public attention.

Festivals and events similar to the Roma Fair have grown exponentially in number since 2002, and have increasingly followed in the footsteps of the success of Gypsy music abroad. However, this growing commercial success of recognizable Roma artefacts has integrated Roma culture into market capitalism without challenging existing power structures, and has left intact the ongoing marginalization of and racism towards Roma. The 2002 Roma Fair took place in the crucible of Romanian nationalism, and offered a multitude of images of Roma that challenged the supposedly neat distinctions between ethnicities; but in 2015, the Museum of Roma Culture was opened in a marginal location, remote from the centre of Bucharest where the 2002 Roma Fair had taken place. The Romanian public's and politicians' opposition to reappraisals of national history, including engagement with Romanian responsibility for Roma slavery and the Holocaust, reflects the fact that even the formal acknowledgement of Roma culture as deserving a separate dedicated public space required a long and intricate process in Romania.

Notes

1. Hasdeu (2008) provides a compelling reading of a similar event held in 2001 as a carnivalesque parody of the nation.
2. For de Certeau (1984), places have the security of institutionalized support, while spaces are temporary.
3. The Romanian branch of American NGO ActiveWatch (www.activewatch.ro) condemned several controversial statements by the President about Roma.
4. 'Integrarea Romilor in lanul de porumb'. *Cotidianul*, 13 May 2003.
5. Andrea Ghita, 'Ziua Dezrobirii – respinsă de Senatul României', *Acum*, 22 September 2010. http://www.acum.tv/articol/17851/ (last accessed 1 March 2012).
6. In Transylvania, Țigani were not enslaved, but were subjected to imperialist assimilation campaigns that sought to turn them into 'New Hungarians'. Young children were taken away from their families to be raised as 'Hungarians'. The majority of Roma in today's Hungary are Romungre, a category of Roma who have stopped speaking Romani and whose name denotes them as a mixture of Roma and Hungarians. Such categories demonstrate that ethnic identities bear the imprint of continuous exchanges and transformations, and are always in flux rather than static.
7. Michael Stewart (1997, 7) stresses that these policies were unsuccessful because, even when the state employed and settled them, many Roma maintained the lifestyle the Communist Party was attempting to destroy.
8. Similar interpretations are common throughout East Central Europe and the Balkans. Alaina Lemon discusses a similar situation in Russia, where Roma are also seen as lacking culture and as needing Russian culture in order to express themselves. 'Soviet scholars,

for their part, claim that Gypsy choirs became so popular *because* their repertoires contained half-forgotten Russian folk songs and ballads embellished in a "Gypsy style'" (Lemon 2000a, 41).

9. Roma (or at least thus-named) institutions may perpetuate the same traps, or fall into others. Alaina Lemon (2000a, 2001), in her discussion of the Teatr Romen in Moscow, critiques the perpetuation of authenticity criteria, as non-Roma continue to control the representations of Roma; Peter Vermeersch (2008) discusses the Czech Roma museum in Tarnow and its ghettoization.

Chapter 2

Living in the Citizenship Gap

Roma and the Permanent State of Emergency in Pod

Everyone treats us like the lowest of the low because we live here.

—Trilingual Romni, Pod, 2009

No matter how smartly dressed you are, you're always a Țiganca.

—Romni in Pod, 2014

In this chapter I use performance paradigms and ethnographic research to discuss coping mechanisms and survival strategies in conditions of extreme precariousness in Pod, a squatting settlement in Transylvania where several hundred Roma lived within walking distance of a major refuse site. Drawing on my co-performative witnessing (Conquergood, 2001, no page number, Madison 2011, 25) conducted over eleven years, I discuss the everyday performances of citizenship of Pod residents against the structural constraints they faced in Pod and beyond; I show that the diverse community of Roma in Pod, who do not fit official definitions of Roma culture and tradition, are relegated to abject Țigani stereotypes. Pod's social conditions between 2001 and 2012 were a materialization of what I have called the citizenship gap, the de facto non-citizen status of most Roma in Romania.

As an ethnographer, I see my role as bearing witness, making visible the fact that Pod is a result of devastating neoliberalism on nationalist terrain – a toxic mixture that maintained the citizenship gap for Roma. Roma in Pod live in a perpetual state of emergency, in conditions comparable to refugee camps.[1] According to Walter Benjamin (1968), 'the tradition of the oppressed teaches us that the state of emergency in which we live is not the exception, but the rule' and 'not men or man, but the struggling, oppressed class is the depository of historical knowledge'.[2] From the perspective of minor history, Pod shows the continuity of the plight of the Roma under post-socialist neoliberalism.

The perpetual state of emergency in Pod operated through state mechanisms, and was facilitated by state employees who oversaw the violations of human rights that were everyday realities: most residents had no access to social or medical services, lived in inadequate housing with no electricity, water or refuse collection services, had no access to public transport and faced segregation in the education system. The citizens of this community were invisible to local authorities; yet at the same time they were under constant surveillance and hypervisible as Țigani to the police. Thus Roma in Pod experienced a complete version of living in the citizenship gap: Pod was both hypervisible and erased from official maps.

Life as a State of Emergency in Pod

In the years following 1989, Pod received an influx of new residents. Most of them moved to Pod because they had lost their jobs, their homes – most often after being evicted from newly privatized properties – or both. Pod residents had travelled from nearby and distant villages and cities, yet their migration within Romania was erased in media representations, which equated them with the rubbish on the refuse site: the implication was that they had always been and belonged there and were to blame for their own deplorable living conditions. Despite repeated reports and alarm signals from international and local NGOs about the proliferation of internal migrant communities in extra-urban areas such as Pod, the phenomenon of internal migration to such sites has increased in the two decades after 1989. While in the first decade Romanian media reports about such places tended to arouse disbelief, in the following decade Pod and its equivalents across the country became the norm, and no longer made news headlines.

Presented as an insoluble problem in the local media, often with intimations that the residents themselves did not want a solution, Pod, and similar settlements across the country, had ceased to be of interest to foreign journalists. After Romania gained EU membership in 2007, Western media reports about state violence against Roma increasingly focused on Roma migrants in the West. Western media presented Roma migration to Western Europe as economic migration, despite reports about the persistence of discrimination against Roma after 2007. Western media and governments' views on Roma from Romania and Bulgaria changed once they became potential migrants to the West, seeing them as a threat rather than an object of compassion.

Armando

In 2001 I went to Pod to visit Armando, a Rom in his mid twenties whom I had met during a theatre project. He had been living in Pod since 2000, when he had joined his parents and siblings, who had been living there for about ten years.

The stench coming from the nearby refuse site and piles of rubbish around the huts seemed overwhelming on my initial visits to Pod. There were several stray dogs in the community, and the many fires people lit to get rid of rubbish also added an acidic smoke smell to the stench. Armando's parents' hut had a pile of metal scraps out in front, from which his stepfather sorted various types of metal to be sold as recyclables. Some constructions in Pod were entirely made of wood, while others had a more improvised appearance. Armando's family hut was one of the simpler ones, made of recycled wood and other recycled materials. From the outside its walls looked like a patchwork of plastic, wooden planks, cardboard and rubber, held together in a delicate balance. Inside there were two furnished rooms with one window in each. The first room had a bed, a large cupboard filled with household ornaments, a stove, a few chairs and a table. The second room served as both living room and bedroom, with a sofa, a bed, a table and four chairs. A portable black-and-white TV, powered by a car battery, sat on the living room table. Colourful fabrics and carpets, with an insulating layer of plastic underneath, entirely covered the walls inside.

After my first visit to Pod, I kept going back. In the beginning I found the realities in Pod disturbing, while at the same time I was surprised by people's resilience. Every time I went back, Pod did not fail to surprise me. Anger mixed with a developing sense of responsibility made me return. During one of my first visits, I was unconsciously holding a camera, and as Armando and I were walking towards his parents' hut, a man came towards us and started shouting that I was not allowed to use a camera. Only then did I realize my naivety and the offence a camera on display caused in a place that the media, often using photographs taken without permission, had turned into a cliché. I probably looked like one of those journalists. I reassured the Rom and promised not to use my camera unless locals asked me to take pictures of them, as Armando's relatives often did. Sometimes residents would ask me to come back at a later date and take their pictures when they were better dressed, not in their work clothes. Given that most of the locals – adults and children alike – worked on the refuse site, they tended to wear old clothes and often looked unkempt, but they did not want to appear in photos in that way.

Over the eleven years during which I visited Pod, a lot changed in its overall appearance, but little changed in the status and situation of its inhabitants. By the end of the decade, visible signs of prosperity were emerging: a few newly erected brick houses now marked the beginning of the settlement on the main road, and a small number of residents saw significant profits from various recycling activities. However, in 2010 many of the residents were destitute, still lived in the same shacks, and still lacked access to basic services.

Armando's trajectory reflected the fact that some Roma were able to find employment because of newly created jobs, including as school mediators in charge of Roma communities, community nurses and local councillors for Roma issues. Always well dressed, Armando took advantage of some of the opportunities available to ambitious young Roma; however, due to his lack of a university education, the few jobs he had access to were temporary and either poorly paid or voluntary; he never worked on the refuse site. In 2001 he was unemployed, although he volunteered with the Pentecostal association, which had built a church in Pod. He also volunteered as a social mediator, and as a community nurse he distributed medication and first aid and took emergency cases to hospitals in the nearby city. In 2005 he was hired as a school social worker. As a relative newcomer to Pod, he was often challenged by other Roma who considered themselves, or were recognized by others, as community leaders. There was no single leader in Pod, but several Roma who enjoyed respect from different sections of the community. Some residents respected Armando's skills and ability to navigate and speak the language of state institutions and NGOs, while others resented and suspected him for the same reasons.

I went to the landfill site for the first time with Armando and his mother in 2001. In the early years, collecting recyclables at the refuse site was lucrative; by 2010, competition had become keen. In 2001, when Armando, his mother and I walked up the hill to the gate that marked the beginning of the refuse site, the site was guarded, and Pod collectors were working there informally, without protection or supervision. Life was a relentless state of emergency in Pod, as most residents worked in extremely dangerous conditions, tolerated and unacknowledged by both the state and the refuse company. The boss of the local refuse company, who managed the landfill site, claimed that he was helping poor people in Pod to make a living. However, as much as they made a meagre living from recyclables, the collectors prevented the site from overflowing and reduced the amount of refuse.

As we entered through the gate, Armando's mother checked with the guard, and we continued up the hill until the site itself was visible. It looked like an ocean of rubbish, plastic bags and unidentifiable objects and remains piled on top of each other. There were also clear paths that divided the landfill into different sections, and dirt roads on which the trucks arrived. Children and adults alike used hooks to sort through the layers of rubbish and find the coveted recyclables for which recycling centres paid well: non-ferrous metals sold best, followed by glass and paper. The collectors, an army of workers of all ages, headed for the site in the middle of the night to greet the new harvest of refuse that the company's trucks would unload in the early morning. Six of Armando's seven siblings, ranging in age from six to seventeen, collected alongside their parents. Market demand for certain products and price fluctuations influenced the monthly incomes of Pod residents. In one month in 2001 Armando's entire household made the equivalent of the average individual monthly wage in Romania (US$100).

Crows were flying overhead, and smoke was rising here and there on the horizon. Fires were particularly dangerous, as flammable substances in the rubbish could ignite without warning. There were numerous sharp and flammable objects in the unsorted refuse that posed serious dangers. Accidents of the most horrific kind happened on a regular basis A few years after our visit, Armando's mother suffered a head injury while working there, and was left with long-term pain and side effects. One of Armando's brothers died from second-degree burns after an accident on the refuse site. Here Armando describes the death of his brother:

> He died at seventeen, burned. He was completely burned, second-degree burns. His legs had burned, his back, hands, face. His hands, I mean the whole fist, like that, all burned and he was in pain for at least five months. He was working with paint, which he shouldn't have; he shouldn't have played with it. He played with paint that contained a chemical substance; once he made a fire, he threw in the paint – the paint tube – and it blew up. And blowing up, he burned.

He suffered for a few months in hospital before passing away. Armando visited him every day.

The main sources of danger outside the refuse site itself were inappropriate materials used as combustibles, including scrap plastic. Armando's parents' hut burned down to ashes, and they were left with nothing and had to start again from scratch.

> I told you that everything they [his parents] had burned down. All my mum had left was the shorts and T-shirt she was wearing. He [the step-father] was in trousers and a shirt. I had gone to the saltwater baths … I didn't know what was going on here. I could see a thick, black smoke, but I didn't know what it was. When I came home, it was all put out. Ashes. Within two months they put it back in place. With everything, with everything that's inside. Just imagine. They're in debt over their heads … They were left like that; it was the second time they have been left like that. The first time it was during winter. That's when their brother-in-law died. Yes, he died in the fire. That's why when you go by these huts there is an earth mound, with a fence. That's where their hut used to be. And both wife and husband burned alive, at night, on New Year's Eve.

I asked whether the neighbours had heard anything, and why they had not intervened.

> They did, but it was too late. It was at night, but they couldn't put out the fire. The firefighters came, they all came, and their very own mother, can you imagine, collected the ashes of her own child.

People in Pod had become accustomed to catastrophes as part of their everyday existence. Not only were their lives a perpetual state of emergency, but death was also a daily part of their lives.

While Pod residents were invisible vis-à-vis the law and lacked citizenship rights, Pod was hypervisible to and strictly monitored by the police. As performance studies scholar Dwight Conquergood (1997, 355) aptly notes, subordinate groups suffer from both too little and too much visibility: 'Either they are willed to disappear or they are rendered hypervisible within the scopic regimes of power. They are shuttled back and forth between erasure and exposure, being ignored and being exhibited by the ruling classes'. Pod residents' encounters with the state apparatus consisted of surveillance and repression, in violent police raids in their community or at the landfill.

According to several Pod residents, including Armando, police often descended onto the landfill, beat up whomever they found and then left. Roma and human rights NGOs had denounced one of these raids and submitted the case to the European Court of Human Rights. Roza, a Romni, described to me how a Rom from Pod had been attacked on his way home after he had been out selling recycled metal. He had been walking on the path that connected Pod to the main road, across railway tracks – the only way of accessing the closest bus station, which was more than a mile away even with this precarious shortcut.

> Those ones, the Corturari [nomadic Roma], mugged him and beat him almost to death. The police came, the hooded ones, went up there [to the refuse site] to ask who had done it. They said, randomly, that it was someone from here, but he was not guilty, because we knew that he had been here when this happened at the railway crossing. And the police came, the hooded ones, and took this man, and threw him to the ground, like that, without asking him anything. And then we all came out, especially the women, children in our arms, and confronted the police about doing such a thing. We had been here with him when it happened, and we knew he was not guilty. We women, we all came out, and the police did not know what to do.

This was one example where the communities fought back against the police, with success. Most other stories about police abuse did not include resistance to police violence.

Recycling: From Survival to Entrepreneurship

Pod was the result of the neoliberal transition in Romania, which continued institutionalized racism against Roma and maintained a complete citizenship gap for impoverished Roma. However, most media representations of places like Pod lacked any structural analysis of the situation. It was rare to find an accurate description of work in Pod in the media, without an ideological slant that abjected people and turned them into the refuse they collected.

In a 2006 local television programme on the TVR channel about the planned closure of the refuse site and its replacement with an ecological waste disposal site, Pod residents were completely absent. Not only were they absent from the discussion between the boss of the refuse company and another guest, but they were never mentioned during the one-hour discussion. In a spontaneous street interview presented during the programme, a passer-by answered the question 'How will an ecological waste disposal site change our city?' by saying that a number of poor people would lose their livelihoods. He was evidently referring to Pod inhabitants. Surprisingly to me, there was no reaction to this statement in the studio. Not unlike state institutions, the discussants chose to ignore Pod, to make it invisible. As the refuse site was the livelihood of most of the Roma in Pod, its closure would have important consequences for them.

Destitute communities, such as Pod, were a result of two key changes: the withdrawal of universal social security and the disappearance of low-skilled jobs after the fall of Communism; and the recognition of Roma and programmes for them (such as the National Strategy for Improving the Situation of Roma (NSISR)), which did not address the institutionalized racism inherited from Communism. Roma in the countryside were excluded from the redistribution of land during post-socialism (Pons 1999). The post-socialist agrarian reform stipulated the return of property to pre-nationalization owners and collective farm members could receive land even if they had not owned land before collectivization, provided they lived in the relevant town (Pons 1999, 50). Many Roma should have benefited from this law, but in fact very few of them did so, despite having worked on collective farms. In many cases the land reserve was insufficient, and Roma – the last priority on redistribution lists – were left out. Even when the land available would have sufficed, the numerous legal provisions associated with land redistribution dissuaded many Roma from applying, as they often lacked knowledge of how the system worked (Zoon 2001; Pons 1999, 50–51). In urban areas, many Roma had lived in nationalized buildings during socialism, and these properties were returned to their owners after 1989, leaving Roma tenants homeless. Unemployment was another factor driving the growth of Roma migration to Pod; after 1989 a high number of Roma were left unemployed because of the bankruptcy of the former socialist factories and plants and the dismantling of collective farms.

There have been repeated attempts to close the refuse site at Pod and replace it with an environmentally friendly one; every year I heard stories in Pod that it was going to close down. Indeed, before 2007, everyone I spoke to in Pod told me that it would have to close by 2007 when Romania gained EU membership, but it did not do so. When I returned to Pod in 2008, after a year's absence – and after Romania had joined the EU – I expected to find the refuse site closed and people gone. Instead, I found Pod bigger than ever, with large new houses flanking the main road and the number of workers on the refuse site had increased as well. There were at least three different categories of people living and/or working informally on the refuse site: seasonal workers, both Roma and non-Roma, travelling from as far as 500 km away, working through the summer and then returning to their homes; those who collected at the site throughout the year but had not been born there and had primary homes elsewhere; and finally, those born there, including many young people under twenty-five who had spent their entire lives in Pod.

Dumitru and Irina

In 2008 I went back to the refuse site with Armando, who at the time was employed as a social mediator in charge of supporting Roma school students. On the back of his scooter I rode up to and across the landfill to Dumitru and Irina's work headquarters. They were part of an extended family of Romungros in Pod. It was a hot August day, and Irina, a woman in her mid to late thirties, sporting a tan and wearing a spotless summer dress, was looking after her three-month-old daughter inside the hut. There were two couches on either side of the rectangle, a large freezer to the left of the entrance, a TV and DVD player, and a table at the back, between the couches, with coffee, cappuccino packets, tomatoes and canned fish displayed in piles. She offered to make me a cappuccino from a packet, which I accepted. Surprised to find this level of conviviality at the site, I apologized for having come empty-handed.

In front of the hut there were about thirty huge sacks filled with scrap iron, collected by people who had sold them to Dumitru or had traded them for some of the goods displayed on the table. Bare-chested and wearing dusty grey jeans and flip-flops, Dumitru washed his face in a basin outside and came in. He was handling a wad of notes: money from the scrap iron, Irina explained. 'These Țigani', as she called them, collected for Irina and Dumitru and sold the material to them on credit, for what I later realized was less than market price. The 'Țigani' also bought goods from their improvised store, on credit or for cash.

Irina called herself a 'Țiganca', so she was not necessarily looking down on the workers; 'Țigani' indexed familiarity with them for Irina, but also the negative connotations of the word for the majority. Most of the 'Țigani' who worked for Dumitru were either young or elderly. As we walked around the hut, we saw some of them, including two young men I had known for a while. One was Armando's brother, who in 2001 had been a little boy collecting alongside his older siblings. Now he collected on his own and sold his harvest to Dumitru. Dressed in jeans and a T-shirt, and wearing headphones to listen to music, or perhaps just to block the external noise, he was an unexpected sight in this location, among the layers and layers of rubbish. He looked like a flâneur exploring an apocalyptic site in a sci-fi film. Not far from him I saw another young man I vaguely recognized and whose eyes struck me: while Armando's brother seemed partially detached and insulated from the realities around him thanks to the headphones, this young man looked sad, with a sadness that was too deep and resigned for his age. Armando told me that this was Radu, who had danced *dans ţigănesc* at a Christmas party I had attended in Pod in 2003. He was now a grown young man and was working at the site. His family, Armando told me, had moved up to the site from down the valley in Pod.

Mirela

As we walked around the landfill we came across Mirela, who had built a small shelter covered with sheets. There was one space where she worked; beyond another plastic sheet, placed vertically like a separating wall, was another space where her children were playing. I entered beneath the plastic sheet and walked into the children's space, where I sat in an old armchair with worn upholstery of an unidentifiable colour. On the ground, among discarded packaging for instant coffee and cappuccino, there were many small, multicoloured animal toys. The little girl seated next to Mirela was in Year Four at primary school; Mirela's other son, also enrolled in school, was not there. Both children went to mainstream schools, unlike most children in Pod, who attended schools for children with learning disabilities. Mirela explained to me that her husband had left her with four children and nothing else, and she had moved to Pod two years ago. She planned on staying and working there until she could save enough to take care of her children and renovate their house in the countryside. She wanted to leave as soon as she could, as 'this' was not a place to stay, she said. It made more sense for her to collect by herself, she told me; although the earnings were never guaranteed, they might be larger than the small income she would earn from an uncertain job out there. She had obtained a mortgage on a house thanks to money earned on the landfill and with Armando's help. Armando told me: 'When you see someone work hard to achieve something, you feel like helping them'. Armando's mother had not sent her other children to school, and he did not approve.

From Mirela's patch I could see cars with licence plates from other parts of the country, some as far as 300 km away, parked on the landfill site. These belonged to seasonal collectors who would spend a few weeks, even months, up at the site and then leave until the following year. Other people seemed to be even more occasional collectors: one middle-aged woman in a straw hat and rubber boots looked more like a hiker than a Pod resident, yet she was obviously collecting, armed with the usual hooked stick. Different Pod collectors informed me that work had become very competitive, and collectors sometimes fought over access to the trucks that unloaded refuse from the city. Some Pod residents – such as Adam, who had converted to Pentecostalism, and Irina's family – owned small houses or plots of land in other parts of the country, where they were unable to survive due to the lack of jobs and the decline in agricultural production. Others had nothing, not even an ID card.

This visit to the refuse site confirmed for me that informal collection was on the rise instead of subsiding. The presence of seasonal and occasional collectors, some from hundreds of miles away, was a sign that a lack of jobs and poor living standards for the retired and other disadvantaged population groups was making more people turn to collection as a source of income. With the exception of success stories such as that of Dumitru and Irina, who had created an informal business on the site and exploited or – depending on one's point of view – managed the work of others, the site was a place of survival with little hope. Mirela, determined to work on her own and not to depend on the likes of Dumitru and other intermediaries, was another example of fortitude and determination.

Nonetheless, to see young people born in Pod become adults there and work on the refuse site was heartbreaking. While Dumitru boasted to me that he was helping the Ţigani make a living and that they would be lost without him, the fact that he was using their labour and making a profit was difficult to ignore. The dozens and dozens of sacks of recyclables packed and ready to go in front of his tent were witness to his entrepreneurial spirit. Dumitru and his family had arrived in Pod during the previous five years, while Armando's brother and Radu had been born there almost two decades ago. Yet it was Dumitru who had reaped the benefits of their work. Armando's brother's father had recently died, and Radu's father had become very ill and so the two young men made a living selling their collections to Dumitru.

Going back, I parted company with Armando once we reached Pod on his scooter. When we spoke again the following day, he told me that after our visit to the refuse site he had gone home and cried. That was why he did not go there often, he said.

Building a Life in Pod

Adam

There were a few other residents who, like Dumitru, had managed to make a decent living in the environment of Pod, while many others lived hand to mouth, unsure what the next day would bring. In early June 2008 I visited Adam, one of the better-off Kelderara in Pod, to discuss the possibility of the community applying for a grant from the EU-financed PHARE projects to improve the situation of the Roma. Like Dumitru, Adam was one of the leaders of the community and one of its most visible success stories – an exception rather than the norm. There were harsh discrepancies among residents, more visible now with new houses like Adam's flanking and towering over the more modest huts. He proudly showed me his new house, built from scratch with materials collected from the refuse site, he explained, or paid for with money earned on the site. I was speechless after the house tour. In a squeaky-clean bathroom complete with bathtub and flushable toilet, Adam pointed to the tiles covering the floor, all in immaculate condition, and told me they had all been found on the refuse site. A large kitchen opened off the main entrance, followed by a large room featuring a washing machine and other amenities. Two exotic plastic trees in the hallway marked the passage into another living room with a large TV, separated from the kitchen by a glass wall. Adam was keen to legalize his situation on the squatted land, as his house could be torn down any day: like all the other houses in Pod, it had been built without permission. Although most people in Pod lived in improvised shacks, with radically lower living standards than Adam, the house was, nonetheless, a stark contrast to the poverty and dirty homes described in the media.

Adam and I sat down as his wife Maia, also known as Eva, brought us coffee in cups decorated with intricate golden metallic flowers in relief. She also brought two long, straight glasses filled with Coca-Cola. We discussed the specially allocated EU funds for Roma and the competition over housing projects for Roma communities. When I asked Adam if he was interested in formal employment, he answered 'not really'. He told me that collecting recyclables from the site would work for another year or two, four at the most, and afterwards that would be that. He admitted that some people would have preferred to be employed, to have a sense of security; he knew that if they should be evicted from Pod, where they had no legal rights to reside, he could lose the house. As I show in Chapter 3, NSISR grants did not make provisions for settlements such as Pod, even though squatting was a widespread phenomenon among Roma because of their lack of access to adequate housing.

Miki

Some Pod residents' ID papers were not from the local area, and as a result they had no access to social services, healthcare or adequate housing.[3] Other Pod residents lacked ID papers altogether, and as a result their experience with institutions was similar to that of refugees and *sans-papiers*, even though they had been born in Romania and lived there all their lives. The lack of local ID papers was consolidated Pod residents' dispossession and lack of citizenship as local authorities used this to justify their neglect of Pod.

Miki, a gentle and soft-spoken young man in his early thirties, was paperless when I saw him in 2009. He had spent much of his childhood in state institutions, and had ended up in Pod after a visit with friends from out of town. He stayed behind and, as the saying about Pod went, he never left. He built himself a shack and found a partner, but had little hope of better times. Armando had been trying to convince him to reapply for his papers: Miki had left his ID with his friends from out of town, and it had got lost. He needed his birth certificate in order to apply for a new ID, but he was not motivated enough to go to fetch it from out of town, two hours away. Miki seemed resigned, and his attitude was very different from Armando's fighting spirit. The next time I saw him he still had not retrieved his birth certificate. Miki worked assiduously on the refuse site, and the hut he had built was no small achievement for someone who had had no possessions of his own all his life. But I felt that Pod was dangerous for people like him, because as much as it lacked pressures and constraints, for those with no extended family in the neighbourhood it was a place with little hope. While Dumitru and Adam had ties to permanent addresses elsewhere, Miki and other paperless residents had gradually become completely detached from the outside world, their contacts restricted to the settlement, where they often traded collected materials for food and drink from entrepreneurs like Irina, or at the bar in the village nearby.

Vanesa

Vanesa, a Romni in her thirties, lived next door to her brother Lazlo and his wife and child. Most people in Pod lived next to their kin, and several extended families lived there. When I met Vanesa in 2006, several new houses had been built, looking smart on the main road. The community had grown and some had visibly prospered, as testified by the new houses, the absence of rubbish heaps among buildings, and the few cars parked there. Inside the simple-looking wooden house where Vanesa lived with her husband and four children, there were two rooms: a kitchen/living room and a bedroom. They had running water, and the house was equipped with refrigerator and freezer (the newest models available in Romania), a washing machine, a TV, and VHS and DVD players. An electric heater warmed the place, and Vanesa told me that two winters before the other Ţigani's water had frozen inside their houses, but her home had stayed warm. Her house had been insulated, and that was why it was not cold, she explained. 'Look there, at the door,' she said, 'it's not even closed properly and it's not cold'. Vanesa reminisced of better times when she lived in the city. Originally from the countryside, she and her family had lived in rented flats in the city for ten years, a prosperous period for her husband's informal trading. She told me that at that time she used to wear expensive clothes and be covered in gold jewellery:

We used to sleep on cash. That's how I got ahead of all the Romanians. I had a golden cross from here to here [shows length, about a finger long], and golden chains also, from here to here, one on top of another. I had so much gold on my wrist that I had to hold my arm like this to be able to write, because I couldn't otherwise. This is how I would hold my hand [she shows me how she would have to prop her arm on the other hand, because of the multitude of bracelets].

Gold and cash were the only ways Vanesa felt she could 'get ahead' in a social hierarchy where she would always be the last. She and her family had moved to Pod after her brother had lived there for two years, as 'nowadays it's hard to make a living'. She often referred to 'our Romanians who work hard abroad'.

Vanesa told me that people like Adam were fools to build proper brick houses without permission, as they would eventually be evicted and lose everything. The following summer, however, her partner rebuilt their hut into a more imposing wooden structure, even though they did not have permission to build. Their house was not as imposing as Adam's, and this difference reflected Adam's better material situation, which Vanesa confessed she envied. She said that she could not help but remember Adam's humble origins in a village near her own, although she used to be so much better off than him. She made fun of the fact that Adam and his wife now hired servants and used gloves to peel potatoes.

A Romungri, Vanesa did not speak Romani, and she had a strong sense of a modern identity, distinct from traditional Roma. She explained about so-called assimilation:

We are Romungros, Romanianized Țigani, that's what they call us. We don't marry our children young, we're not like that. I wear mini and long skirts. Here there are Țigani who only wear long skirts, to the ground. We're not like that. I recognize a few words, that's all.

As highlighted in the introduction to this book, the term Romungre denotes a mixture of Roma and Hungarian, and initially referred to so-called assimilated Roma who spoke Hungarian and whose main occupation was music. In Romania, Romungre like Vanesa speak only Romanian. Vanesa was not an 'authentic' Romni, as she did not speak the language and did not identify with Roma tradition. She looked down on other Roma because she considered herself 'modern' and their tradition backward. She saw herself as more civilized than Roma who married their children young. She discussed her 'modernity', 'civilization' and 'education', all attributes that differentiated her from other Roma:

We're Romungre, we do not follow tradition. And the others think we're stupid. But our women have more freedom. Their women work for their men. Our women, after they get married – you stay home with the kids, and you work if you want to.

Her comments on gender referred to Roma traditions such as early marriage and sartorial codes. She expressed her preference for voting for Romanian politicians, as she said she did not trust some of the Roma politicians.

While she emphasized at times that she could not escape being recognized as a 'Ṭigancă', and she distinguished between non-Roma and other Roma or Ṭigani, at other times she used 'Romanians' inclusively, to denote citizenship: 'Nowadays it's hard to make a living; our Romanians have to go and work hard abroad to make money,' she told her lawyer, a line that illustrated her changed circumstances since moving to Pod. Here Vanesa was speaking of 'our Romanians' as including all Romanian citizens, irrespective of ethnicity. Her multiple self-identifications did not fit the normative monoethnic performativity that was hegemonic in Romania, nor the definitions of Romanian citizenship that excluded Roma.

Black versus White: Gendered Racialization and the Citizenship Gap

The racialization of Roma is based as much on physical markers, such as darker skin tone, as it is on class or its visual markers such as clothing. Collectively, the whole of Pod was racialized as a place where Ṭigani lived, even though some individual residents sometimes escaped such labels when away from Pod. Intentionally or unintentionally, some Roma passed as non-Roma when they were wearing formal clothes or looking like professionals; some, like olive-skinned Armando, were taken for foreigners such as Arabs on the basis of class or status markers. Usually Roma are considered 'swarthy', but this is not a necessary marker of Roma identity. Olive skin can also signify someone from southern Romania, where a large percentage of the population – Roma or not – present this physical characteristic, while Roma can be fair-skinned.[4] The suspicion of abjection, of being a Ṭigan, can hang over anyone on the basis of a variety of factors: darker skin, shabby appearance, and address or place of origin. The racialization of perceived class indicators and/or skin tone may have been unreliable, as I show in the examples below, but it still led to experiences of discrimination and abuse in encounters with staff at state institutions.

Vanesa, Giani and Mona

In Vanesa's family's interactions with the police and the justice system, the racialization of Roma, slippery and context-dependent as it was, had direct negative consequences. When I first met her, Vanesa was surprised by my interest in Pod and often exclaimed, 'You come here to visit us, in our miserable situation!' However, she had Giani call me and ask me to meet them in town to tell me what had happened to them. Vanesa's father had died the previous year, run over by a car whose driver, a non-Roma priest, had fled the scene of the accident. Vanesa and her brother had decided to sue the driver. The initial investigation dragged on for almost a year because, according to Vanesa, the police had tried to cover up for the perpetrator. Vanesa's family decided to demand a new inquest a year after the accident, and they hired a new lawyer, who asked them to pay in advance for her services. This was not the usual practice, as payment is routinely required at the close of a legal case. Vanesa explained that she had been apprehensive from the beginning of the new investigation, as one of the police officers had said to her at the first hearing: 'Do you know who ran your father over? I was surprised when I saw who he was. He's a priest. I was very surprised'. Vanesa told me that she had replied: 'Sir, priest, whatever he is, we all pray to the same God. God judges us all. It does not matter'. But the police officer insisted: 'Do you realize he's got connections?' Vanesa was undeterred, despite the police officer's attempts to intimidate her.

The new lawyer was present for Vanesa's hearing, and Vanesa's testimony was accurately recorded; but the lawyer failed to attend most other witness hearings, including when Vanesa's son Giani and his fiancée Mona testified. Giani had dark hair, dark eyes and light olive skin, while Mona was a very fair young woman. The police officers misread Mona's ethnicity, assuming she was an ethnic Romanian, but they identified Giani as a Rom; they called him 'black' and taunted her for having a black boyfriend. This invocation of blackness as a slur intersected with gender stereotypes in the police intimidation tactics. Vanesa described what happened:

> When they [Giani and Mona] called me, the girl said, 'I was ashamed. I did not know what I was saying'. After they treat her like that, that she likes Moroccans and – 'you white ones like Moroccans'. Unbelievable. After that, they make her swear on the Bible. They gave her a cross and a bible. Everyone else who testified, myself, my brother, my child, none of us had to swear on the bible, and they made the girl swear on the cross and bible that she was telling the truth, nothing but the truth.

Vanesa was very upset that the police had mocked Mona and Giani, and that one of the police officers had called Giani black. She kept repeating that her son was not black, and stressed that the police officer was in fact darker than Giani. Whiteness here is different from, for example, whiteness in the US. The terms 'white' and 'black' are shifters – they are context-dependent (Lemon 2000). In Romania they can be used to differentiate Roma from non-Roma, and Roma often discuss African Americans in the US as similar to them, a transnational imaginary kinship based on the shifter 'black'. For example, these *manele* lyrics identify President Obama as a Țigan because of his blackness: 'The Americans have realized/What a great heart Țigani have/And they brought to the White

House/A good man with black skin'.[5] However, in the case of the police officers, the identification of Giani as black was negative:

> Mona: They asked me my name. I told them. As I went in, they asked me if he [Giani] was my boyfriend and I said yes. And he [the police officer] said: 'How come you're white and he is black? Do you love him?' 'Of course I love him'. Then he said: 'Nowadays, Romanian women go after – ' It was quite ugly, what he said.
>
> Ioana: And you're ashamed to repeat it.
>
> Mona: Yes.
>
> Vanesa: Even if she [Mona] had been a street worker, they had no right to talk to her like that. We paid a lawyer – she must come and defend us, not leave us alone. Otherwise the police can call us into their office and they can take a big stick and beat us, do whatever they want with us, because our lawyer stopped attending the hearings and didn't do anything.

The police officers expressed a fear of miscegenation, invoking a scenario where 'black' foreign men were supposedly corrupting 'white' ethnic Romanian women, here cast as the 'powerless sex'. The invocation of blackness was supposed to mark Giani and his family as not Romanian and as foreigners, even though they were Romanian citizens.

The police officers' mistaking of Mona's ethnicity confirms the lack of reliable physical markers to read ethnicity in Romania. Nonetheless, Vanesa believed that her face and accent marked her as a Ţigancă. She told me that when she had been searching for a flat to rent before moving to Pod, she used to call to arrange to meet prospective landlords.

> Vanesa: OK, we met and after they saw me they would say, sorry, it's no longer available. And I would say, 'if I was Romanian, I would be OK, right?' Some did not say anything, others laughed or said 'that's not true'. They thought I was one of those Ţigani who can't count to two.
>
> Ioana: How did these strangers know you were a 'Ţigancă'?
>
> Vanesa: Well, they could not tell from my voice, only when they saw me. No matter how smartly dressed I was, they would still recognize me. From your face, the way you speak, they can tell. And your darker skin.

Vanesa was convinced that no matter what she did, she would always be identified as a Ţigancă – 'I have the face and the accent,' she said. One experience was not necessarily like another, but together they all contributed to Vanesa's sense of how *gadge* racialized her. Despite the fact that she owned the term 'Țigancă', she dis-identified from the uneducated poor Țigani. Thus she further displaced the abjection contained in the slur onto the other Țigani, those from whom she thought she was different.

Vanesa's fears of police abuse were compounded by events she had witnessed in Pod, including police raids and violence. Because of the state of emergency that was life in Pod, Vanesa and her family rarely disclosed their address. Hiding one's address was a common strategy among Pod residents to avoid identification with 'the lowest of the low', as one woman in Pod said they were considered. For example, Vanesa used her previous address when dealing with the police and lawyer. In this way she and her family were unlikely to be racialized as Țigani living amid refuse. However, even though Pod residents rarely disclosed where they lived, sometimes their ties to Pod surfaced, even if they passed at other times as non-Roma or more 'civilized' Roma. Giani told me that he had never told anyone at his school that he lived in Pod but one day a woman from Pod saw him on the bus and gave him away, which caused him embarrassment:

> She started speaking Romani to me, and I do not speak it, and because I said I did not understand, she started yelling so that the whole bus could hear: 'You pretend you're not from the rubbish dump, don't you?' Can you imagine how I felt? All those cute girls on the bus.

Being a 'Țigan' did not bother him, Giani explained, but he did not like being associated with Pod, because of the negative associations it had for most non-Roma. Giani wore immaculate clothes, including all-white outfits or shiny suits and tight shirts; he sometimes wore large necklaces and sunglasses, and would not have looked out of place in a *manele* video; even though he might be read as Roma or 'black', as happened with the police officers, he had never been identified with Pod. The woman on the bus had assumed that he could speak Romani and that he was only pretending otherwise in order to avoid her. This was partially true, because even though Giani did not speak Romani, he did not want to be associated with her, especially as she may have looked unkempt. Giani's potential cachet with young women, with his flashy and immaculate clothes and playful persona, had been temporarily compromised on the bus.

Armando, on the other hand, told me that he was not ashamed to be living in Pod, and would gladly bring his friends there. Like Giani, he always looked well groomed, and he always wore a suit jacket or even a full suit. Both Giani and Armando resisted abjection through their everyday public performances, using dressing up as a powerful tool. Vanesa too always took care in how she dressed, and often wore immaculately white outfits. However, these instances did not change the racialization of Pod residents in most other situations, when non-Roma treated Roma in Pod as non-citizens.

Despite instances of passing, either in state institutions or in other contexts, everyday encounters in public for most Pod residents who ventured outside Pod were shot through with racism. Many in Pod had given up fighting for their citizenship rights. However, Armando was determined to fight against racism and demand his rights. Vanesa was less hopeful than Armando, and less knowledgeable, but determinedly fought against injustice when it happened to her family.

Vanesa wanted to find another lawyer, and to ask their current lawyer to refund the fees they had paid in advance. Giani had found out that, with police approval, they could access the recording of a conversation with the lawyer during which the latter had verbally abused Vanesa, a fact the lawyer later denied. Vanesa needed to consult with her relatives to make a decision, and she was upset because they did not want to hear about her complaints. Her brother and partner told her she was too sensitive, and that she needed to recover the money they had already paid if they were to change lawyers. Her family had chosen Vanesa as their representative in charge of interacting with the lawyer and the police. She was caught between her own anger at the discrimination her child had experienced from the police and her relatives' apparent indifference to these occurrences. Eventually she decided to go to see the lawyer, and I accompanied her.

We entered the handsome, newly built house where the lawyer lived and worked. An elderly white-haired woman with a slightly hunched back, the lawyer, showed us into a small room that served as her office. She seemed very friendly and asked Vanesa if I was her daughter, a question that seemed absurd given that we were roughly the same age. Vanesa was unfazed and introduced me as her friend. My presence changed the lawyer's attitude, as her ostentatious friendliness demonstrated. When Vanesa complained about discrimination, the lawyer claimed: 'black, white, it does not matter – look at America, now they have a black president. Now that we're in the EU, that [discrimination] is no longer possible'. She sided with Vanesa against the police officers, exempting herself from any blame for what had happened.

Invoking stereotypes of sexualized, mysterious and dangerous women, she called Vanesa a 'beautiful Țigancă': 'I have told you, it does not matter that you are a Țigancă; I told you from the beginning that you were beautiful, very beautiful'. This remark came in response to the accusation that she had failed to do her job by not attending the hearings and had then verbally abused Vanesa on the phone. Like the question about whether I was her daughter, this remark revealed the stereotypes about Roma women that filtered her perception of Vanesa.

The lawyer's anti-discrimination tirade illustrated how some *gadge* had absorbed the language of diversity and could cynically switch it on when necessary. Vanesa – who had told me, 'I'm not afraid of her' – did not fall for the lawyer's apparent change of heart. She said that as a 'Ţigancă' she could not compete with the lawyer's status and social capital: 'They say we Ţigani, we have a loud mouth. We're Romanianized Ţigani, we're educated. Don't think, madam lawyer, that education is everything. If I haven't got your education – there's a God'. Vanesa told the lawyer that they would hire someone else, because she had not done her job. Even though she and her family ultimately decided not to file a formal complaint against the lawyer, they changed lawyer and eventually managed to successfully sue the driver.

'You Are where You Are Coming from': Racialization by Contagion

While usually whiteness is considered incompatible with Roma, in this section I show that phenotype is overridden by location in the racialization of Roma, which is primarily based on social and cultural markers. I regard the process through which individuals were identified as Ţigani because of their association with sites like Pod as racialization by contagion. When Pod was marked on someone's record as their place of residence, or when someone was identified as coming from Pod, they could not escape racialization as Ţigani, regardless of their complexion.

Alex and Mira

In the summer of 2007 Alex, Giani's friend, who was blond and blue-eyed and would not normally be taken for a Ţigan or a Rom, was run over by a truck while riding a scooter on the main road near Pod. Lorries carrying refuse from the city drove at high speed in the vicinity of Pod, and because there was no pavement, pedestrians and riders were often at risk. Because the ambulance had gone to pick him up from Pod, the hospital staff assumed that he lived there, and he faced discrimination. Had the ambulance not picked him up from Pod, his experience at the hospital might have been different.

Despite the fact that medical assistance was supposedly universal in Romania, Pod residents lacked family doctors and people had to travel miles to the nearest hospital, which was in the city. They only had access to emergency medical assistance, as most of them were unemployed and therefore uninsured. Ambulances often refused to come to Pod, because it was supposedly outside city limits and so Armando took emergency cases to hospital himself. Even though he was sometimes looked down upon at these institutions, he had attended a training programme for community nurses and felt empowered by the experience, determined to fight discrimination. Adults and children who worked on the refuse site had no protection and no insurance, but they often needed medical assistance as they were often victims of horrific accidents. Those without IDs, and those with IDs from other localities, were often refused assistance by municipal authorities because they did not have proof of residence. Therefore, if and when they reached a hospital, they entered the sordid game of expectations and bribes to which everyone in Romania was subject, despite the officially free health system.

Cases of negligence and malpractice in hospitals were frequent, and not limited to Roma. The patronizing attitudes of medical staff, their lack of communication with patients and their use of obscure technical language were widespread problems in the health system in Romania. As anthropologist Michele Rivkin-Fish (2005, 211) explains, in the post-socialist context new ways of relating to the state and of building on the secondary economy were consistent with, yet different from, socialist modes: 'If evading official procedures through arrangements based on personal connections was central to the socialist system's very functioning … "democratic" reforms have done little to make such practices anachronistic in the realm of healthcare'.

Armando and I went to visit Alex in hospital with Mira, Alex's mother. We found Alex in a three-bed ward, one leg in plaster and one eye covered with a patch. He was lively and in good spirits, and said that he could not wait to get back onto his scooter. Despite Alex's optimism, Armando found out from a nurse that he had no chance of being operated on the following day. He had not even been scheduled yet, even though he had been in hospital for three days. Mira lifted his eye patch and Armando asked the nurse who was on the ward at that moment to change it, as it looked rather old. The nurse replied angrily that Alex was not her only patient and she would change the patch when his turn came. I had had similar experiences with nurses in Romanian public hospitals, who were notoriously unfriendly and refused to do their job unless they got bribes, just as doctors would refuse to operate unless they were paid informally. Hospitals in Romania were also infamous for lacking the most basic equipment and medications, and patients often had to bring their own.

Racism compounded the hospital's staff attitude towards Alex and Mira. Mira complained that Alex's sheets looked dirty, which they did, and that the wet wipes she had left for him on his bedside table had disappeared. I stepped outside and waited for her. When she came out of the ward, she was wiping away her tears and still crying. Alex had told her that the doctor had asked him if his parents knew he was in hospital. 'How would they not know?' Mira exclaimed, upset. 'Is that the bedside table of someone who no one visits?' she continued, alluding to the different things he had on it. She told me that the doctor had asked Alex where he was from. Even though Alex had said that he was from the village where his family had a house, the doctor had insisted: 'but where did the ambulance pick you up?' 'Pod,' Alex replied. This information functioned as the stigma from which one could not hide, one that trumped all other categories of identification. The doctor asked what his parents did there, and Alex replied that they worked with non-ferrous materials. 'Do your parents steal?' the doctor allegedly asked. A chain of assumptions and stereotypes followed as the doctor marked Alex as a Ţigan from Pod, even though he could have been a visitor there. Mira was outraged:

> They saw I was a Ţigancă and they treat him like that. They tell him he is stealing. When the nurse took away his wet wipes, she said they belonged to the patient who had left. They took one of his toilet rolls. Why? They think we're that kind of Ţigani. If I ask Mihai, he'll come and kick them all out of the hospital. We work with non-ferrous materials; that's what we do.

Mira thought she was the reason the staff associated Alex with Ţigani, as Alex did not fit the Roma stereotype. However, it was Alex's association with Pod that had caused him to be racialized even before he had arrived.

The following day I spoke with Armando. He was upset because he had met the doctor, who had told him that they would not be able to operate on Alex until the following week, claiming that they did not have the necessary materials for the operation. Armando warned the doctor that if he treated Alex differently he would call in television crews to make a fuss about it. Armando was determined to fight for the young man's basic rights as a citizen. According to Armando, the doctor had replied that it would not be a good idea, but he had not seemed too frightened. Mira had also seen the doctor, who had asked her if she was Alex's sister. When she said she was his mother, the doctor replied: 'How can you be his mother? You're so young. How old were you when you had him?' Alex was sixteen and Mira was in her late thirties.

The doctor's condescending tone was not only a reflection of class and status difference, as it would have been with peasants: his remarks stemmed from stereotypes about stealing and teenage motherhood that racialized both Alex and Mira. The tone was modulated by a slight fear of the unknown: the foreigner within, the Ţigan. These were subtler instances than the blatant anti-Roma racism and stereotypes in right-wing publications in Romania, but they betrayed similar preconceptions. When virulent attacks appeared in the media against unidentified violent gangs of Ţigani, they built on stereotypes latent in viewers or readers and 'verified' by fragmentary and often rare encounters with Roma, such as that between Alex, Mira and the doctor.

In the end, after consulting other people, we realized that the operation was being delayed not because of a lack of materials, but because the doctor had not been informally paid. Armando's colleagues at the school advised him that the doctor expected to be paid the usual bribe before doing anything. Without paying bribes to doctors, one risked being left on the operating table, even in a very serious condition. Armando refused to even think about paying; he had never bribed anyone in his life, he said. Eventually Mira paid the doctor seven million lei (around €200) and Alex had successful surgery, with a temporary metal implant in his leg. He never returned to have it removed.

Conclusion

These individual stories, and the collective experience of Pod as a community, illustrate how places like Pod have become the materialization of the citizenship gap. Pod is similar to a refugee camp, but one for legal citizens who are de facto non-citizens; here, a state of emergency operated, although some individuals were able to escape it temporarily by leaving Pod. The Romanian state had pushed its own citizens to the margins of society and recycled the abject Țigani category, even as 'authentic' Roma were being officially recognized. As gender, skin tone and other external markers compounded the racialization of Roma during post-socialism, the relative subjective nature of this racialization did not make it less permanent for those Roma whose lives had little chance of improving. Their invisibility as citizens and their hypervisibility as Țigani, in encounters with the police, state institutions and non-Roma, continues during post-socialism.

Another consequence of the specific nature of the racialization of the Roma, who are often undistinguishable from other ethnicities in Romania, is that professional and middle-class Roma are easily assimilated into the majority and their contribution thereby rendered invisible, unless they declare and promote their own ethnicity. The following two chapters show how the discourse employed in social programmes has circumvented the most disenfranchised Roma and discuss young Roma in Pod and their experiences in the school system.

Notes

1. Their de facto non-citizen status is also comparable to that of some ethnic minorities in other parts of the world, such as Aboriginal people in Australia and, to some extent, African Americans in the United States.
2. Written in the aftermath of Hitler's election as German Chancellor in 1933, Benjamin's discussion of the state of emergency reflects a specific historical moment, as well as the permanent condition of the 'oppressed', for whom history is not a linear narrative of progress.
3. Reports such as Ina Zoon's (2001), list the lack of local IDs as one of the main causes of lack of access to services among the Roma.
4. Scheper-Hughes and Hoffman (1998, 385) discuss the relationship between race and class in Brazil, which is similar to the racialization of poverty in Romania:

   Traditionally, race was determined, at least in part, by class identity. While physical features and color differences were noted, money lightened the skin, just as its obvious lack darkened the skin. In a certain sense, then, there are no (social) 'whites' in a favela, and all street children are 'black,' that is, socially blackened by their marginality and distance from 'white' and 'polite' Brazilian society.

5. 'Şi-au dat seama americanii/Ce suflet bun au ţiganii/Şi-au adus la Casa Albă/Un om bun cu pielea neagră/Vrem şi noi unul la fel/Ca să ne bazăm pe el'.

Chapter 3

Too Poor to Have Culture?
The Politics of Authenticity in Roma NGO Training

In this chapter I discuss the training of Roma activists as self-sufficient citizens, and I demonstrate the streamlining of civil society around Roma culture and ethnicity through EU- and government-funded PHARE programmes designed to improve the situation of the Roma. PHARE programmes were one of the main components of the 2001–2010 National Strategy for Improving the Situation of Roma (NSISR), and included three main strands: income-generating activities, housing and healthcare. Roughly 70 per cent of the funding came from the EU, and the remainder from the Romanian government. Through an analysis of a training session for Roma activists and a close reading of PHARE documents, I show that the session, and the programmes more generally, excluded most poor Roma and recycled Ţigani stereotypes. Focusing on performances of citizenship in relation to constraints imposed by policy framing, I argue that the collaboration between the Romanian state and the EU in PHARE programmes that claimed to 'improve the situation of the Roma' in fact maintained the citizenship gap for Roma and racialized hierarchies in Romania.

Setting the Scene

In June 2008 Armando and I attended a training session for activists working with Roma communities, which had been organized by the local authority and an NGO partner of the Open Society Institute. I had heard about the PHARE programmes in the media, yet in Pod almost nobody seemed to know about them. Armando and I were invited to this training session after I had asked the local Roma affairs councillors to support an application for a PHARE project for Pod. When I asked Vanesa to join us, she answered that she would not go:

> I am crazy. I tell it like it is, to their faces, and then they'll come and take me away in an ambulance. I have got no education; I'm learning from the others [pointing to Armando]. I've only finished eight classes. In the eighth year I had to repeat the year to continue, but I didn't.

When I asked Adam from Pod to come and join Armando and me for a one-day workshop about the PHARE programmes, he answered: 'I gotta make money in that time'. Adam told me that he had had enough of those who only visited the community when they needed something, such as politicians from the Roma Party for Europe, who would come seeking the votes of the roughly sixty (out of 400) people in the community that had local IDs and were therefore able to vote. Dumitru, who had a thriving recycling business on the refuse site, likewise told me that he did not have enough 'idle time' available to attend the session, which was to start in the morning and end in the late afternoon. In the end just Armando and I went.

The training session's stated goal was to inform participants about and prepare them for a new call for project proposals, the deadline for which was fast approaching. It became clear during the session that Roma with little education had not been expected to attend. Most of the participants – apart from Armando – shared the cultural and social capital gained through higher education. There were ten Roma university students in visual arts, psychology, economics and philology, all members of Roma NGOs; two non-Roma economics students; one international relations student; and a non-Roma schoolteacher. The session leaders were two trainers, Victor and Corina; they were in training themselves, as we would find out later. There was also an observer from the NGO that had co-organized the session, who later revealed that he was Victor and Corina's appraiser. The session took place in the regional council's headquarters, where Victor worked.

We spent an hour at the beginning of the training session identifying the characteristics of underdeveloped and developed communities. Victor then drew a diagram showing a dramatically falling gradient line, with 'an underdeveloped Roma community' at one end, and at the other end the Romanian city of Sibiu, 2007 European Capital of Culture, symbol of modernity and civilization. As he had already done a few times during the session, Armando protested that it would be better to name a concrete example such as Pod in the diagram. 'You'd better put our [local] city down, why put Sibiu? Because that's exactly how it is. I'm fed up with discussions, there's nothing practical in these sessions,' Armando continued. Somewhat unenthusiastically, Victor changed the two names as per Armando's request. After these adjustments,

Victor regained his composure and exclaimed confidently: 'Getting from Pod to an ideal city like Sibiu is the task of our session'. Despite having changed the names in the diagram to refer to Pod and its nearest city, Victor continued to talk about 'an ideal city', and kept calling it Sibiu. Victor asked participants to name four problems in underdeveloped communities and identify solutions for them. He explained that these solutions would help to level out the gradient line in the diagram. However, Armando's remark –'there's nothing practical in these sessions' – pointed to what I identify in this chapter as a growing discrepancy between rhetoric and practice that paralleled the abyss that Victor had pictured between the two types of community.

The PHARE Programmes: Improving the Situation of which Roma?

A close reading of the PHARE programme description shows that its rhetoric facilitated the processes of giving value to some Roma communities while denying value to others. The large percentage of funding for the programme that came from the EU reflected the Romanian government's secondary role and the structural power of transnational governmentality in the streamlining of cash flows (Elyachar 2005; Wolf 1982). PHARE programmes presupposed collaboration between local authorities and Roma NGOs, and the notion of civil society thereby constructed was a hybrid rather than an independent sphere. It was also a notion of civil society that did not challenge the core of state institutions in Romania or their embedded racist structures. The discourse of Roma culture, as it was implemented in schools, at local and international festivals, and in this case in social programmes, reflected how EU definitions were adapted at national and local levels, and how they upheld the citizenship gap for Roma. Roma cultural identity was assumed to lie in the traditions of the underdeveloped communities that participants in the training session I attended were being taught to develop.

Some of the PHARE social programmes specifically focused on entrepreneurship. These programmes defined activities eligible for funding according to traditional Roma occupations, which included metalwork, woodcrafts, brick making, and gold and silver artisanship. Roma whose work comprised activities other than these did not qualify. Despite a rhetoric that encouraged entrepreneurship, these programmes did not promote independence, but were overlaid onto existing informal networks between local authorities and companies. The resources offered (i.e. non-reimbursable credit) were much sought after, and the most disenfranchised people did not have access to them. In fact, as I show later in this chapter, the programme participants did not have access to them either, despite the rhetoric and the certificates.

The PHARE programmes were vigorously mediatized in Romania, as were the social and development components of the ten-year NSISR, the government's EU-backed strategy for Roma discussed in the introduction to this book. With some scepticism, Romanian national media reflected on international reports on the persistence of Roma poverty and marginalization. This was often coupled with local reports that offered no structural analysis of the causes of abject poverty in Romania, instead offering stereotypical representations of such poverty and suggesting that the Roma were to blame for their own destitution. These parallel signals, about EU funding programmes for Roma on the one hand and continuing Roma poverty on the other, produced a public perception in Romania that Roma did not take advantage of the opportunities available to them, and that the Roma in charge misspent the funding.

The phrase 'improving the situation of the Roma' in the names of both the NSISR and PHARE programmes gave misleading signals to the public at large, Roma and *gadge* alike, who were unlikely to have read the lengthy documents and may therefore have taken it at face value. The name of the NSISR did not specify which Roma were its target; however, one might have surmised from the accompanying media reports on poverty that the poorest Roma were the NSISR's and PHARE programmes' main targets. Indeed, I naively assumed from media headlines that the PHARE programmes were meant to 'improve the situation' of the most disenfranchised Roma, and I knew that Pod residents were certainly among them. I was certain that Pod residents would qualify for at least one of the strands: the community lacked access to healthcare, many lived in precarious housing, and they were engaged in recycling, an income-generating activity. After attending the training session, however, I realized that its goal had little to do with poor Roma directly, and a lot to do with turning participants into neoliberal subjects.

My subsequent analysis of some NSISR documents and PHARE programme descriptions suggested that their main goal was the creation of a Roma infrastructure of state functionaries and NGO workers who would help to govern Roma who 'might be excluded', rather than the alleviation of poverty among the most disenfranchised Roma. The PHARE programme description identifies specific goals: 'specific measures include improving collaboration between local authorities and Roma representatives, continuing the recruitment and preparation of school and medical mediators for Roma communities, vocational training, and valorization of traditional occupations' (Ministerul Economiei și Finanțelor 2006, no page number). Thus collaboration between local authorities and NGOs, and the training and recruitment of school-community mediators and voluntary community nurses, appeared as two main foci. Already apparent in these few lines is the division between the training of leaders and functionaries on the one hand, and vocational training and traditional occupations on the other. The last two items listed, 'vocational training and traditional occupations', referred to two different sets of community members.

The programmes envisioned Roma culture in terms of traditional occupations, prioritizing them and promoting entrepreneurship based on them, even though only a small minority of Roma actually practised them. The grant scheme thus failed to take into account the large diversity of Roma communities in Romania, not just in occupational terms but also as nomadic or settled, assimilated or semi-assimilated, and so on. Moreover, the programme strands that funded housing projects assumed or required land rights; but a large number of Roma did not have papers, and many of them had no ownership or other rights to the land because they had been evicted or had left their homes to look for work. These Roma therefore could not benefit from the housing programme. Equally, the programmes seemed to ignore the situation of the numerous migrant Roma within Romania who lacked IDs, or whose IDs did not match their places of residence. In short, the programmes failed to address the multiple aspects of Roma exclusion from actual citizenship.

A 2008 PHARE programme outlined the Romanian government's strategy for several years to come. This programme emphasized collaboration between local administrative institutions, social services and Roma communities. The requirement that local public institutions should collaborate with NGOs, preferably Roma ones, could be seen as a commitment to inclusivity. However, Roma NGOs constituted a small fraction of the Roma population, and those who were not in NGOs were not eligible as organizers. While the text stipulated as a precondition that Roma communities should be involved in the development of projects, the authors of grant application documents needed to have experience of such applications and a familiarity with bureaucracy and budget-planning; the presence of Roma themselves in the devising of projects was not listed as necessary. Moreover, the document used the general term 'Roma communities', thereby erasing differences in class, Roma group, gender or age.

The grant schemes in this 2008 programme, including those focused on impoverished communities, had three strands: income generation, infrastructure and health. The funding of these three strands was detailed as follows:

> Of a total €20.5 million (of which €6 million represent the Romanian government's contribution, and €14.5 million represent PHARE funds), [the programme] estimates an investment scheme of a total value of €18 million (of which €12 million [represent] the European Union's contribution) and the second phase of the information and consciousness-raising campaign (continuing the 2004 initiative). The grant scheme will finance projects in the fields of housing, small infrastructure, health, vocational training and income-generating activities, the main concept being community development. (Ministerul Economiei şi Finanţelor 2006, no page number)

The complicated bureaucracy around some of the grants supposedly targeting impoverished Roma meant that very few people were able to fulfil the necessary conditions even to apply. The 'main concept' recommended for the PHARE grant scheme was 'community development', but some activists had very specific definitions of 'community' that did not include places like Pod, as I will show later in this chapter.

The grant schemes described above were coupled with an institutional component covering training and assistance for local authority partnerships with Roma NGOs and initiatives, Roma experts in regional districts (*prefecturi*) and medical staff:

> Within this component, an investigation was initially conducted into the training needs of the target groups, represented by Roma experts in *prefecturi* and Roma NGOs, and among health organizations' staff and family doctors. Between 2004 and 2005, through a series of courses and training workshops, over 500 individuals were instructed, some of them belonging to regional institutions, local authorities and Roma NGOs/ initiatives. (Ministerul Economiei şi Finanţelor 2006, no page number)

These programmes focused on adding new functionaries to existing structures, such as Roma experts employed on local councils, as social workers and as Roma specialists in schools. The session I attended with Armando was one example of this kind of training programme.

At their most successful, as reports on the NSISR suggest,[1] the PHARE programmes created new middle- and lower-middle-class functionaries. Class differences among Roma were absent from the document cited above; the only time 'poor Roma' were mentioned was in the following sentence: 'qualitative and quantitative research brings relevant information about poor Roma communities in Romania, and the information and consciousness-raising campaign has reached three target audiences – the majority population, the Roma, and opinion leaders' (Ministerul Economiei şi Finanţelor 2006, no page number). Nonetheless, it would be wrong to suggest that no poor Roma benefited from these programmes. Mariea Ionescu, former leader of the National Agency for Roma, developed a successful income-generating project with a Roma community involved in the traditional occupation of brick making, who developed their own businesses under Ionescu's guidance. An important aspect of Ionescu's project was consultation between project organizers and community members during the project's devising stages, and the fact that the project started from activities in which community members were already competent and engaged (Palade 2005).

Training the Trainers: Performing Neoliberal Civility

For many Roma, the process of the 'NGOization of Roma rights', (Trehan 2009, 56) represented a unique opportunity to find a space for their concerns and to forge national and international connections. However, these opportunities were not available to the many Roma who did not share the educational and social capital necessary to become NGO members or activists. Roma studies scholars Elena Maroushiakova and Veselin Popov (2001a) note the almost overnight development of an opportunistic 'Gypsy industry' of NGOs in East Central Europe in response to Western funding for 'Roma issues', an 'industry' rarely guided by real concern for Roma people. Anthropologists Steve Sampson and Ruth Mandel have argued that lower-ranking bureaucrats adept at playing the system during socialism were the first to benefit from Western funding and programmes designed to build civil society in post-socialist East Central Europe. Rather than focus on concepts such as 'corruption' in this process, however, I start from Steven Sampson's (1996, 126) observation: 'the transition has many agents, both foreign and local and we need to unravel their mutual complicity'.

As this chapter will demonstrate, through activist training participants become citizens/volunteers at the expense of the communities they are being trained to develop.[2] Firstly, the workshops reproduce stereotypes of deserving and undeserving poor Roma communities: some Roma are worthy of the trainers' efforts, while others are 'judged not to have such tradable competence or potential' and become 'devalued and thus vulnerable to exclusionary practices' (Ong 2006, 7). Secondly, during the sessions the trainees reinforce their own difference through performances of 'culturedness' and professionalism that distinguishes them from the Roma masses. A university education and fluency in English and in 'project talk' are among the many conditions for achieving activist credibility and status.[3]

Through the collaboration between the state and NGOs in the crucible of neoliberalism and nationalism, the Roma identities performatively deployed during the training session I attended were activists performing civility, i.e. culturedness, and traditional Roma performing authentic culture. However, these are not citizen identities, but rather two ways of becoming visible and recognized as Roma by the state and PHARE programmes in Romania today. The performative coming-into-being of Roma professional ethnics as citizens is limited to their cooperation and performance of civility. The latter may allow Roma activists to appear as citizens; but their recognition and modernity are predicated on their not being the Roma who do not fit the framing of the PHARE programmes, who are cast as the abject, undesirable Other, and whose very existence the activists ultimately agree to ignore.

The focus on 'culture' as ethnic authenticity, and indirectly on 'culture' as culturedness or civility, becomes a mechanism of exclusion.[4] While activist training and PHARE programmes may seem like springboards for social mobility and the creation of a Roma middle class, they exclude those who are judged as lacking either type of 'culture'. Culturedness is a requirement for participants to become accepted and efficient activists, and lack of cultural capital bars one from success. As Sarah Phillips (2008, 111) shows for Ukraine, 'a certain amount of cultural capital is still crucial to qualify as a member of the elite, or even as "middle class"'. For example, Armando struggled to get to grips with the language and conventions of the training programme precisely because he lacked the other participants' educational background. They were all university educated, while he was completing his secondary school education in his thirties.

These distinctions were reproduced in the training session we attended through the participants' clothing styles, mannerisms and speech patterns (see Englund 2006). Most of the Roma students present had benefited from the quotas for Roma in universities. These quotas for secondary schools and universities allowed better-off Roma to enter institutions they otherwise would not have been able to access, but the most disadvantaged Roma did not benefit from these policies. For example, in Pod, where many children attended 'special' schools for children with learning disabilities, of the few who had finished Year Nine and enrolled under the quotas for Roma in secondary school, none had graduated.

Participants in the training session performed 'culture' as 'culturedness' to distinguish themselves from the masses that they were supposed to help develop, while the trainers invoked 'culture' as 'tradition' to distinguish between authentic Roma and those who had 'no culture': some kinds of poverty and conduct were not Roma; and Roma authenticity was not necessarily separate from poverty, but a kind of noble, primitive Other. In this way the training session recycled stereotypes and racial prejudice. For example, one Roma activist, who had arrived carrying a briefcase and wearing a suit, complained about Pod residents who allegedly had not cooperated with an ID campaign for the undocumented, exclaiming 'they have no culture'. 'They have no culture' in this instance meant that, for the speaker, Pod residents lacked both civility (i.e. were selfish and had no community spirit) and tradition, where 'tradition' referenced the ideal, unthreatening, exotic Roma who spoke Romani and lived in remote locations rather than in places like Pod. Given the stereotype prevalent in Romania that Roma had no culture and were an underclass, it is perhaps not that surprising that this activist dismissed Pod and did not want to associate it with 'Roma culture'. However, if one accepts such exclusions, even temporarily, one becomes complicit with the neoliberal commodification of culture that leaves monoethnic nationalism untouched. The acceptance of such exclusions also means that the cultural identities recognized by the state and NGOs cannot lead to actual citizenship, and that all Roma symbolically remain outside citizenship.

An incident involving a small group of participants later in the training session further illustrates how poverty was discussed. The group had been asked to draw an image of an underdeveloped community, and they focused on an imaginary community they named Poorfellows. Their depiction presented Poorfellows as unthreatening and remote, situated outside the city in a badly kept open space that was littered with rubbish (although not excessively so) and lacking infrastructure. Their drawing was pinned to the wall in front of the whole group, and the schoolteacher introduced it. She said that the people of Poorfellows had their culture, their songs and dances, and were in touch with their traditions, unlike people living in the city. I could not tell whether this was her view of Pod, or if she had deliberately invented an idealized version of Pod. Either way, she had never been to Pod, so her impressions were based on hearsay, media reports and her work at school with Roma children. Even if she was idealizing the real Pod as a place in touch with song and dance, Poorfellows seemed to be frozen in time and space, as if the people there were waiting to be discovered by activists. Real Pod residents worked hard on the refuse site, and did not loiter in front of their shacks. Whether based on Pod or not, this stereotypical image fitted the general misunderstanding in the PHARE programmes, according to which Roma needed training in order to do something, and which failed to recognise their ongoing activities as work because they were not in formal employment or traditional occupations. At least this speaker's image was a step up from media stereotypes of dirty, thieving and aggressive Roma, albeit a patronizing one. In Romania many Roma themselves aspired to meet the stereotypes of Roma as passionate, hot-blooded, innate performers.

The focus on culture as tradition framed the rhetoric of the training workshop and obliterated social issues. The discrepancy between the stated goal of the session (learning how to solve social issues) and its actual outcome (the imposition of the rhetoric of 'culture' as the engine through which social change, i.e. development, could be implemented) illustrated the erasure of political economy in the post-socialist recognition of the Roma. The organizers strove to replace 'Communist' talk with a 'culturally sensitive' discourse distinct from the 'wooden language' of socialism; in the process they reduced culture to an unchanging tradition, and erased political economy from a programme that claimed to address social issues. In other words, the trainers were very careful to emphasize the focus on Roma culture in order to align themselves with postsocialist ideas and 'Europe', and to distance themselves from socialism.

As the session ended, one of the organizers, who had been silently observing in a corner, stood up to say a few words, and revealed that he was the trainers' evaluator. He took a moment to critique some of the participants' use of a specific word: 'integration'. He was troubled, he confessed, by 'integration', because it was almost synonymous with 'assimilation', the socialist policy regarding Roma. Instead, he drew attention to the new era that emphasized multiculturalism and cultural difference. Current policies, according to him, were in stark contrast with socialist assimilation policies, which had denied the existence of Roma as an ethnic group. The organizer's dismissal of socialist rhetoric was a statement about progress, as he was trying to present himself as being in tune with Western standards. However, the new policies were only superficially novel: they left untouched the institutionalized exclusions of socialism, as did the session he had organized. The training session naturalized collaboration between NGOs and the state, and erased the systemic exclusions to which Roma were subject as the new ideologies preserved the racialization of poor Roma and the depiction of Țigani as cultureless. By emphasizing the difference between socialist assimilation and post-socialist recognition, the organizer and the session, just like the policies they promoted, were erasing the impoverishment of Roma communities caused by the shrinking of the state's role and the ongoing racism many poor Roma continued to encounter. In this respect, post-socialist recognition and socialist assimilation policies were strikingly similar.

At the end of the session, Victor encouraged everyone to come up with their own project proposals. According to him, drafts could be submitted to appropriate institutions if participants wanted to get involved. This was ironic on several counts, the most obvious being that the PHARE projects were extremely complicated, verbose and competitive, and involved complex partnerships between local government agencies, NGOs and private companies. It was not enough to write a grant application; one had to identify partners with which to work, including local authorities. Despite Victor's positive message, proposal writing also required familiarity with a certain jargon, or 'project talk' (Steven Sampson 1996). Jon McKenzie (2003) has described the 'forced quantification of the nonquantifiable'[5] as part of what he calls the 'perform or else' imperative of neoliberalism, and this imperative was visible at the training session in the concern with results-based criteria – not only in the draft proposals we wrote during the day, but also in the certificates we received at the end – and in the general disregard for process and participation. After the session I realized that Pod residents, including Armando, could not write such proposals; nor were they meant to. Armando and I had asked for guidance beforehand, but as we left the session I still felt as confused as when we had started.

Finally we all received our certificates, and were encouraged to apply for the upcoming round of grants on the PHARE programme to improve the situation of Roma. The certificates were arguably rewards for the participants' consent to the ideology of post-socialist recognition; their acquiescence was recoded as civility. Here we came full circle, from the diagram described at the beginning of the chapter to the closing ceremony, as participants were offered certificates that emblematized the gap between theory and practice, and between activists and the 'underdeveloped'.[6] As Armando received his certificate last, Victor jokingly suggested that they had almost run out of copies. Armando replied that it did not matter to him if he did not receive one, as he had already collected a thick stack of them from other workshops, and they had been of no use. Despite having attended many similar training sessions, he was under no illusion that he could initiate a PHARE project. Armando's negative reaction reflected his frustration that he still lacked the social capital and knowledge to write a grant proposal.

Indeed, Armando had been making critical comments throughout the course of the session, interrupting Victor and Corina several times. He reminded the instructors that he came from Pod, and he evaluated most of their claims against failures or successes there. He had told me that politicians and NGO workers often refused to discuss Pod, either because there was nothing they felt they could do or because it failed to provide the kind of success story they would want to endorse. The trainers did not welcome Armando's questions, and seemed annoyed by his disruptions. (Some of this behaviour may also have been down to his personality and the self-aggrandizing tendencies that resulted from his otherwise admirable sense of responsibility for Pod.) Armando irritated the trainers, both because he refused to perform according to the pre-established course of the session, and because he blurred the distinction between the activists and those who needed help. Technically he belonged to both categories: as a Pod resident, he was from an underdeveloped community of Ţigani; as a trainee he was, at least theoretically, a future project leader.

Armando's critique represented a refusal to endorse the artificial separation between participants and Roma masses, or to comply with the equation of civility and compliance. Despite the trainers' confident tone about the value of grants for improving living conditions for many Roma, Armando's example told a different story. As someone who had tried and failed to use the skills acquired in similar sessions to write successful grant proposals, Armando was proof that access to grant funding was prohibitive on many counts, including education, knowledge of project talk, and last but not least connections – the informal networks of the secondary economy.

Given the limited resources available and the fierce competition for grants, it would be naive to assume that any of the participants would go on to be successful, even if they felt encouraged to pursue a project. The training mirrored the recognition of the Roma under post-socialism: by performing civility, Roma activists could make claims on the Romanian state, and could collaborate in the development of Roma communities as defined in these sessions. The participants' performance of culturedness, the streamlining of grant proposals, and the organization of social reality into projects (problems and their solutions) based on 'project talk' (Sampson 1996) were aligned with neoliberalism, and did not disrupt the biases of monoethnic nationalism within existing structures. The session trained participants in civility, the very definition of which excluded Roma from the Romanian imaginary: civility is 'exclusive, defined against the assumed ignorance of the masses. Concepts of human rights, personal manners, styles of clothing, and the language of everyday life are all implicated in producing these distinctions. The making of individual subjects, in a democracy no less than under colonialism, depends on objectifying others' (Vaughan 1991)' (Englund 2006, 9). While the claim to civility and culturedness by Roma intellectuals and young people is an important political statement that potentially destabilizes ethnic and racial hierarchies in Romania, programmes such as PHARE have disciplined young activists into a civility that acquiesced with the monoethnic nation-state. They are recognized by it only when they are no longer recognizable as Roma.

During a break from the session, I engaged in conversation with two participants. They were both first-year university students, one in visual arts, the other in economics; they told me they had enrolled through the quotas for Roma. The art student was wearing combat boots and had long, wavy hair; the other was dressed more formally. One of them remarked that it was difficult to distinguish the Roma among the participants based on the way they looked: most participants wore casual or formal urban clothes and could pass as non-Roma, a far cry from Ţigani stereotypes. The other mentioned that Armando was the only one who looked like a Rom. This was ironic, because Armando did not consider himself a Rom; but his appearance, with his slightly darker complexion and in particular his moustache and black hair, made others identify him as a Rom. The two students complained that Armando talked too much and was too loud, sometimes taking over the session. These participants read Armando's interruptions as proof of his lack of civility and 'culturedness', which made him grate with the polite and educated participants, and indirectly confirmed the stereotype of loud, quarrelling Ţigani. As I have shown, the trainers did not welcome Armando's questions and interruptions, and through their responses they implied that following the established course of the session was the right way to behave as an activist.

Armando, who considered himself a mixture of Roma, Romanian and Jewish, once said to me: 'if only my mum had made me a true Rom'. His distinction between 'a true Rom' and a less-so mixture like himself reproduced the dichotomy between authentic and abject Roma that media phenomena such as Gypsy soaps on TV engendered in parallel with post-socialist discourses of culture and diversity. These discourses not only influenced non-Roma and their perception of Roma, but also shaped how Roma thought of themselves: Armando's hybridity did not make sense within post-socialism's regimes of authenticity.

However, one day Armando and I were standing outside the Cultural House in the city, where festivities for International Roma Day were about to take place. A journalist went straight up to him without hesitation, picking him out from among a group of Roma and non-Roma to ask: 'can you tell me why you are proud to be a Rom?' Without blinking, Armando responded: 'I am proud, because I am a European citizen, and our customs are even richer than those of other nationalities'. I was surprised to hear him comply with being called a Rom, and I asked him what had happened. He gestured with his hand, as if to say, 'what can I do, that's how things are'. In my view, Armando's change did not reflect opportunism or insincerity, but rather his realization of the subject position that was open to him under the wide common denominator

'Roma'. While for Armando this was an ongoing process of self-identification, the journalist's understanding of who was Roma was more straightforward: using visual markers, he had probably assumed that Armando's olive skin and moustache were signs that he was a Rom, given the context, i.e. the celebration of International Roma Day. Armando identified as a European citizen rather than Romanian. He may have chosen to do so because being 'European' is seen as more positive than being 'Romanian'; Armando was steeped in the European discourse on Roma, and his statement reflected the fact that it was easier for Roma to be identified as European citizens, especially in Romania, where they lacked actual citizenship.

Armando always wore a suit when in town, and his metal-rimmed spectacles gave him an intellectual aspect that many in Romania do not associate with Roma. For example, one day I was with him when he met a non-Roma electrician who asked him whether he was an Arab. Images of Roma professionals and intellectuals are still rare, and the majority associate Roma or Ţigani with abject poverty, or with colourful skirts and costumes. At other times, and especially when he was not wearing spectacles, Armando's moustache marked him as a Rom. I was in a pharmacy with him once when he was buying medication for someone in the community. He was holding a fifty-lei[7] note in his hand, and put it down on the counter before the salesperson gave him the product. The sales assistant took the note and went to find the medicine. When she came back with it, she asked for the money as if she had never taken it. Armando explained calmly that he had just given her a note and she had taken it away. She denied it. The sales person refused to serve him until he paid again. I intervened, stating that I had seen her take the note. She refused to see my point. We threatened to file a complaint and asked for the store manager, but we were told that the manager was not on the premises. The salesperson removed her name badge and ignored us. Later that day I filed an online complaint with the company, a big pharmaceutical chain. We never heard back. I believe the episode happened because the woman had identified Armando as a Ţigan, i.e. a thief and crook. Whether she took the note on purpose or genuinely forgot she had taken it, we will never know. Many non-Roma are convinced that all Ţigani steal, whether poor or rich; it is one of the prevalent stereotypes about Roma. These stereotypes position Roma as Ţigani scapegoats for the corruption prevalent in the country.

Closing the Gap: Authentic Artisans and Selfish Entrepreneurs

As already discussed, the training session I attended with Armando assumed that the target communities were somewhere else, not present. It created a distinction between activists and communities, erasing the links between the trainees and their own environments, and the knowledge that could be brought from people with direct experience in those communities. By not attempting to engage with the communities who were the target of the development projects, the training session was implicitly teaching students the 'appropriate technology' approach to development. Feminist and post-colonial scholars have argued against decentralized, small-scale approaches to development that exclusively emphasize local resources. They have shown that development agencies following this trend display patronizing attitudes, assuming they only need to bring technology to a place that lacks it in order to effect positive change. This appropriate-technology approach consists of a top-down practice in which Western-trained international experts and state development agents work to assess which technologies to develop locally. On such projects, communities are only consulted at the dissemination stage of the process, and this well-meaning paternalism often leads to failure (Warren and Bourque 1991, 195).

This appropriate-technology approach shaped trainers' and participants' attitudes during the training session. Describing her own experience, Corina, one of the trainers, stated that often a community's biggest problem was not the same for everyone, and it would be necessary to ask several community members; she said she had often received different answers from members of the same community. She explained that it was important to ask the underdeveloped community members what they wanted to achieve, as one might make the wrong assumptions when deciding whether access to transport or water constituted their priority. Implying that activists had no prior knowledge or experience of the community, she nonetheless established that the trainees were the decision makers, with only minimal input necessary from communities – a lack of input from the supposed targets of development that reflected the methods discussed in the documents from the NSISR. She implied that it was up to the activists to decide priorities on the basis of possibly conflicting answers, but she did not offer any suggestions as to how such decisions might be made. Corina also mentioned that she knew of quite underdeveloped Roma communities with satellite dishes. Her remark sounded like a warning: underdevelopment may hide behind flashy surfaces, and such cases blurred the clear demarcation between modernity and underdevelopment.

In the second half of the session we were asked to break into smaller groups and identify four problems that occurred in Roma communities, and then to name partners, interested parties and sources of potential financial support to solve those problems. I joined three university students, all members of a Roma student NGO: Ana, a young woman with long wavy hair; Cristi, a sturdy young man wearing a T-shirt bearing the logo of the National Agency for Roma, the only state institution explicitly in charge of Roma affairs; and a thin young man who was an economics student. Ana suggested the lack of ID papers as one of the four issues, and mentioned that she had participated in an ID campaign in Pod:

Ana: We went there; they registered everyone. Some of them did not even know their date of birth.

Cristi: Can you imagine, when you've got ten children …

Ana: Many did not show up the next day. Those who have their ID done often lose it, because they leave it as a security deposit in shops where they buy on credit and things like that. Some don't want IDs because if they run into trouble, it is more difficult for the police to track them down if they don't have one.

Ana's description of the ID campaign in Pod illustrated some of the difficulties and complexities of people's lives there. I suggested that it might be helpful to think about why the campaign Ana mentioned had not worked. Despite addressing the shocking reality that over a million people in Romania did not have ID cards and consequently were excluded from basic citizenship rights, the plan to create IDs for all undocumented people had failed to take into account Roma who had migrated within Romania. Many in Pod feared that new IDs would not grant them the right to stay there, and would allow authorities to chase them away more easily. However, such complexities, including police abuse, which lay behind the Pod community's lack of trust in state institutions, were not discussed during the training session. We had to focus on our exercise and produce solutions and possible partners for each problem (the other three were school attendance, lack of infrastructure, and employment). Each group shared their problems and solutions at the end of the time allotted.

The four small groups in the session had each produced a drawing that was subsequently pinned to the walls – two drawings of developed communities and two of underdeveloped ones. When participants were first split into groups and assigned to draw an example of a developed or an underdeveloped community, Armando's group focused on the latter topic, and he convinced his partners to focus on Pod. They drew it together, and he chose to present it to the whole group once we had reconvened. But despite Armando's constant reminders that Pod was a concrete example to address, the trainers stayed determined to stick to abstractions.

When I suggested to Victor that the local authority headquarters where he worked should do more for the Pod community, he complained that the community had no leader and no NGO, and that it was difficult if not impossible to work with them. 'You go once, one person says "I'm the leader", then someone else comes and says, "no, I'm the leader"', exclaimed Victor. Even a cursory examination of the anthropological work on Roma in East Central Europe would reveal that Roma often challenge notions of leadership through what Michael Stewart (1997) calls 'brotherhood equality' in communities that constitute themselves as groups of equal men (*Rom baro*). Victor also complained that in Pod people did not even know their own names: 'you ask them their name; they tell you it is Viorica, then they say, no, sorry, it's something else'. Anthropologists working in both Romania and Hungary have shown that many Roma use nicknames more often that their officially registered names (Stewart 1997; Engebrigtsen 2007). In Pod, for example, as for many Roma elsewhere, many people did not have IDs, and their weddings were rarely officially recorded. It would therefore make sense that, when asked their name, someone might first give their nickname (or Roma name) and then, realizing that their inter-locutor wanted to know their ID name, would provide a different one instead. Thus Victor's complaint was paradoxical, given that one of the characteristics of the NSISR was supposedly to promote Roma culture. Victor's critique of Pod implied that community members did not make enough of an effort to lift themselves out of their lack of organization (they had no NGO), did not collaborate with activists, and therefore did not deserve his further attention.

Despite Victor's dismissal, the entrepreneurial spirit was not missing from Pod. As I showed in the previous chapter, although media descriptions per-petuated the stereotype that Ţigani did not work, various kinds of informal work took place in Pod, including recycling from landfill, brokering between scavengers and recycling companies, and trading in collected scrap materials. Some, such as Dumitru and Adam, thrived, even if the majority did not. While Dumitru and Adam might well have been reluctant to engage in PHARE pro-grammes, the younger residents on the refuse site would have certainly ben-efited from a legal framework and social and healthcare protection in relation to their work.

Recycling practices received praise in other contexts, especially in the recent push for ecological waste disposal, in which recycling constituted a top priority. Artists and activists led campaigns to recognize the innovative aspects of recycling and other ecological practices in impoverished Roma communities like Pod, dubbing the shacks of people in such communities 'eco-architecture' because all the materials used to build them are recycled (Orta 2010). But these initiatives were more visible abroad, and unfortunately they did not affect the PHARE programmes' definitions of Roma culture as grounded in traditional occupations.

When I suggested that recycling work should be recognized and that PHARE programmes might provide a framework to do so, Victor replied: 'if they continue to work each for themselves, I'm not going to be able to help. If they get hired, they need to follow a schedule. They can't be doing every-thing on their own. Their work would be regulated'. He claimed that Pod entrepreneurialism was too selfish and insufficiently collective, even though in fact the whole country was then undergoing a process of privatization, and enterprise was the new buzzword. People in Pod were not waiting for anyone to help them, and they were already displaying the values of individualism and self-reliance that neoliberal ideologies were teaching the former socialist countries. The difference, however, was that they refused to be regulated. They were already engaged in income-generating activities, without the input of councillors or social workers. The kind of work they did, which in other contexts was being promoted in the EU as recycling, was unthinkable within the rigid frames of EU funding.[8] Their self-reliance and individualism were not in line with the NSISR, and they were not engaged in any of the traditional crafts that would be valued as 'culture'.

Ironically, many of the Roma involved in scavenging scrap metal displayed all the elements of business-making that some of the PHARE programmes were supposed to help them develop. As I have shown, successful entrepreneurs like Dumitru and Adam saw themselves as helping the community members who worked for them. However, instead of taking their ongoing activities as starting points and working with them to develop a legal framework for those activities, activists like Victor insisted that these Roma only wanted to work for themselves, were selfish, and did not care about the community. All these values were at the core of the capitalist work ethic, but when presented as part of Pod residents' behaviour they took on negative undertones.

For Victor, Roma in Pod were not authentic enough to be traditional, and needed vocational training to discipline them into becoming employees and 'team players, not entrepreneurial figures' (Ong 2006, 221). As I showed in Chapter 2, recycling practices in Pod benefited the local refuse company, which did not have to provide security or decent working conditions for the pickers, who were exposed to incredibly high levels of risk. Waste disposal practices in Romania at this time did not involve recycling, a situation that was supposed to change after EU membership and Pod residents were already recycling goods even before Romania joined the EU. The object of their work – vast landfill sites – was supposed to disappear with the introduction of ecological practices and there would have been many ways to encourage them to stay involved in those practices and to recognize that the work they were already doing brought many benefits to different parties, including the city and the refuse company.

In the PHARE programmes there was space for informal labour only as long as it complied with 'authenticity' definitions of Roma: the revival of traditional crafts was a recurring theme in these programmes and the larger NSISR. However, while some Roma groups were successfully working as coppersmiths and silversmiths, other traditional Roma crafts had become completely marginal and their productivity minimal, and many Roma had stopped engaging in traditional activities. An example of how the PHARE programmes assisted 'authentic' Roma informal labour is the National Agency for the Roma's poster-child PHARE project with Roma from a Cărămidari (brick making) community: this focused on Roma who were engaged in traditional crafts and could start productive businesses. Traditional crafts were envisioned as the object of income-generating activities, with Roma NGOs, local state authorities and other third parties working together to support authentic Roma craftspeople. Such a definition was easily applied literally, thereby excluding people like Pod residents and this exclusion was exacerbated by the use of informal funding networks: the much-coveted non-reimbursable credit from the EU, which was available for a limited number of grants, was directed as much through informal networks in Romania as it was through the PHARE programmes' application procedures, and there was no publicly available information about the grants.

So far I have shown the widening gap between labour practices in Pod and the focus on tradition, as well as the failure to address the links between poverty and exclusion in the NSISR. Ultimately, I believe, Pod residents were disqualified from PHARE programmes simply for being insignificant in light of larger interests at local authority headquarters. It would therefore be very easy to read the PHARE rubrics and find no space in them for Pod residents. For example, the medical facilities opened under a similar programme a few years before had remained closed for a long time. The official explanation was that there were not enough people in Pod to qualify for a family doctor – a preposterous proposition given the number of people in the settlement. According to Armando, the real reason was that no doctor was willing to go to Pod. In contrast, local authorities had found sufficient resources for the recently opened new police station on the site and, as I showed in Chapter 2, Pod was heavily surveilled by the police, despite local authorities' apparently uninterested and laissez-faire attitude towards residents.

Conclusion

The structural limitations of the PHARE programmes and their intersections with informal networks of power in Romania constituted a mix that made it very unlikely that the poorest and neediest Roma would benefit from these programmes' resources. As I have shown, this was partially due to the programmes themselves, which focused on culture and authenticity, and on the training of activists and their display of civility. The failure was also partly due to intersections with the secondary economy that created new sets of exclusions, such as the lack of access to information. Most significantly, most Roma had no access to the resources available through these programmes, as local networks of power, including government and NGOs, competed for these resources. This did not make it impossible for any projects to reach those in need; it only made it very unlikely.

The failure of social programmes to treat the situation of the Roma in Romania historically, and their embrace of the triumphalist discourse of neoliberalism and 'culture', led to the dominance of authenticity criteria and differentiation based on a contrast between 'good', deserving Roma and 'bad', undeserving ones. In the current political configuration, Roma deserve attention only insofar as they are 'authentic', and the undeserving ones have only themselves to blame. The problems of homelessness, eviction, squatting and the lack of IDs, which are all endemic in places like Pod, are ignored.

Between the reprivatization of nationalized properties, gentrification, and the closing of plants and collective farms during post-socialism on the one hand, and the emphasis on traditional occupations in social programmes on the other, urban working-class Roma have been left out. Despite the fact that status distinctions were among the actual outcomes of training processes, such as the one I attended, any discussion of class differentiation was completely obliterated, and the poor Roma who were targets of these social programmes were constructed as cultureless or inauthentic. The absence of class analysis during the discussion at the training session of the living conditions and hardships of impoverished Roma was further aggravated by the activists' need to distinguish themselves from socialist practices, which were all lumped altogether as negative. The casting of the socialist period as a failure with regard to Roma obliterated the instrumentalization of culture in neoliberalism as well as considerations of social justice.

The overall dismissal of class analysis as socialist-sounding rhetoric is somewhat ironic, as many poor Roma under socialism had benefited from housing provision and free education, and many had been employed, albeit in low-skilled jobs. Many Roma from Pod described pre-1989 times in more nuanced ways and emphasized that they had been better off in those days. The rhetoric of PHARE programmes has reinforced abject stereotypes and has not allowed any discussion of the causes of poverty under neoliberalism, such as discrimination or racism.

Notes

1. An official report on the strategy is available at www.publicinfo.gov.ro/library/10_raport_tipar_p_ro.pdf. (last accessed 21 June 2010).
2. Some activists may find creative ways to bring about change despite such processes (see Keck and Sikkink 1998; Hemment 2007; Phillips 2008).
3. See Englund (2006) on a similar situation in Malawi.
4. As John and Jean Comaroff (2009, 49) argue, in neoliberal capitalism culture equals 'the quintessential site of self-construction', as 'ethnic consciousness has become the socioeconomic vehicle of cultural diversity'.
5. Jon McKenzie (2003) explains: 'Thus under performativity, public accountability increasingly entails the forced quantification of the nonquantifiable, the qualitative, and this forced quantification, I would argue, accounts for many of performativity's perversities'.
6. Harri Englund (2006, 72) critiques the production of certificates on human rights training in Malawi: 'Through certificates, closed workshops, common appearance, and human rights jargon (often in English), a commitment to the project and its particular world-view was generated. Crucial to this emerging quasi-professional identity were

those disadvantaged and poor Malawians – the grassroots – who were excluded from the group'.

7. The equivalent of £1.

8. As Kelsall (2003, 198) argues, 'The leading donor agencies, such as the European Union and many bilateral donors, prove to be highly rigid in envisaging the forms that their engagement with democratization could take. Various indigenous practices, in particular, remained unthinkable as targets of external funding'.

Chapter 4

Performing Bollywood

Young Roma Dance Cultural Citizenship

At a show in the local Cultural House, three young Roma men stand onstage, legs apart, chests pushed forward, heads turned to the right. They are Giani, Tibi and Cosmin, members of Together, a group of young Roma and non-Roma[1] people from Pod and elsewhere. With his hair slicked back, Giani is wearing a skin-tight, black sleeveless T-shirt, tight black trousers with a big metal-buckled belt, and two thick chains around his neck, a large cross hanging from one; he is flanked by the other two young men, also dressed in black shirts and black trousers. As the Bollywood tune 'Mohopet' starts, they begin to dance: arms flexed and hips thrust forward, heads tilting and rolling from side to side, they go through undulating arm and body movements and vigorous sideways jumps. As the song reaches the refrain, Giani lip-synchs to the recording and walks backwards, arms in the air, body undulating, to welcome three young women from upstage. Giani's partner wears a sequined bra top with hanging coins, and a split skirt covers her leggings; the other two young women wear black tank tops and tights. All three sport high heels, and scarves with beads and coins wrapped around their waists. The women join their partners, and the six dancers step forwards in unison, shimmying and leaning back and forth, then step left and right to the rhythm of the tune, and shimmying in place with their arms flexed, lower their torsos close to the ground.

—Field notes, June 2008

In this chapter I argue that Together's intercultural and cosmopolitan dance practices, which included Roma, Romanian and Bollywood-inspired dances such as that described above, represent embodied expressions and performances of cultural citizenship – defined as the right to be different while belonging to the nation (Rosaldo 1993) – and offer a critique of hegemonic monoethnic identity paradigms in Romania. Drawing on an approach to children's rights that takes into account living rights (rather than abstract rights) and the importance of social justice principles in judging the success of rights implementation (Hanson and Nieuwenhuys 2012), I analyse Together's dance practices as a response to the citizenship gap they experienced and the failure of their rights as children, including the right to education. Despite new initiatives to improve the educational experience of Roma children, most such children (including the dancers in Together) continued to face discrimination and a lack of equal opportunities. As one of the studies in the international project Edumigrom ('Ethnic Differences in Education and Diverging Prospects for Urban Youth in an Enlarged Europe') found:

> The accounts of Roma students in Central European countries ... brought up a wide range of examples of regular and severe discrimination and openly prejudiced and even racist remarks of teachers, peers, and others in the close surroundings. Still, interviews with students and parents showed that Roma adolescents often did not interpret such behaviour as being discriminated against but as something that is a regular, and therefore 'natural' concomitant of daily life. (Szalai 2011, 20)

In my discussion of resistance in Pod, here and elsewhere, I am mindful – following Foucault (1978, 95–96) – that where there is power, there is resistance. Some of the forms of resistance identified in this chapter, such as Together's dance practices, were more productive than others, and I see these different forms of resistance on a continuum, as forms of expression of these young people's subjectivities. Using ethnographic research carried out between 2006 and 2011, I show that while some of the Roma students I interviewed had indeed normalized the discrimination they experienced, most of them had not, and they resisted the system in a variety of ways, including through low engagement at school, and in some cases through refusal to be enrolled in 'special schools' for children with learning disabilities, a common fate for Roma children. The young people in Together critiqued both the discrimination they experienced in school and the commodification and current success of Roma performances in dance festivals and television soaps, which some of them saw as an appropriation and exploitation of Roma culture.

In the first half of this chapter I discuss how Together members experienced and resisted the citizenship gap in the classroom in the larger context of the

Romanian education system; in the second half I focus on their resistance and subjectivities as expressed through their dance performances.

The Citizenship Gap in the Classroom

In this section I focus on the educational experiences of several young Roma in Together, including Giani, Tibi, Cosmin, Gabi and Gelu, all from Pod. Giani and Tibi, who were sixteen and fourteen respectively in 2008, when I recorded most of my interviews with them, attended a mainstream school; Gabi, aged fourteen, and Cosmin, aged eighteen, attended or had attended segregated schools officially designed for poor Roma students, as well as special schools for the disabled, which are attended by a disproportionate number of Roma students. Gelu, aged six, had finished his first year in a mainstream school. All of the girls in Together bar one were non-Roma and attended the same mainstream school as Giani and Tibi, where Armando also worked.

In 2005 Armando became employed on a part-time basis in a mainstream school as a school mediator for Roma communities. His job was to encourage attendance among Roma students. Between 2006 and 2010 I visited several schools, mainstream and special, that young people from Pod attended. I also accompanied Armando on trips to visit families whose children were at risk of dropping out of school or were failing academically, often because of poor attendance. Young men from Pod tended to attend school for longer than young women, who were often forced to leave school to help at home with younger siblings and other chores.

My own data, as well as sociological and education studies research, shows that Roma students continue to experience discrimination in the educational system in Romania as well as in most other East Central European countries (Miskovic 2009; Vincze 2011; Szalai 2011; Edumigrom 2011). The 2004 European Roma Rights Centre (ERRC) study 'Stigmata: Segregated Schooling of Children in Central and Eastern Europe' provides ample detail on the discrimination Roma children suffer in the educational systems in five countries, including Romania. The study lists as the main encroachments on children's rights the enrolment of Roma children in schools for children with learning disabilities (so-called special schools in Romania); segregation in all-Roma schools or all-Roma classes; denial of enrolment in mainstream schools; and the generally inferior quality of education for Roma children (ERRC 2004). The ERRC's 2006 report on the situation of Roma in Romania highlighted that the National Strategy for Improving the Situation of Roma (NSISR) had had a limited impact, and that in most areas discrimination continued despite the creation of kindergartens to prepare disadvantaged Roma children for mainstream education, and of bursaries and Roma quotas in secondary schools and universities (Council of Europe Report on Romania 2006). As mentioned in Chapter 1, the curriculum taught and continues to teach the history of ethnic Romanians only; only Roma children had the option of studying Roma history and Romani language in optional courses.

In a 2011 report on the education system in Romania, Enikő Vincze presented the tensions that had been at work over previous decades. These included on the one hand progressive policies put in place to address the disadvantage faced by Roma children, and on the other hand the failure to attend to larger issues such as the values of multiculturalism promoted in the system, which did not encourage interculturalism or the mixing of students with different ethnic backgrounds: 'without an intersectional approach and without structural transformations aiming to redress socio-economic inequalities, educational policies do not have the strength to generate sustainable changes. Moreover, during times of economic crises they are endangered by being neglected and cut' (Vincze 2011, 9). New initiatives, such as the introduction of quotas for Roma students, Roma school mediators and inclusive policies, were superimposed onto ongoing institutionalized racism in the education system.[2] These progressive measures had had different results at the schools I visited during fieldwork in Romania, but overall their outcomes were not successful.

In 2008 Roma students from Pod were still overrepresented in special schools, and only around 10 per cent of the child population attended a mainstream school. Many had started the first year in a mainstream school, but after a couple of years had transferred to a special school. Despite being a pervasive practice, not only in Romania but across East Central Europe (ERRC 2004), Roma children's enrolment in schools for the disabled was and remains little known to the general public. Social workers, psychologists and teachers tacitly accepted, rationalized and perpetuated this practice, which predated postsocialism. During Communism, the official mission of the education system was to 'civilize' and 'modernize' Roma through assimilation policies that acted as 'technologies of governance' (Ong 2003), rooted in a racist and totalitarian ideology that saw Roma children as having learning disabilities because they were bilingual. These practices continued after 1989, in parallel with and despite the new quotas for Roma students in secondary schools and universities (Vincze 2011). Non-Roma sometimes critiqued Roma quotas as arbitrary and unjustly favouring Roma, without being aware of the ongoing discrimination in the educational system. While some Roma children did take advantage of the quotas, many of them experienced discrimination in primary and secondary school, as was the case with children in Pod.

In 2008 Giani was in his first year at a vocational school, after having completed eight years in a mainstream school. He described how poor (or poor-looking) Roma students were treated as Țigani and racialized on the basis of a variety of external markers:

So because of their clothing, or maybe because they were not well groomed, they were looked at differently. And anyway, this word Ţigan was something absurd. As if one wasn't a person. Even the teachers would discriminate.

In a conversation in 2008, Mira, a Romni and mother from Pod, showed that she was also aware and critical of the discrimination Roma children faced, succinctly describing the processes of racialization of poverty that underpinned how the citizenship gap for Roma children was maintained in schools. She explained how it was possible that many Roma children in Romania continued to be sent to special schools, just as they had been during socialism:

If they see you're cleaner, they send you to the D school [mainstream school]. If they see you're a little dirty, they say you won't make it and they send you to the school on B road [special school].

The school system would equate a child's low social status with disability and prevent them from attending a mainstream school. Mira's assessment reflected the shocking reality that eighteen years after the end of socialism, and one and a half years into Romania's EU membership, Roma children continued to be discriminated against and pathologized. The difference between 2008 and Communism, she pointed out, was that in those days 'they would only take these kids to the special school'. Now some of them, the 'cleaner-looking ones', might actually be allowed to enrol in mainstream schools. School personnel assessed the public performances of the child and parent and racialized them as Mira described, playing an instrumental role in maintaining the citizenship gap for Roma in education.

From All-Roma Schools to Special Schools: The Persistence of Discrimination

In 2006 I visited the Roma-only remedial section of the mainstream school, which was organized for Pod students. For five years the section had been part of the school where Armando currently worked. It had a reduced curriculum, like the special schools for students with learning disabilities, but it catered to poor Roma students only, and provided a school bus, free meals, and help with homework to encourage them to attend school more regularly. (The journey to the school, about two or three miles from Pod, was long and dangerous for a child, as it involved crossing railway lines and climbing a hill to reach the closest bus stop.) In effect, this school section was a smaller version of the special schools, where Roma students were also offered free meals and free transport to and from school. Designed to remedy material inequalities, these provisions came at the price of treating young people as having learning disabilities.

Ironically, poor Roma children such as Giani, who stayed in mainstream education against the odds, were not encouraged in the same way, and school buses only came for students who attended non-mainstream schools.[3]

During my visit I spoke to two teachers and visited two classes. There were blatant differences in the treatment of remedial and mainstream school students. The remedial classes were very small, with four or five students each, and followed the curriculum for students with learning disabilities. The two teachers, both young women, complained about the students' poor discipline; students in this Roma-only school section had a bad reputation as violent and recalcitrant, and there was an emphasis on policing them. Over 90% of the students in this section were male, and fights between them often broke out in the hallways and classrooms. Teachers regarded this behaviour as proof of the young Roma's bad character and lack of respect for authority.

I interviewed several young Roma about their experiences within the education system. In 2008 Cosmin was employed by a refuse company, as was his father. He told me how he had been tested and sent to a special school. He called the special school a Roma school, thus changing 'special' from a derogatory into a more positive qualifier:[4] 'There are only Ţigan kids there. That's why they call it Special School Number Eight. It's a school for Roma kids only'. His interpretation of the school's name reflected the reality that special schools had become synonymous with Roma schools, and that recruitment was based on ethnicity rather than intellectual ability. Some of the parents I spoke with associated 'special' with the material conditions offered, rather than the reduced curriculum. Some told me that they had never been told that educational standards and achievements would be lower in the special school, while others knew about the school's reduced curriculum. As Cosmin pointed out, parents did not expect their children to become doctors or teachers, and many had little faith in the education system.

Even though he and his parents did not dispute the test committee's verdict about his alleged learning disabilities (harshly expressed as low IQ), Cosmin subsequently resisted the system in many ways. Despite pressure from his family to continue, he left school after Year Nine and went to work for the local refuse company. His younger brother was also enrolled in a special school, and, like Cosmin, attended erratically. Despite stereotypes about Roma refusing education and parents not encouraging their children to go to school, my research found the opposite: I see the students' so-called bad behaviour as resistance to their treatment as second-class citizens. This knee-jerk reaction was ultimately detrimental to the children themselves, but it was the result of their mistreatment in the education system. Their recalcitrant behaviour, which also performatively indexed countercultural masculinity, was passed down among siblings and friends and although apparently defiant, in fact it colluded with the institutionalized racism of the system, keeping Roma students away from education.

With Romania's EU membership and the official recognition of the Roma, measures were implemented to encourage Roma children to stay in education, including the addition of Roma elements, i.e. people, courses and cultural performances. However, the values and practices embedded in the school system remained unexamined, and obviously discriminatory practices continued, hidden under positive labels. Following Romania's EU accession and membership, starting from 2007, schools that officially catered for Roma students, including the one Cosmin had attended, were closed down because they were seen to encourage segregation; this in turn caused an invisible traffic in discrimination, as children from these schools were sent to the special schools, which officially catered for students with learning disabilities and were seen as inclusive (see Vincze 2011). Official discourse claimed that Roma had the right to an inclusive education based on multicultural principles and because special schools admitted students with learning disabilities, they were seen as inclusive, even though Roma children without disabilities continued to be enrolled in them. When Cosmin's school was closed down, the students were automatically transferred to a special school – without being asked – rather than to the mainstream school within the same premises. This is only one example of the persistence of institutionalized racism in education, despite legislation against it.

In 2008 I visited one of these special schools for children with disabilities. The school enrolled a high percentage of poor Roma students, including many children from Pod, who were registered as intellectually deficient but in fact were there because they were Roma and poor (a situation that continues today). Ironically, the school had recently received EU recognition as a 'European inclusive school' for its allegedly progressive and inclusive educational practices.

The school had a social mediator in charge of teaching Roma culture and language to Roma students. She told me that students were required to take an IQ test every four years. Some Roma children were listed as 'intellectually deficient' or having a 'liminal intellect' only four years after being declared apt for mainstream education. In fact, according to the school mediator, Roma children initially enrolled in mainstream education would subsequently be transferred to a special school because of poor attendance or 'bad behaviour'. An IQ test would serve to justify the transfer. The school mediator described these Roma students, most of them male, as misbehaving and unmanageable, and explained that young, inexperienced, female teachers were unable to cope with a class of mainly male students. Some of the teachers did not even try to discipline students and during class time many students would be outside, playing in the playground.

Blaming the Parents

Romanian media often blamed parents for poor Roma children's lack of attendance and low success rates in school; as mentioned above, the general discrimination engrained in the school system was not known, including the disproportionate number of Roma students attending special schools, and the invisible traffic of Roma students to these unofficially segregated special schools from the more openly segregated mainstream schools. The blaming of Roma parents erased the pervasive institutionalized racism that Roma experienced, and of which the education system was only one instance. Most of the Roma parents from Pod whom I met wanted their children to study and supported them as much as they could. A very few did not want to send their children to school, and these were the exception rather than the rule. Most parents were also aware and critical of the segregation in the school system, and rated their children's chances of success as very low.

Cosmin told me that his mother used to pay him to stay in school, but he did not stay. He had been attending a segregated remedial school whose curriculum did not engage him, and he confessed that he had been frustrated that they were studying easy subjects. With hindsight, he felt that he and his fellow students had been treated like second-class citizens and had studied less than their peers in mainstream education, but he said that at the time they had enjoyed the free meals and numerous breaks. Most students from Pod worked outside school hours; they collected scrap metal and other recyclable materials, helped their parents with household chores and did odd jobs and so had little time to study. Students in Cosmin's school were supposed to stay in school after hours to do their homework for the following day. Despite the schedule being designed to support Roma students to complete their homework before they returned home, Cosmin found the homework basic and unchallenging, and said that students would spend the afternoon listening to music rather than study-ing. The education system treated these Roma children as academic failures, and their cultural and socio-economic differences as learning disabilities.

As the 2004 ERRC report on Roma children's education and other reports on discrimination highlighted, testing methods that determined children's enrolment in special schools were often culturally biased and did not take into account many Roma children's bilingualism. Psychological and IQ tests took (and continue to take) place in intimidating conditions, often without parents' knowledge.[5] The only way for a student to transfer back from a spe-cial school to a mainstream school was for the parents to appeal against the committee's decision but given many Roma parents' low expectations and lack of knowledge of how the school system worked, most were unlikely to appeal. Financial incentives also made many parents accept special schools more readily: the cost of clothes, stationery and the school fund was covered by the state in special schools, but not in mainstream schools; for this reason it was more difficult for some parents to support their children in supposedly free mainstream education. Giani reflected on Roma parents whose children attended special schools:

Even shoes, clothes, they received aid of that kind at those schools. I can't say myself that I had great conditions. We used to live in a rented flat. I lived in a rented flat from the age of seven – with my mum and dad. But even so, I still preferred to go to the ordinary school. If I'm wasting my time in school anyway, at least I should attend a proper school.

Giani's teacher had attempted to transfer him to a special school in his first year but he stayed in the mainstream school because of his mother's intervention. Vanesa and other mothers described to me how they had to fight with teachers to prevent their children from being transferred to special schools, which would often be suggested by the teacher for no other reason than that the child was Roma and from a disadvantaged background. Despite his attending a main-stream school, Giani's engagement was low, and he did not feel that the school could help him to fulfil his aspirations. For him, dance was a way to 'get ahead' and show his worth to teachers who looked down on him because he was a Rom.

Another example from Pod illustrates how children judged to be underper-forming would be transferred to special schools, and their parents' dilemma in the face of contradictory messages. In 2008 I accompanied Armando on a trip to Pod to deliver warning letters to parents about their children's school progress. The first stop was to see a first-year pupil who had not passed into the second year. Gelu was a little blond boy with green eyes. Dressed in a green T-shirt and tracksuit bottoms, he was seated on the floor in the single-room construction. He was eating soup with bread, and had a kitten beside him. Both his parents were at home. His father, who seemed younger than his mother, was employed by the city hall to collect detritus from demolition sites. When Armando handed him the letter, Gelu's father read it aloud and then started screaming at Gelu, who was now seated on the sofa with his plate next to him. The father said that 'while these folk are here' Gelu had to decide what he was going to do, as he, the father, was working hard to keep him in school, while Gelu was scatty and did not study properly. The father said:

> I did ten years of school, my wife can't read, and when I come back tired from work, not once did he [Gelu] ask me for help with his homework. He comes home from school, drops his bag, and that's it, he's out. And I made the mistake of buying him a bike. His clothes are dirtier than if he were from the dump. It breaks my heart to send him with clean fresh clothes. By the time he gets to school, he is covered in mud. Even the teacher said she could not cope with him. She did not know what to do.

Gelu's mother said that she would be ashamed to go back to school in the autumn with him in the first year again, as he would likely have to repeat the year. 'You will be one of those who were enrolled in the first year until age seventeen',[6] she said. Gelu's father added: 'You will end up in jail or at the dump, over there. At least those at the dump work. They work hard. You will end up in jail'. 'Like Păcală,' said Gelu's mother, referring to a trickster character in folktales. 'Look,' she said to me, 'his sister, who will be in Year Five, is at the seaside. She got first prize'. The sister's diploma was on the wall. His mother said that maybe she should take him to the special school. 'He's not stupid,' said his father. 'It would be a pity to take him there'. His sister, however, attended a special school. When I asked the mother if she knew that they studied a reduced curriculum in special schools, she nodded. She said she was afraid to send her daughter there again, as one never knew what might happen. She seemed to be suggesting that children were not appropriately supervised in that school, but she did not elaborate. Gelu then spoke for the first time and said he would prefer the special school.

After we left, I asked Armando whether he could take Gelu to the preparatory kindergarten, which was designed for impoverished Roma children about to start their first year of school. Armando said that he would not take him, because he had tried before: 'There's no way with him. When he is sent for punishment he laughs; it does not help. He's got a reduced IQ. Maybe he needs to be taken to the special school'. Gelu's father had also confirmed that he had tried physical punishment several times, but it had not worked. Gelu's mother said she wanted to transfer their daughter out of the special school, so he would not be going there either, because money was taken out of their wages every month for transport and food.[7]

Armando, who was against IQ tests, invoked Gelu's test results as if they had been a reflection of his aptitudes, and confessed that he was at his wits' end because Gelu was difficult to manage. Hegemonic practices, even when questioned, could be internalized in circumstances when people had no other explanations or solutions. Children like Gelu preferred to go to special schools to join their siblings, and among Roma children from Pod these schools had a reputation for being easier and more fun than mainstream schools.

Many of the children whose families we visited on that trip had very poor attendance. While Armando did his best to alert state institutions, his previous experiences with such services gave him little faith that any of the children with poor attendance would receive help. Local authorities replied to Armando's letters when he alerted them about problem cases, but little was done. Social interventions carried out in this system were unlikely to encourage students to stay in mainstream education. Parents' most frequently invoked reasons for their children's poor attendance were the lack of shoes and clothes, as well as poverty: many parents took children to work with them on the refuse site. Each case was complex, requiring attention from specialists; but first and foremost it required fair treatment from an education system that did not place value on these children as human beings.

Even when cases of discrimination in the education system go to court, the results are limited. Following an unsuccessful action in the Czech courts in 1999, a discrimination case from the Czech Republic was taken to the European Court of Human Rights in 2000 on behalf of eighteen Roma children represented by the ERRC and local lawyers. The evidence before the court was based on ERRC research in the city of Ostrava, where over half of the Roma child population were educated in schools for children with learning disabilities. As the ERRC report showed:

> Over half of the population of remedial special schools is Romani. Any randomly chosen Romani child is more than 27 times more likely to be placed in schools for the learning disabled than a similarly situated non-Romani child. Even where Romani children manage to avoid the trap of placement in remedial special schooling, they are most often schooled in substandard and predominantly Romani urban schools ... Tests used to assess the children's mental ability were culturally biased against Czech Roma, and placement procedures allowed for the influence of racial prejudice on the part of educational authorities. (European Roma Rights Center 2007, no page number)

The case was eventually successful in 2007, and the defendants were awarded €4,000 in damages. However, the money could hardly make up for a world of lost opportunities, and these results have not actually led to a change in the school system.[8]

Quotas for Roma Students: Resistance and Lack of Information

The quotas for Roma in Romania's secondary schools and universities were a positive discrimination measure designed to encourage Roma educational success. However, even when Roma students did well in mainstream primary and secondary education, there was a lack of information and guidance to help them take advantage of the quotas.

In 2008 I attended one of the regional annual meetings for students applying to secondary or vocational schools under the quotas for Roma students. As school mediator, Armando was accompanying Together dance group members Tibi and Alina, both Roma students in their final year at the mainstream school where Armando worked. Giani, who had graduated the previous year, was now studying in a vocational school under the quotas for Roma students, and he accompanied his friends to the meeting to give them support.

The meeting was postponed by half an hour without any explanation. Eventually the regional inspector and the inspector on Roma issues and education arrived and let everyone into a meeting room at the Ministry of Education's regional headquarters. About forty people – parents, students and school mediators – sat down at a long table headed by the two officials. They read out the names of each school and asked the students who were applying to those places to come forward and bring their supporting documents.

Tibi, a skinny, slightly shy young man, had chosen the same school as Giani, who had promised to defend him if other boys tried to beat him up. 'Giani made me go there. He said they would not beat me if I go there,' said Tibi. Tibi had a good overall mark, above the pass mark required to be able to enrol under the quotas, and could have chosen secondary school instead of vocational school. He told me that he had heard that secondary schools were boring and you needed a good head for study. I told him that he was capable of studying, as far as I could tell, and that secondary school could open up more opportunities for him in the future. Tibi was convinced that secondary school was not for him.

Alina, who lived in a foster home sponsored by a German NGO, was determined to go to a secondary school with a very good reputation in the humanities, because she wanted to go on and get a law degree under the quotas for Roma students, in order to become a lawyer and then a judge. Armando told me: 'See, I like Alina: she knows what she wants and is determined'. She had advisors who encouraged her at the foster home, unlike Tibi, who lived with his parents and did not get any guidance from home or school. Alina was surprised that Tibi, who had a higher average mark than hers, was not considering secondary school: 'It's better in secondary school, isn't it?' Nobody had explained Tibi's options to him, the difference between secondary school and vocational school, or the existence of quotas in universities. Armando, who was very supportive of his students, was not aware of all the available opportunities either.

I urged Tibi to at least consider the secondary school option. Giani initially laughed off the suggestion, but then agreed that one had better future prospects if one graduated from secondary school. Tibi decided to choose the secondary school section of the institution where Giani's vocational school was located. He wanted to know whether the secondary school and vocational school were in the same building, and when Giani told him that they were, he said: 'That's fine, we [Giani and he] would not have been in the same class anyway'. He then decided to apply for a place in the secondary school section of that institution.

Several young people from Pod who attended a special school gave explanations similar to Tibi's for preferring the special school, despite knowing that they were studying a reduced curriculum. One girl told me that the special school was better, because they played more and her siblings went there as well, and the children were not as mean as in other schools. Roma students faced discrimination not only from school officials, but also from other students, who often called them names, ostracized them or bullied them. Going to school with one's friends (as in Tibi's case) or siblings ensured a level of protection – including from other Roma students. One young man told me that some Roma students, not from Pod, were very mean at his school.

Educating and Informing via Roma-led Television Programmes

The lack of information and awareness about the quotas among Roma children and parents in Pod was not surprising. In fact, the only instance during my fieldwork when I heard practical information about the quotas for Roma being discussed in the media was on the *Roma Caravan* (*Caravana Romilor* in Romanian) programme, the oldest TV programme with and about Roma on Romanian television. For a long time most Roma in Pod could not watch this programme, because it was broadcast on a small private channel that could only be received with a special antenna. As I show in the next chapter, Roma-run television programmes such as *Roma Caravan* addressed an emergent Roma counterpublic and discussed issues such as the quotas in education, which although legally supported by the government, were highly controversial among the majority of Romanians. The mainstream media were more likely to perpetuate stereotypes of Roma parents and children as refusing education than to inform their viewers about ongoing discrimination or quotas for Roma students.

On a 2009 *Roma Caravan* show dedicated to Roma quotas in education, there was a discussion of the application process for quotas in higher education. Participating in the discussion were two Roma politicians: Cătălin Manea, vice-president of the Roma Party for Europe, and Iulian Paraschiv, president of the party's youth organization. 'Two future university students', as the moderator called them, Mirela Radu and Leonard Fieraru, also participated.

The two politicians stated that their party had issued approximately 320 letters of recommendation for higher education in 2009, around 100 of them for Bucharest. (These letters of recommendation were necessary for Roma students to prove that they were Roma ethnics in order to enrol under the quotas.) Manea emphasized that the letters of recommendation did not guarantee a place unless the student had a pass mark; if there were more candidates than places, those with higher marks would be admitted. The moderator asked Manea whether Roma students suffered discrimination because they were studying under the quotas. He replied that for the young people he knew it was not an issue, because they were well prepared, proud to be Roma and determined to graduate, but he emphasized the need for counsellors in secondary schools who could advise students about the quotas in universities; Radu then explained that she had found out about the quotas through a *Roma Caravan* programme, and had consequently enrolled in secondary school under the quotas.

Paraschiv highlighted the need for the majority to understand that Roma had real values and to put an end to the stereotype that all Roma were impoverished or beggars. The moderator asked the two young people if they had ever encountered discrimination in secondary school. Radu replied: 'Discrimination exists, but I can't say it affected me, because I adapted and I was in a nice class'.

The moderator asked her if anyone had complained about her studying under the Roma quotas. Paraschiv intervened:

> See, miss, even you have a wrong perception, forgive me for telling you straight. You are studying under the quotas – what is the problem? Mr Păun[9] himself has been telling us that admission does not boil down to the letter of recommendation, that many can be top of their class on graduation. It no longer matters if you're Chinese, American, an Aborigine from Papua New Guinea or a Romanian citizen of Roma ethnicity.

Here the Roma politician was projecting a positive vision of a future that was possible in Romania, but mainly for the well-informed and better-off Roma. He was also keen to move the discussion away from discrimination.

However, the moderator had a point, because the quotas for Roma students were seen as unjustified by many non-Roma, who did not share the view that Roma were discriminated against and therefore regarded the quotas as discrimination against non-Roma. As much as Roma needed to be informed about opportunities that existed for them, there was also a need to inform and educate non-Roma, including teachers, about the discrimination in the education system and the role of the quotas in changing the long history of anti-Roma discrimination. For example, in 2011 *European Rom*, a programme on the public television channel TVR1, the only public TV show that focused on Roma, advertised an open competition for scholarships and tutorships for Roma students who wanted to pursue a medical career; this was part of an EU-funded campaign to encourage Roma students to become health professionals and prepare them for admission to medical school. But neither the advertisement nor the programme explained why such campaigns were necessary. I did find one instance where the quotas for Roma students were explained, but only one: on the website of the NGO ActiveWatch, there was a testimonial from a successful candidate, who stated: 'We were slaves for 300 years'.[10] Roma history remains little known, and more reminders like this may help to teach non-Roma about the past, linking the past to the present, and to the quotas in education.

Together: Dancing across Cultures, in Mainstream and Special Schools

Together was formed as a result of the recent success of Roma dance in and outside schools. With the post-socialist recognition of the Roma by the state and the NSISR, Roma students were encouraged to perform their culture in schools, even as that culture was defined in the problematic terms described in Chapters 1 and 3. At Armando's school, a mainstream school with a relatively large number of Roma students, the Roma students who danced 'Roma dance' at school festivities were very popular.

The ideas and dance techniques of Together came from the dancers themselves, and Armando acted as the group's advisor and manager, whose role was mainly to find them gigs. Initially comprising students from the mainstream school only, as they started to perform elsewhere the group was joined by Pod Roma students who attended special schools, including Cosmin and Gabi. Their repertoire and style were mostly set by Giani, who had previously danced at various festivals. The other dancers had had less experience onstage before joining the group; some, like the non-Roma, had danced in the mainstream school's Romanian folk dance group.

Most of the Roma members of Together danced at parties in their own communities, and they often collaborated with Giani in choreographing their numbers. Given their fraught experiences in schools, dance represented a way to communicate on their own terms, and to express their subjectivities and cultural citizenship while being successful and appreciated by others. It became clear from talking to them that dance was important to all of them. All of them were aware of the different kinds of discrimination they faced in schools, including the young people who accepted or allegedly preferred special schools.

The multicultural principles in the education system did not encourage intercultural exchanges among children from different backgrounds. Children who came from mixed backgrounds had to choose which ethnic identity to endorse performatively in their choice of school and dance. The normative monoethnic performativity pervasive in the curriculum was further reflected in the practice of ethnic and folk dance. Only Romanian dances were technically called 'folk' dances in Romania and, as I discussed in Chapter 1, the construction of the 'Romanian folk' did not include other ethnicities: in schools, Romanian students performed Romanian folk dances, Hungarian students performed Hungarian folk dances, and so on. In most schools, authenticity criteria regulated Roma ethnicity: only Roma students performed 'Roma dance', and they never mingled with other ethnic folk dance groups. This interpretation of heritage bred segregation, locking students within their own cultural backgrounds. The essentialism of the definitions of citizenship in Romania was thus reproduced on school and festival stages and in the promotion of national folklore.

Departing from these practices, Together performed a variety of styles, from Roma to Romanian and Bollywood-inspired dances. Given the hegemonic essentialist views of identity in the school system and beyond, Together's multi-ethnic constituency and multicultural repertoire were significant. They had consciously chosen to go against these hegemonic practices, and their dances reflected the discrepancy between the imaginings of Roma culture imposed through the official discourse of recognition and the ways in which young Roma people thought of themselves and their culture. Young Roma in the group, all of whom were from poor backgrounds, were claiming a Roma identity that was influenced by global cultural movements and capital flows, but which went against the authenticity criteria imposed during neoliberal post-socialism.

Inspired by their consumption of Bollywood films, Together's Bollywood dances disrupted simplistic definitions of culture and ethnicity, and displayed their affective transnational connections to a global Roma diaspora represented through India as an imagined place. Their Bollywood dance performances were a critical commentary on the citizenship gap they experienced, both materially and culturally, in their daily lives and in school, as well as an expression of belonging to Romania while claiming cultural capital through affective connections outside Romania.

In their diasporic identifications through Bollywood, they were rejecting the language of rights imposed by the state and the normative monoethnic performativity of the school system. Discussing Macedonians in Greece, Jane Cowan (2001) highlights the complexity of identifications that cannot be accounted for within simplistic minority-ethnic identifications or the discourse of rights to culture and ethnic identity (the imperialism of multiculturalism, as she calls it). As Hanson and Nieuwenhuys (2013) suggest, the discussion of children's rights needs to focus on living rights, which take into account how children experience officially sanctioned rights. In Romania, many Roma see themselves as both belonging to their country and different from the majority. Roma children have the right to culture, but this is rigidly understood and applied: the new culturalist discourse imported from the EU envisions cultures as bound, immovable entities, and fails to account for the diversity of Roma experience or for multiple identifications within one individual. Together's dance practices were an expression of their right to culture as a living right, and in their rejection of imposed identifications, they directly and indirectly critiqued the discrimination they experienced on a daily basis.

From *Csingeralas* to Bollywood: Rejecting Authenticity and Claiming Cultural Citizenship

Here I analyse Together's dance performances through the prism of what anthropologist John L. Jackson (2005) calls 'racial sincerity', which turns its focus on people as racial subjects rather than racial objects.[11] This shift in perspective is important given the authenticity criteria according to which Roma identities were sanctioned during post-socialism. A focus on their sincerity in relation to the dances they practised highlights young Roma people's connections with the types of dances they chose and their reasons for choosing them, rather than external expectations about what their cultural performances should be like.

Together students who attended the mainstream school where Armando worked presented a version of *csingeralas* at school festivities. *Csingeralas* was the name of what many Pod residents considered 'their' dance. Giani taught *csingeralas* to other students, including non-Roma and it became known in the school as the 'Roma dance' or 'Ţigan dance'; the term *csingeralas* was never mentioned at school, even though this term was commonly used among Roma. The dance has a particular history in the multi-ethnic Austro-Hungarian Empire, to which Transylvania belonged until 1918 and the footwork and hand-slapping in *csingeralas* are characteristic of a number of other dances found in the territories of the former empire. One of them, the male dance *Slovacko verbunk*[12] from the Czech Republic, was recently declared an item of UNESCO's Intangible World Heritage. It has its origin in the recruitment of young men into the Austro-Hungarian military, and it is an improvisatory dance form with many styles, sometimes starting with a song and a slow rhythm of higher leaps and continuing with smaller, faster leaps and slaps. Similar dances can be found in Hungary and Transylvania, where the Romanian name is *bărbunc*.[13]

Significantly faster than the other versions, the Roma version of this dance, *csingeralas*, and its accompanying music are known as *bărbunc ţigănesc* in Romanian. Unlike *verbunk* or *bărbunc*, *csingeralas* is danced in pairs, and the footwork is close to the ground.[14] Some of the male improvisations in *csingeralas* use similar leaps and slaps to the *verbunks*: one could say that there are Roma *verbunks*, just as there are Roma *horas* and other types of dance, or Romanian versions of *csingeralas*. None of these forms is the 'original': they have all influenced each other. The repertoire has shifted and cross-fertilized among groups of different ethnicities in the Transylvanian space, and therefore it is problematic to use ethnic-national denominations for these practices. However, it is equally important to underline that there is a repertoire in the folklore of the region that is specifically Roma, despite the exclusion of Roma from hegemonic nationalist definitions of folklore in Romania and elsewhere.

Together danced a version of *csingeralas* at an end-of-year school event at Armando's school in June 2007:

> Four young women wearing long, colourful wavy skirts and shirts, and four young men, including Giani and Tibi, dressed in red silk shirts and black trousers, enter in pairs, to the audience's rapturous applause. Giani and his dance partner, a non-Roma girl, followed by the other three pairs, make a semicircle upstage, and Giani walks about and shakes hands with each of the boys. Then he signals with his right hand that they may all sit down. Once seated, each pair engages in a traditional Roma activity, as Giani explained to me later: palm-reading, card-reading and welding (one young man was hitting a metal plate with a hammer). The soundtrack is the Roma anthem 'Gelem, Gelem', which starts with a slow lament. As the rhythm changes to a fast-paced Transylvanian Roma tune with violin and bass, the dancers stand up and start dancing: each pair takes it in turn to have their moment centre stage. The boys slap their thighs and chests as they leap and perform

rapid footwork in improvised moves; for their centre-stage solos some kick both legs in the air, while others jump low to the ground, legs open, and then hit the ground with one hand. The rapidity of the footwork and the originality of the jumps vary with each performer; the girls make waves with the full fabric folds of their long, wide skirts. Giani and his partner are the last pair to take centre stage, to the audience's applause. As their moment ends, all the female dancers form a line at the back, while the male dancers step forwards in single file and slap their hands together, then slap their legs and chests, increasing the rapidity of their foot- and handwork in unison, to the audience's delight. (Field notes, June 2007)

For this number, Together's performance included little Gelu and a young girl; children in Pod grew up dancing *csingeralas*, and they were all familiar with the form. The performers also danced a Bollywood number similar to that described at the opening of this chapter, and a Romanian folk dance for the same event, again to the audience's enthusiastic cheers and applause. Overall, the movements in *csingeralas* and the Romanian dance were similar, even though the costumes and speed of the movements differed. Although choreographed, the Roma dance number included improvised sequences, such as the boys' individual solos.

While Roma dance proved immensely popular with audiences at every public Together performance I attended, its reputation was not the same in all schools. For example, in 2008 I attended the end-of-year festivities at another mainstream school, where the Roma dance group did not have any boys. The Romani language teacher, who managed the group, had asked Armando to bring boys from Together to dance with the Roma girls in this group. The girls and boys danced together, enjoyed great success, and were the most applauded act at the school event. However, I could not help wondering why they could not find any boys in the school to dance with the Roma girls: there were Romanian folk dance groups in the school with plenty of boys who had performed at the same event. However, they were not Roma, or at least did not identify as such. Ironically, the boys in Together were not all Roma either, but they danced *csingeralas*. At this school the lines between who could dance which folk dance were clearly drawn, and only Roma were expected to perform a Roma dance. Another reason may have been that the non-Roma did not know how to dance *csingeralas*, which included different, much more rapid movements than the Romanian dances. Nonetheless, non-Roma students in Together had mastered these movements and danced as skilfully as the young Roma people.

Together dancers engaged with one another in a dialogical way as they learnt a variety of folk dances and invented their own eclectic routines. However, Together's reception often reiterated stereotypes about Roma, such as that their performance talent was supposedly innate, not based on work or training. Moreover, the non-Roma in Together were taken for Roma, for the simple reason that they danced Roma dances. Giani mentioned that at one dance show the presenters introduced the group as 'the Roma from Siesti' (a neighbourhood in the city), despite the fact that half of them were not Roma: 'For example, we had a show where we were presented as the group of Roma from Siesti, so they called them [the Romanian ethnics in the group] Roma, and they didn't mind'. Ironically, a school caretaker once remarked in conversation that she had not been all that impressed with Together's most recent performances at school festivities because not all of the dancers were authentic, i.e. they were not all Roma. Both reactions revealed essentialist understandings of ethnicity and erased the dancers' labour. They reflect expectations that ethnic boundaries should not be crossed in stage representations, and that one should be the ethnicity that one performs onstage.

Because they were seen as a Roma group despite their name, Together encountered resistance and prejudice from some audience members:

Giani: Not everybody likes this style. Some even make a difference between ethnicities. That is, if you're a Ţigan, you're not seen like someone else who's Romanian.

Ioana: Even when you dance?

Giani: Yes, when you dance. So I've even seen Romanians, Romanian ensembles [who would treat Together differently because they were Roma]. I've had many shows where, so some spectators would gossip about [the dancers being Roma], or – but this would happen with one or two people. Not in an exaggerated way. But even those ones, after we came out onstage and they saw the crowd reaction to us, they saw us differently, they would even congratulate us.

Giani was proud to mention that the group's performances had elicited non-Roma audiences' praise despite their initially disdainful attitudes. He rejected the simplistic identification of ethnic identity from the outside, a process of racialization that I discuss earlier in this chapter. He equally criticized the exoticization that sees all Roma as wearing colourful outfits:

Giani: So I behave normally, I don't dress – because I am Ţigan, I don't dress in Ţigan clothes. I dress normally like anyone. I dress how I like it. It does not mean because I am Ţigan I have to wear Ţigan clothing. I am the same as everyone else. I have done shows with folk dances, and I did not mind that they were [Romanian] folk dances. To me it seems obvious that everyone be considered equal. That people are not seen as above others because they are Ţigani or Romanian.

Giani owned the term 'Ţigan', as many Roma do in Romania, neutralizing its negative connotations. At the same time, he did not approve of *gadge* using this term. I see Giani here as claiming not authenticity but Jackson's (2005, 18) sincerity, which 'recognizes that people are not simply racial objects (to be verified from without) but racial subjects with an interiority that is never completely and unquestionably clear'.

Bollywood Dance and Roma Counterpublics

Whereas Together's performances of Roma dance were received within regimes of authenticity, despite the group's multi-ethnic constituency, their Bollywood performances opened up a space for the expression of their subjectivities, as they clearly did not perform officially recognized identities in Romania. Hegemonic readings of their Bollywood dances reduced them to 'ethnic chic', a superficial and commercially driven endorsement of ethnocultural difference; but to a Roma counterpublic, the dances spoke of sincere (in Jackson's sense) Roma self-identifications, and invoked alternative views of citizenship.

Following Rosi Braidotti's (2004, 139) call for more work 'on the role of contemporary global media in both colonizing and stimulating the social imaginary of global cultures', I argue that India, as reflected in Bollywood films, shaped the social imaginary of the young people in Together. While it commented on the erasure of Roma from the Romanian nation, their Bollywood dance also reflected a diasporic imaginary in the sense articulated by Aiwha Ong (1996, 25):

> Whether nurtured by nostalgia for vanishing cultures, fired by consumer restlessness, or impelled by spiritual homelessness, such alternative imaginaries can cast identities beyond the inscriptions and identifications made by states. The concept of imaginaries therefore conveys the agency of diaspora subjects, who, while being made by state and capitalist regimes of truth, can play with different cultural fragments in a way that allows them to segue from one discourse to another, experiment with alternative forms of identification, shrug in and out of identities, or evade imposed forms of identifications.

The diasporic dimension that I identify in Together's members' subjectivities and their Bollywood dance performances derived from their sense of disenfranchisement and lack of citizenship rights. Roma activists and scholars, anthropologists and political scientists see Roma as a global diaspora (see Hancock 1987; Gheorghe and Acton 2001; Lemon 2000a; Silverman 2012). Backed by linguistic evidence, the theory that Roma originated in India is widely accepted today (see Matras 2002). Roma activists have used the connection with India, from where Roma migrated towards Europe as early as the twelfth century, to claim a unified Roma identity, without advocating a return to India. Together's use of Bollywood therefore differed from the mainstream trend of ethnic chic in the Romanian media; the latter was evidenced in media phenomena such as Gypsy soaps on television and the consumption of Bollywood films, and glossed over material realities and fetishized difference, ultimately reinforcing hegemonic cultural norms.[15] A Roma counterpublic would read the performance of Bollywood and the indexing of India in Together's dances as relating to Roma identifications.

Bradeanu and Thomas (2006) have shown that for most of its Romanian consumers, Bollywood has become a combination of exotic tourist object, Oriental Other and socialist nostalgia. The recent revival of 1980s Indian films that were popular during Communism has caused a new trend of performers capitalizing on ethnic and Developing World chic. Bradeanu and Thomas (2006, 144) call this new genre 'Hindi turbo-folk', part of a new type of cosmopolitanism and an economy of métissage in which Romanians have become consumers of 'a new transnational popular culture' characterized by 'fusion, quotation, irony, parody and hybridization'. I argue that ethnic chic in Romania can be an endorsement of difference from a position of privilege, mirroring or aspiring to be like the West, where one's 'not-quite-European-ness' might become less visible through difference from the performed Other.

Diverging from this position, young Roma in Together used India discursively to make an intervention in their own marginalization and to claim their cultural citizenship in Romania. Giani's sense of kinship with India and Indian actors was enabled by popular culture and based on affective identification with the songs, dance and spirit of Bollywood films. For Together, India became a diasporic, transnational symbol that functioned as a way of thinking beyond the monoethnic nation and expressing cultural citizenship. While it did not solve these young people's experience of disenfranchisement, the diasporic imaginary refused the authenticity regimes of 'coercive mimeticism' (Chow 2002) – the recognizable identities that are imposed upon minorities.

The young people's affective connection with India and Bollywood can also be traced back to state policies. The consumption of Indian films by the Together dancers' parents during Communism played a role in the young people's predilection for India and Bollywood films: Giani watched the latest Bollywood films that he could get on legal or pirated DVDs. He was an avid fan of Bollywood star Salman Khan, and his slicked-back hair and sartorial style channelled his idol; on one wall of his parents' house he had created a mural, a black ink lithograph portrait of Salman Khan. In 2006–2007 his mobile phone screensaver was a portrait of Salman Khan, later replaced with a picture of Giani himself in a pose emulating the Bollywood star.

Together's consumption of popular culture thus pointed to a symbolic India not as the Oriental Other, but as a form of self-identification. Together's dances summoned up an imaginary homeland to counter the mistreatment experienced in the real homeland. Giani's mother Vanesa once remarked: 'if only I could send him over to India. Send him on a magic carpet across the seas'. Whereas the consumption of ethnic chic reinforces the difference between Self and Other, Together summoned Bollywood as cultural capital that they lacked in their own country, and as an avenue of expression that resisted the citizenship gap and the simplistic binary of post-socialist recognition, where one could be either Romanian or Other (Roma) but not both:

> Giani: In Indian films they sing love songs, they are action-filled, and there's compassion – they have many qualities, compared to other kinds, which are either comedies, or action movies only. Indian films have something special. For example, that film, *The Chain of Memories*, was quite something. I think it is the most successful film. I've got it on DVD.

> Ioana: I've seen it in the cinema. I still remember it.

> Giani: With three brothers, so it was the most successful, how they were left orphans; it was a global success. It had pity, and love, and music and dancing. For me it is one of the most important films. For example, our Romanians, if they were to make, like they made these films [Gypsy soaps], if they made them, why don't they try to do it with – to have them sing in the fields, when they fall in love, when they see their loved one, a love song, and she would answer through a song. I think it would be successful. It would certainly have some success. But no, they don't think about such things. But we've still been noticed, although not in our country, in a different country. For example, in India, the actors had huge success, Salman Khan or Raj Kapoor.

> Ioana: Is he a Rom?

> Giani: Us Țigani, in fact, we come from India.

Giani identifies with both 'our Romanians' and 'us Țigani' who come from India, thus expressing his sense of cultural citizenship and belonging, despite the difficulties and discrimination he faces as a Rom. Romania is 'our country', and India is 'a different country'. These multiple identifications show that for him the investment is not in India per se, but rather in using it as cultural capital in Romania.

I will conclude this chapter with an anecdote from the field demonstrating that Together's Bollywood-inspired performances did not elicit the same ethnicity-based readings as their folk dances and had the potential to resist the normative monoethnic performativity of identities in Romania. Asked to speak on a local television show about the success of 'Gypsy music' abroad, I invited Giani and a non-Roma girl from Together to perform live in the studio during the show. (Due to restricted studio space, the television channel was unable to accommodate more than two dancers.) They chose to perform a Bollywood-inspired piece, which included belly-dance style movements and Bollywood moves, such as the undulating of the head and arms, and the brusque thrusting forward of the hips. The dancers lip-synched to the lyrics of the songs and mirrored the performances in the films: they raised their arms and gestured with the song lyrics, which they only knew phonetically. The show hosts were visibly surprised by the dance, and were curious about the dancers' choices. Unlike their Roma dances, which were read through the prism of authenticity, Together's Bollywood dances broke the mould of what audiences expected to see in folk or ethnic dance shows. Rather than evaluating whether the dancers were talented or not, as many commentaries on Together's Roma dance performances did, the hosts asked who the performers were, and about their choice of dances and their sources of inspiration. The Bollywood dance opened up the possibility of these dancers being read as 'sincere' in Jackson's sense, and addressed both non-Roma and Roma as a counterpublic.

Notes

1. Five out of the ten regular Together members were non-Roma: four young women and one young man.
2. In 1980s Britain, Paul Gilroy argued that racism could not be eradicated through policies, but was a matter of politics (1992). According to Gilroy, it is not enough to criticize a government's lack of will to address racism if politics are not addressed. Hazel Carby (1999, 219) calls for an examination of 'not just courses and curricula, but also the social relations of classrooms and schools in relation to the wider material and ideological structures within which both teachers and pupils are located'.
3. This changed in 2015. Now all students from Pod can take a school bus, including to mainstream schools.
4. Michael Stewart (1997) discusses how Roma said they went to the 'crazy school' during Communism in Hungary.
5. Carby (1999, 213) describes a similar practice in relation to black students in 1980s Britain: 'Underachievement is assumed and then tested to be proven ... Educational policy and practice actually constitute black children as an alien group that present "problems" that are external to "normal" schooling'.
6. In fact a child is only allowed to repeat a school year twice in mainstream education.
7. Special school fees were taken directly from the salaries of parents in employment, so they were not actually free for such parents.
8. However, in a BBC interview conducted in 2008, a teacher in a Czech school explained that Roma children needed to be sent to 'special schools': http://news.bbc.co.uk/1/hi/programmes/crossing_continents/7581969.stm (last accessed 2 November 2012). Reports carried out subsequently and published by ERRC show how despite the adoption of anti-discrimination legislation in the Czech Republic and other countries, the

discrimination of Roma children in education continues. http://www.errc.org/article/racial-segregation-continues-in-czech-schools-despite-landmark-european-court-ruling/2992 (last accessed 2 November 2012).

9. Nicolae Păun was president of the Roma Party for Europe, the only Rom in the Romanian parliament, and sponsor of *Roma Caravan.*

10. See www.activewatch.ro (last accessed 30 November 2011).

11. Jackson discusses African American subjectivities in his work; 'racial sincerity' is relevant in the Roma and Romanian context, as both African Americans and Roma face similar scrutiny and objectification in relation to a supposed authenticity.

12. From the German word *werbunk*, meaning 'recruitment'.

13. Because the dance was performed by men, through folk etymology the name of the dance became associated with the Romanian word *bărbat* (man), with which *verbunk* has no connection.

14. Among the recent dance groups that have focused on *csingeralas* while calling it *verbunk* is Roma Fest, an all-male dance group with a Japanese manager, who have enjoyed success outside Romania. They dance in a circle, in a set way, and the form of the dance is closer to stage renditions of *verbunk* by Romanian and Hungarian folk groups than it is to Roma events. See http://www.youtube.com/watch?v=DxoNZciiQo0&feature=related (last accessed 15 November 2013).

15. I discuss these television soaps at length in the next chapter.

Chapter 5

Consuming Exoticism/Reimagining Citizenship

Romanian Nationalism and Roma Counterpublics on Romanian Television

A rose in her long black hair, Roma actor Zita Moldovan, presenter of *Roma Caravan* (*Caravana Romilor*) – Romania's only long-running TV show by and about Roma – was dressed in a long, wavy skirt and a top with bare shoulders of the kind typical of Roma dancers in Russia. Beside her was her co-star from the Gypsy soap[1] *The Sprânceană Clan* (*Clanul Sprânceană*), the non-Roma actor Marius Bodochi, wearing a long black suit jacket with a dark shirt casually unbuttoned to show his chest. Together they were hosting the 2008 Gala for Roma Excellence, an event organized by the National Agency for Roma and the Roma Party for Europe, a Roma political party with just one representative in Romanian parliament. The gala's declared mission was to honour known Roma talent, reward successful Roma of whom non-Roma might not be aware, and recognize non-Roma who promoted Roma values.

Roma and non-Roma artists were award winners that evening. For many TV soap stars, acting in the soaps involved dressing up in colourful outfits, mispronouncing Romanian words, and wearing heavy jewellery. Non-Roma pop star Loredana and her fellow cast members from the TV soap *Gypsy Heart* (*Inimă de Țigan*) won a special prize for promoting 'authentic Roma values'. Carmen Tănase, Doinița Oancea and a few other actors from the soap stepped up onto the stage to collect their award. Tănase said: 'Thank you for allowing us, every night at 8.30 pm, to become part of your ethnicity'.[2] Oancea followed Tănase to the microphone and added: 'Some of us already are,' reminding everyone that there were some actual Roma, including herself, in the show's overwhelmingly non-Roma cast.[3]

Four years later, at the Gala for Roma Excellence's 2012 edition, the segment 'I Too Was Born in Romania' from the Roma-produced *Roma Caravan* won the media programme award. The two producers went onstage, thanked the jury, and declared that they were happy to have stepped into normality with their programme. Later, Varujan Vosganian – a Romanian politician of Armenian descent – declared as he collected his award for contribution to the Roma cause: 'Someone said earlier that you had stepped into a period of normality. No, your ethnicity is only now emerging'. In this chapter I show that both Vosganian and the producers were right. The producers were right because *Roma Caravan* and other Roma-led media had created a Roma counterpublic that shared a safe space and took Roma cultural citizenship for granted; but Vosganian was also right because, in the larger landscape of Romanian media and society, such views were only just emerging, and were often ignored, challenged or denied outright.

I will discuss the representations of Roma on mainstream Romanian television, which continues to be the major media platform in Romania and is run overwhelmingly by non-Roma. I analyse these representations in relation to a Roma counterpublic – the 'us' invoked above by Oancea, which was also the 'you' addressed by non-Roma actor Tănase – and the mainstream public in Romania – the 'us' indexed by Tănase. Focusing on commercially successful televisions soaps such as *Gypsy Heart*, on debates and talk shows about current affairs, and on the very few Roma-led television programmes, I analyse the intertextual relationship between fictional and non-fictional Roma representations, the latter including performances of citizenship, where Roma activists and artists claimed both a Roma identity and Romanian citizenship. Paying attention to class, gender and ethnicity both on and off the screen, my media ethnographic analysis combines textual analysis of the soaps and television talk shows in which Roma participated, with my fieldwork in Pod and Internet evidence about the soaps' reception among Roma and non-Roma (although this is not a detailed study of television consumption).

Consuming 'Gypsy Chic' and Scapegoating Roma in Gypsy Soaps

Broadcast on private television channels, Gypsy soaps brought 'traditional' and recognizable images of Roma onto television screens for the first time in Romania since before socialism. The passionate, extravagant singer and dancer Rodia (played by Loredana), the 'free spirit of the community' who sang the 'tortured soul of the Ţigan',[4] and Roza, the rebellious, hot-blooded daughter of the *bulibasha* (clan leader), State, were two examples of romantic stereotypes in *Gypsy Heart*. Boasting famous ethnic Romanian actors on their cast lists, the soaps received top audience ratings, launching what I call 'Gypsy chic', the superficial endorsement of Roma cultural difference under the influence of Western capital, consumerism and global media concomitant with Romania's entry into global capital flows. These soaps predated reality shows featuring Roma Gypsies in the UK and US, such as *My Big Fat Gypsy Wedding* and *American Gypsy*

While the soaps represented the beginning of a wave of Romanian TV programmes featuring Roma characters played by non-Roma, Roma had long been among the most popular entertainers in the Romanian music industry:[5] several popular Roma singers featured in reality shows that aired on private TV channels; the reality show *Clejanii*, on the Turkish-owned private channel Kanal D, featured Roma musicians Viorica and Ioniță from Clejani – a village in southern Romania famous for its generations of Roma Lăutari – and their children Margherita and Fulgy; and a reality show on the private channel Antena 1 featured *manele* producer Dan Bursuc, who created a school for *manele* singers.[6]

The display of Gypsy chic and the focus on wealth in Gypsy soaps reinforced stereotypes that had been persistent during socialism about excessive Roma wealth and criminality – the flipside of the poor, abject Țigan, the Other of the nation. Sara Ahmed's (2000, 116) observation about the figure of the stranger as Other is particularly apt for understanding how the soaps exemplified the appropriation of Roma culture in the service of capital: 'Consumer culture involves the production of the stranger as a commodity fetish through representations of difference. Differences are defined in terms of culture, and culture, as in the official discourses of multiculturalism … is restricted to the privatized and expressive domain of style'.

The first Gypsy soap broadcast on the private channel Acasă, *Gypsy Heart (Inimă de Țigan)*[7] was launched during the 2007–2008 season (Figure 5.1). It registered high audience ratings, peaking on 29 May 2008, when it was the most watched show among women aged between fifteen and forty-nine years in urban areas, according to the Acasă website. Its sequel, *The Queen (Regina)*, which ran from autumn 2008 to spring 2009, fared even better; according to the Acasă website, on 15 May 2009 it recorded the highest ratings for prime-time television in Romania, surpassing a national football derby between the Bucharest teams Steaua and Rapid, which was being shown at the same time.[8] *The Queen* was followed in 2009–2010 by a new series, *State of Romania (State de România)*, featuring the characters State and Flacăra from the previous two series. A fourth sequel, *The Inheritance (Moștenirea)*, modelled on *The Queen*, was launched in autumn 2010.

These soaps had little to do with real Roma, and mostly presented aspects of Roma culture in stereotypical ways. Their depictions of Roma reflected a larger trend in soaps: from North American soaps to Latin American and Turkish tele-novelas, such shows tend to focus on wealth and luxurious lifestyles.[9] However, *Gypsy Heart* did address anti-Roma prejudice in Romanian society through the character of Medalion, the main protagonist, who faced racism in both his career and his love life. Medical student Medalion was the son of *bulibasha* Aurică Fieraru, the leader of a Roma community and the owner of a huge house and caravan; Irina was the daughter of rich ethnic Romanian Gigi Dumbravă, who hated Roma. Medalion fell in love with the *gadgi* Irina, but his family had planned an arranged marriage for him with State's daughter Roza, who had been

Figure 5.1. Gypsy Heart promotional advert, featuring Medalion (Denis Ştefan), flanked by Irina (Andreea Pătraşcu) and Roza (Nicoleta Luciu); television still.

born and raised in Paris. The climax of *Gypsy Heart* was the death of Giuvaeru, Medalion's brother, whose heart Gigi Dumbravă received in a transplant operation at the hospital where Medalion worked. The sequel, *The Queen*, focused on the clash between traditional Roma and those who had 'lost their identity' and became mafiosi, such as State and newcomer Don Luciano Antonucci. The stories also featured the *stabor*, a traditional Roma court, which passed judgement

Figure 5.2. State (Gheorghe Visu), in State of Romania; *television still.*

Figure 5.3. Flacăra (Carmen Tănase) and Rodia (Loredana Groza), in The Queen; *television still.*

on Roza for her extramarital affair with State's Moroccan bodyguard, and also sentenced the magician Sulfina to two lashes for casting a spell on Medalion.[10]

The soaps presented a range of images regarding Roma: from exotic images during the opening and closing credits, such as the caravan in the yard, the big turreted house, the braided and colourfully clad women, and horses roaming the fields, to more parodic depictions focused on excessive consumption and *manele* imagery in the characters of State and Flacăra. The Acasă website described *bulibasha* Aurică Fieraru and his wife Spania as traditional, Flacăra as 'not so traditional', and State as urbanized.[11] Wearing a gold tie, a large golden crucifix, heavy rings on his fingers and bulky bracelets, and flashing two gold front teeth, State was a gangster involved in human trafficking from Romania to Paris, and he controlled an army of beggars on the streets of the French capital. State's colourful persona and his illicit international business borrowed from Bosnian-born film director Emir Kusturica's *Time of the Gypsies* (1987), while *Gypsy Heart* used some of the motifs from Emil Loteanu's film *Tabor* (1975), including the theme of forbidden love between Roma and *gadge*. The *Gypsy Heart* theme tune, sung by popstar Loredana in her character as Rodia, also featured Roma singer Connect-R. For *The Queen*'s theme tune, Loredana/Rodia sang a version of 'Erdelezi', a Roma song from the former Yugoslavia that was famous in Romania from Kusturica's film. *The Queen* also introduced a Roma *manele* singer, child prodigy Babi Minune,[12] while Jean from Craiova, another Roma *manele* singer, joined the cast for *State of Romania*.

Starting with the performers, who (like Loredana) revelled in the opportunity to dress outrageously or (like Tănase) took speaking in stereotypically broken accents to new heights, the soaps displayed consumable Roma culture, making it fashionable as Gypsy chic or as a source of humour. Describing the huge investment behind the *Gypsy Heart* sets and costumes, the Acasă website revealed that the more than 300 costumes had been inspired by traditional outfits and were 'accessorized with massive jewellery'[13] and the sets had been built from scratch for the production and included 'houses with turrets, wagons, carts and a miniature Eiffel Tower'.[14] *The Queen* was promoted with a special emphasis on the new sets, which were 'fascinating, impressive, luxurious, the most expensive ever made for the Romanian TV market, and this is not the only premiere. The Acasă team has managed another feat in the field of television: it is the only team to have recorded in the Sahara Desert!'[15] The huge success of the soaps, and their status as a popular-culture phenomenon in Romania, assured brisk sales of notebooks, pencils and other themed merchandise emblazoned with images of stars wearing Gypsy costumes.

Confirming that Gypsy style had potential as fashion, the actors inhabited their soap personas on multiple occasions off set. For example, Carmen Tănase gave an interview in character as Flacăra, who in the soap was preparing her daughter's arranged marriage. Wearing a string of coins on her forehead, long painted nails, big rings on every finger, heavy bracelets, necklaces and a shiny black dress, she spoke in Flacăra's broken accent: 'I am tired, my dear, my daughter is getting married. It took me a long time to get my nails done and everything'. Asked where she had got her dress from, she answered that her husband State had bought it in Paris, and it was from Coco Chanel's latest collection: 'I got diemonds [mispronounced]', she said, showing off her rings.[16] Loredana also often dressed in character as Rodia, in a long colourful skirt and fake plaits, with roses in her hair, coins on her forehead and lots of jewellery (Figure 5.3).

Figure 5.4. State and Flacăra, questioned by police at their home, State of Romania; television still.

Figure 5.5. Opening credits of State of Romania with State and Flacăra waving like a presidential couple; television still.

While these actors' over-the-top adornments as Flacăra and Rodia off set represented an opportunity to be extravagant and/or ungrammatical, they equally illustrated the obsession with Roma wealth within the post-socialist media's overall focus on excessive consumption. Loredana revelled in the opportunity to adorn herself and become a seductive Gypsy, while Tănase's Flacăra was a parody of the nouveau riche in general. By focusing on wealth, the soaps made the Roma scapegoats for corruption in the country, and encouraged the general populace to ignore Roma poverty and anti-Roma racism.

The characters of Flacăra and State reinforced the parody aspect of the soaps and carried the comic weight of the four series. Their broken accents – stereotypical of Roma speaking Romanian – and their ghetto-fabulous garb, with bling and unorthodox mixtures of traditional costume and urban clothing, made them the soaps' most picturesque and most popular characters. In one example of how these characters embodied the stereotypes of ungrammatical, ignorant Țigani, the episode of *Gypsy Heart* on 20 May 2008 showed Flacăra, State, their daughter Minodora and her partner Stiven in an electronics store, where they were trying to buy a computer without knowing what it was called or what it was for.[17] Ridiculing the characters' poor command of Romanian, the episode shows State mumbling to the shop assistant that he wants a 'coordinator'; correcting him, Flacăra asks for an 'ordinator' (both words are based on the French word for computer, *ordinateur* – State had spent a long time in Paris). State asks if the computer is the most expensive product in the shop, and the assistant says no. Flacăra replies in offended tones, as State puffs and huffs contemptuously: 'Listen, you *gadgo*, this is State Potcovaru, you think we handle such cheapness?' They want a machine that connects to the 'ethernet'; the assistant tells them that they have a choice between a modem and a wireless connection. The four have no idea what he is talking about and look at each in utter confusion. Stiven takes a step towards the shop assistant, warning him that if he has cursed them they will get very upset: 'What are you saying there?' he asks. The assistant explains the meaning of the English word 'wireless' and shows them an Apple computer. State looks at it and asks: 'Have you got one with an uneaten apple?' Later, at home, they hide and are afraid of the computer, and State asks for his rifle so as to be ready to defend them against their new machine.

Always the cunning fool in these soaps, State was voted the most beloved character on the Acasă website, ensuring his reappearance alongside Flacăra in the third series, *State of Romania*. In this sequel, State – freshly returned from Paris, where he has been heading a child- and sex-trafficking network – becomes a mayoral candidate in the imaginary village of Cloncatele. His dress, his speech, and his blonde, ethnic Romanian lover Lili all borrowed in parodic style from the imagery of *manele* videos. This series, exclusively focused on State, Flacăra and their children, was perhaps the brashest in its dystopian implications: it presented a Rom as President of Romania – the ultimate nightmare for *gadge*, and a revival of the rumours during socialism that Ceauşescu was in fact a Rom. State never became President, but he did win the local elections and became Cloncatele mayor. This dystopia not only undermined current Roma politicians – of whom there were only a handful with national visibility – by implying that Roma were hopeless at politics; it also targeted Roma as scapegoats for the current situation in Romania.

On blogs and in online comments about the soaps, some non-Roma audience members alleged that the 'racism' of the Roma/Gypsy characters encouraged anti-Romanian racism and was a threat to a nation that was already Gypsified.[18] For example, one viewer was offended that in *State of Romania* non-Roma were called 'washed off', and that Roma on the show were encouraged to marry only among themselves while State had a non-Roma lover. Even though *State of Romania* was an exaggerated dystopia that presented power relations between Roma and non-Roma that were a far cry from reality, some viewers took it seriously and feared that the majority might really become victimized. In society at large a similar sense of national victimization prompted many ethnic Romanians to refuse to see that Roma might have been facing a worse fate than they were. The Western media's obsession with Roma migrants and its

Figure 5.6. Roma Caravan, *December 2011; members of the National Association of Roma Women; in the background,* Roma Caravan *poster; television still.*

conflation between Romanians and Roma, which had started in the early 1990s and continued in 2008 and 2010, had made Roma more unpalatable than ever to most non-Roma in Romania. Although the soaring ratings for Gypsy soaps seemed to reveal a countermovement to such attitudes, audience interpretations like those above showed that some saw the Roma characters in the soaps negatively, scapegoating Roma for social problems such as corruption and disregard of the law, and even accusing Roma of racism against the majority.

Roma Caravan: *Roma-led Romanian Television*

The lack of institutional representations of Roma was reflected in the fact that, in parallel with the wave of entertainment programmes about Roma on private television channels, there were only two television programmes in Romania that aimed to inform Roma themselves and that featured or were produced by Roma. These were *Roma Caravan*, a two-hour weekly programme on the private channel OTV that started in 1998, and the more recent *European Rom*, a half-hour weekly show broadcast on the public television channel TVR1 from 2008 onwards. These programmes, and the presence of Roma activists and personalities in mainstream media, made visible a growing Roma counterpublic.

Roma Caravan included a news bulletin that provided information on government initiatives regarding the Roma, Roma opportunities (such as the quotas in higher education, discussed in the previous chapter), and other activities led by NGOs or the Roma Party for Europe that were not publicized elsewhere. In the early years of the programme, a segment called 'Model Roma Families' focused each week on a different successful Roma family, and promoted family and religious values. A more recent weekly *Roma Caravan* segment, 'I Too Was Born in Romania', featured Roma individuals who were successful professionals in various fields, and aimed to highlight the countless Roma who had been appropriated as Romanians. The focus on positive Roma role models was unprecedented on Romanian television, and aimed to change the perception, shared by some Roma and non-Roma alike, that Roma intellectuals and professionals did not exist.

In one such programme, for example, the 'I Too Was Born in Romania' segment featured an interview with twenty-seven-year-old Silvia Constantin, an intern in a public relations agency and a volunteer for the Alternative Education Club. She mentioned the multitude of reasons why Roma children who attended the club lacked an education. She also told her own story: 'I am of Roma ethnicity and I've started feeling good in my own skin. This is not a negative thing'. When she was at primary school, other children had said to her, 'You are a Țigancă, that's why we don't play with you'. She went on to study political science at university under the quotas for Roma, and always felt that she could do more. She decided to take the general admission exam for a master's course, so that she could avoid what she called the stigma of the quotas.

'I've had to prove myself twice, three times as much as anyone else, just because my skin colour was different'.

An October 2011 edition of *Roma Caravan* presented a short report about the Roma Student Ball in Bucharest, 'The Roma Student Behind the Mask'. The playful name of the ball indicated that Roma students were invisible to the majority by virtue of the very fact that they were both students and Roma – supposedly an impossible contradiction – and they therefore had to 'come out' in order to make their Roma identity public. Skin colour was no longer a visible Roma marker in this context, as it was when associated with stereotypical Țigani circumstances such as poverty, mendicancy and so on, or with the quotas in education: class and status 'whitened the skin'.

The ball featured Connect-R, a Roma football player turned singer, who had revealed a T-shirt bearing the slogan 'I am a Țigan' while collecting a prize at the 2010 Romanian Music Awards. He had explained the significance of this 'coming out' in the following way: 'I am a Țigan who has surpassed his condition ... It is nonsense to use the word "Țigan" as an insult for someone like myself, who can do things differently. I wanted to show my fellow citizens that there are alternatives'. In the same interview he mentioned the walls of racism and discrimination that he had faced, and how his work had been judged in the past on the basis of his ethnicity: 'It is a good song, he sings well, the dance is good, the message is good, too bad he is a Țigan'.[19]

As he took to the stage for the Roma student ball featured in *Roma Caravan*, he greeted the audience: 'A few years ago I tried to find a Rom among Romanians. I didn't find anybody. How many of us are here?' The majority of those present raised their hands. One of the students interviewed for the show declared: 'We are proud of who we are. The profile of the Roma student: a student who has overcome his condition, who wants to study, who wants to be involved and help Roma communities'. These were successful Roma individuals whom non-Roma might believe to be non-Roma, and whose achievements had been appropriated as Romanian. 'Coming out' from behind the mask of respectability that assigned them a place as citizens, but that did so only as part of the majority – not as Roma – these Roma students countered the erasure of Roma from citizenship and aimed to close the citizenship gap. Contrary to media reports that discussed Roma personalities who chose to 'come out' and declare their Roma ethnicity as if they were confessing a sin, these students emphasized pride in their Roma identity.[20]

Between Țigani and 'Palaces with Turrets': Can Roma Speak on Mainstream Romanian Television?

Despite these more positive representations of Roma, dominant images were perpetuated in soaps and the media in general, including images that criminalized Roma men and focused on the oppression of Roma women. Roma were scapegoated for both corruption and domestic violence in a patriarchal society, and real-life Roma proved far less popular than soap characters when they appeared on current affairs programmes, other than the Roma-led shows. Mainstream television reflected Varujan Vosganian's remark at the 2012 gala that the Roma were only just emerging into public life in Romania.

Until recently, most news shows in Romania routinely identified people by ethnicity. Even when Roma were not named directly in news stories related to crime, Roma were metonymically named through objects or practices associated with them. For example, in a talk show from 2008 that I will discuss in detail later in this chapter, when a speaker mentioned 'palaces with turrets' everyone knew that she was referencing architectural icons of stereotypical Roma wealth and tastelessness – symbols of desirable and watchable wealth in the soaps, but an invocation of negative stereotypes in most other instances. In another example, a reporter on the private channel ProTV in 1999 used the phrase 'certain patients' to describe the perpetrators of antisocial behaviour. Without naming Roma directly, the report metonymically identified the patients as Roma through their actions: damaging medical facilities and threatening people. In this media landscape, entertainment ranging from Gypsy soaps to reality shows presented Roma as rich, and maintained the lie about the extent of racism in Romania. They reassured the majority that if Roma fared poorly in Romanian society, the Roma themselves were to blame.

In the few instances when Roma represented themselves in mainstream Romanian media, they encountered resistance from non-Roma. Non-Roma patrolled the politics of representation to keep Țigani in their place as objects of representation rather than equal subjects. For example, two Roma activists on a talk show rejected the term 'Țigan', which the non-Roma moderator had used to refer to them, and asked to be called 'Roma' – to no avail, as the moderator insisted that the former was an acceptable term to most 'Țigani'. This talk show, entitled *Rom from Romania* (*Rom de România*), was broadcast at the end of December 2007, the first year of Romania's EU membership, on the private news channel Realitatea. Three non-Roma journalists were also present in addition to the two Roma guests. The show addressed questions such as 'Why is there tension between Roma and Romanians?', reinforcing the dichotomy between Roma/Țigani and Romanians and erasing the meaning of 'Romanian' as citizenship. The moderator assumed the *gadge* privilege of representing Others, calling her interlocutors Țigani and refusing to treat them as subjects. The Roma activists identified themselves as Roma *and* Romanian citizens, and resisted this objectification. The moderator blatantly refused to listen to them and continued to use the term Țigani, which the activists had identified as a slur.

On the same talk show, the moderator discussed the coronation of a new Roma king in Costești, a village famous for its rich Kelderara communities. A short clip, with no commentary, showed the new king standing beside a throne, a large crucifix hanging from his neck; he picked up a golden crown from a cushion and placed it on his head. Near him, a woman, her head wrapped in a scarf, was screaming and weeping as the king lifted the crown. The clip played on the screen for several minutes on a loop, in an absurd repetition, and was shown several times during the talk show, with no explanation, as if it spoke for itself. Presented as alien, and therefore as having nothing to do with 'us', the coronation was undermined and exoticized through the repetitive showing, and rendered strange and derisory.

The clip represented Roma tradition as backward, alien and out of touch with the present. Several communities of Kelderara have leaders who identify as kings; however, they represent and are recognized by only a small number of Roma. Against such images of tradition, the soaps might be seen as adding a layer of complexity, as they showed Roma involved in practices with more logic than this video clip. In the soaps, the community's internal judgments were impartial, and *bulibasha* Aurică Fieraru was a fair community leader. In the talk show, the coronation clip was allowed to have the final say in the debate on the state of the Roma communities in Romania and their supposed backwardness.

Between Good and Evil (Între Bine și Rău), a talk show aired on the public channel TVR1 in October 2008, focused on media scandals that had erupted in Italy and Romania regarding Romanian criminals in Italy. The year 2008 was when the Italian government initiated a fingerprinting and expulsion campaign that targeted Roma, many of whom were Romanian citizens. The programme discussed criminality in Romania and Romanians in Italy, and featured one Roma guest: Nicolae Păun, President of the Roma Party for Europe and the only Roma member of Romanian parliament. He spoke for less than two minutes at the end of an hour-long show. Among the guests was also the then Minister for Foreign Affairs, Adrian Cioroianu, who in 2007 had refused to grant recognition as Romanian citizens to individuals whom the government had identified as Roma and who were being threatened with deportation from Ireland for squatting. By 2008 Cioroianu had adopted more 'politically correct' language, claiming that he would count anyone with a Romanian passport as a Romanian citizen. While the talk show participants attempted to steer away from explicitly equating criminality with Roma ethnicity – a standard practice in Romanian media – these stereotypes were barely disguised, and surfaced through innuendos several times during the show.

Another segment of the same show demonstrated how racialized hierarchies framed everyday encounters from the point of view of non-Roma who identified Roma on the basis of unreliable external signs and excluded them from the collective 'us' of the nation. The incident I go on to describe was prompted by an intervention by one of the guests on the show, 1960s pop star Mihaela Mihai. I will focus on her participation in this show in detail, because it illustrates a subject position that is very frequent among non-Roma in Romania and is reinforced in the media as a dominant view. I do not mean to imply in what follows that all non-Roma share this view; however, the incident shows how easy it was to present such views in the media, and how difficult it was for Roma to counter them.

Mihai described an incident that had happened to her, which, she claimed, had prompted her to send out a plea to Roma communities. She alleged that a citizen of Roma ethnicity had stolen her bag from her car. A man in the audience raised his hand and spoke into the audience microphone, asking: 'Am I a Rom?' Mihai replied that she did not know, as she could not see that far into the audience. The man stood up for her to see him better. Mihai replied that only he knew his ethnicity; she had seen blond Roma. The man retorted: 'Madam, that's it: you recognized a criminal as being a Rom, for the mere reason that you thought so. I am a Rom'. Mihai insisted that she should be allowed to finish her point. After defending herself against accusations of racism by claiming that she had Roma friends, she proceeded to differentiate between decent Roma and bad Roma. This differentiation perpetuated the citizenship gap for Roma, in that Roma who performed civility (were 'decent') could be assimilated as citizens while the others were 'bad':

> Somehow, us Romanians, including decent Roma, are fed up with being Europe's shame of sorts. We've just joined [the EU] and all the time this nail is being hammered – Roma citizens, Romanian citizens. I am the last person who can be suspected of racism, because throughout my career I had musicians of Roma ethnicity beside me, we studied together at the conservatory … Because of fear of being accused of racism, nobody dares say certain things. So I addressed the Roma community because I realized that the causes of the situation needed to be addressed. The Roma community is profoundly macho.

She went on to claim that 'clan leaders' had no respect for women, whether as sisters, daughters or wives. The man stood up again and exclaimed: 'You are speaking about Roma. They are very diverse, and I do not belong to a family like that'. 'You do not belong,' said Mihai, 'neither does Mr Păun [the only Roma guest on the show]'. 'There are very many Roma in Romania who do not belong to traditional families,' the man replied.

Despite the self-identified Rom's protest that he and Păun did not belong to traditional families, Mihai was adamant about her generalization. Her point about 'machismo' in Roma communities and 'clan leaders' who lacked respect for women reflected a widespread stereotype about Roma, which was reiterated in the soaps. To accuse Roma of machismo in this way was part of a symbolic construction of Self and Other in which the Other served as the Self's negative mirror image. In addition to making a generalization, Mihai's description of

Roma women as lacking a voice and oppressed by traditional values is problematic because it erases the patriarchal values of Romanian society in general, presenting only Roma as backward, a separate society stuck in traditional values.[21] A recent report on the image of women in the Romanian media at large revealed the discrepancy between men and women in professional positions, and the large percentage of women presented as sexual objects, as succeeding through their association with powerful men, or as housewives.[22]

Soaps and talks shows worked intertextually to perpetuate stereotypes about Roma: the Gypsy soaps reinforced stereotypes that circulated elsewhere, including on the talk show discussed above, such as the prevalence of domestic violence among Roma and the oppression of Roma women. For example, they presented frequent scenes of domestic violence between the couples Zambila and Giani, and Flacăra and State and the Acasă channel website invited viewers to vote for 'the best beating' in the series (placing domestic violence and gang violence on an equal footing); the vote was won by a fight between State and Flacăra. The two female characters who suffered the most domestic violence in the soaps, Flacăra and Zambila, were both very vocal, reproducing the stereotype of the loud, bickering Ţiganca, yet both women were silenced by their husbands, who always had the final say. With the exception of languorous, seductive Rodia and hot-blooded, rebellious Roza, most Roma women in these soaps were traditional and/or dominated by their husbands, even when (like Flacăra and Zambila) they were as loud as the men and fought back. Thus the soaps reinforced patriarchy and the status quo. Children were also victims of domestic violence in the soaps: Flacăra often hit her children when they upset her.

The stereotype that equated all Roma with criminality surfaced in the discussion of the 'Romanian criminal' abroad and at home on the 2008 talk show *Between Good and Evil* analysed above. One of the guest journalists discussed the generic term 'criminal', then replaced it with the pronoun 'he'; later it became clear that he meant male Roma.

> Mihaiu [the show host]: People leave the country, because abroad there are more consumer goods that can be tempting. That's why: you don't steal – you don't steal from the poor.
>
> Guest journalist: He [the criminal] finds [consumer goods to steal] here as well, however, now here we have this problem. Because for seventeen years he [the criminal] has seen groups [mafioso types] come back from abroad and build villas, and they have become clan names.
>
> Mihai [interrupting the previous speaker at the mention of villas]: No, palaces with turrets.

As mentioned earlier, 'palaces with turrets' referred to Roma architecture in affluent Roma neighbourhoods, famous – mainly in the West – for their hybrid and creative style, and reviled locally as the epitome of kitsch and bad taste. Mihai's remark was not necessary, as the guest journalist had already signalled that the supposedly generic 'he' was a Rom with the mention of 'clan names'. From *Gypsy Heart* to *State of Romania*, the soaps confirmed these stereotypes through the character of State, whose human-trafficking business had built his wealth and career in Romania. This was the type of story the journalist and Mihai were indexing in their exchange. These examples represent the public scripts through which Roma are embedded as Others within the normative construction of the monoethnic Romanian nation.

Roma activists who intervened in this public discourse sometimes had a hard time speaking against the grain, as they had already been assigned subaltern or silent roles in the majority's scripts. When Roma spoke from a subject position as both Roma and Romanian citizens, they challenged most non-Roma participants' assumptions. The self-identified Rom in the *Between Good and Evil* audience stood up again to question the speakers' equation of criminals in Italy with Țigani:

> Audience member: They have not yet invented a machine called a Țiganometer for us to know who is a Țigan and who is not. The Minister and Mrs Mihai have mentioned the word 'Roma' [referring to the so-called criminals in Italy]. Wait a minute, how do you know they are Roma? How does anyone know that I am a Rom or not, if I do not declare it?

> Mihai: Why should it be a reason for being upset, if you call someone a Rom? It should make people proud.

> Audience member: A criminal has no ethnicity. He is a Romanian citizen, a criminal.

In Romania, the automatic association of the performance of respectability with non-Roma and the racialization of Roma as Țigani assign the Roma the role of Other. The Țigan label (in the masculine version of the noun) identifies one as criminal, dirty, macho, disreputable, and de facto not a citizen. In this example, Mihai could not let go of the 'Țigani' Others who were necessary for the construction of the Romanian Self. Her refusal to allow Roma to self-identify – reflected in her exclamation 'Why is it an insult to call someone a Rom?' – came from the same unwillingness to let go of one's privilege as was revealed by the moderator of the 2007 talk show discussed earlier. The audience member in this incident was also challenging the racialized hierarchies that guided many non-Roma in their public encounters or their reading of media images. Discussions and gossip often focused on 'spotting' or 'giving away' someone's attempt to hide their being Roma. Public figures were closely scrutinized in the media, and rumours often circulated about personalities' hidden Țigani backgrounds.

Roma Counterpublics: Watching Gypsy Soaps in Pod and Beyond

The runaway success of the soaps, when most Roma were living on or below the poverty line, was perplexing to me. After witnessing the struggles in people's lives in Pod, I found the soaps deeply problematic. The soaps erased class differences among Roma and non-Roma, as well as the racism and discrimination many Roma experienced in their daily lives in Romania. They suggested that Roma were thriving under current economic conditions, and made all other news about them inexplicable. Discrimination was reduced to the dichotomy between tradition and modernity: Roma who were open to modernization risked less discrimination, while those stuck in traditional values were choosing to remain different. For example, the soaps implied that if more Roma were not becoming doctors like Medalion, it was not because of racism and exclusion, but because they did not want to take up an education and preferred to embrace tradition instead. Although Medalion could be seen as a positive role model for Roma, he was the only character in the soaps to succeed through education; all the other characters either refused to engage with mainstream values or sought success through illicit means, like State. The soaps glossed over institutionalized racism at earlier stages in the school system and the harsh realities of many Roma children and parents' lives that sometimes made school an impossible choice. But perhaps I was reading them too literally? Had I lost my sense of humour?

Many Roma in Pod and elsewhere, including at the Gala for Roma Excellence, accepted and/or identified with the images in the soaps, stereotypical though they were, and read them as positive representations of Roma. A critical reading of these soaps therefore needs to take into account Roma people's investment in such images and their potential to stand as cultural signifiers in the continued absence of institutional cultural repositories for them. The appeal of positive or benign Roma stereotypes for Roma people themselves should not be overlooked.

In a 2011 edition of *Roma Caravan*, the moderator, Zita Moldovan, talked to the founding members of the new National Association of Roma Women (Figures 5.6 and 5.7). The association president started by explaining that 'one of my friends from Spain says that Roma there are seen as passionate, hot-blooded, sensual people'. 'We are too,' exclaimed Moldovan. 'No, you know how they see us Roma women here?' replied the president. 'They see us as backward, always three feet behind our men, married as young girls and with a yard full of off-spring'. As I have already discussed, the romantic Roma stereotypes that were pervasive in countries such as Spain and Russia (and to a lesser degree in Hungary and former Yugoslavia) were still rare in Romania. By the end of this edition of *Roma Caravan*, each Roma guest had joined in to agree that Roma women were passionate, hot-blooded and loving, good mothers and hard workers.

The self-exoticization of the Romnja on this show was aspirational, and was a response to the lack of positive images in Romania of Roma in general and Roma women in particular. The thirst for positive images or benign stereotypes was equally present among Roma activists and Roma in Pod and I suggest that this explains the success of Gypsy soaps among Roma. Education, gender and class did not affect the persistence of aspirational romantic self-construction.

Thus Roma in Pod received the soaps favourably, as rare instances of an (apparently, at least) positive focus on Roma in the media. Although it puzzled me initially, the success of the soaps in Pod is not entirely surprising. Until very recently there was no Internet in Pod, and television was a major source of information and entertainment. Most people in Pod did not watch *Roma Caravan*, because it was broadcast on a small private channel that required a special antenna that the majority in Pod did not have; but the soaps were widely accessible, and I had already noticed a predilection for them. In the early days of my visits there, many residents would watch daytime American soaps; several residents, especially women, used to gather in one room to watch soaps such as

Figure 5.7. Roma Caravan, *December 2011; the President of the National Association of Roma Women; in the background, CRED (Romanian Citizens with Equal Rights) campaign poster: 'Get to know the Rom next to you'; television still.*

Young and Restless, with one person reading the subtitles aloud for everyone's benefit. While telenovelas and American soaps were popular, Gypsy soaps were more accessible because they were in Romanian and so did not require the reading of subtitles. In the early 2000s Armando's parents would watch television on a small battery-powered black-and-white portable TV and Armando did not have a television set in his own home, and often watched the soaps with neighbours; in 2008, however, Vanesa's household had a large-screen colour TV, a DVD player and a computer. At the time when the soaps came out, from 2008 onwards, most of my fieldwork was taking place outside Pod, in schools, NGO training sessions, local festivals and so on but I still visited Pod regularly. Once I realized the appeal of Gypsy soaps among residents, I discussed them with fans and non-fans from Pod.

Young Roma Counterpublics and Gypsy Soaps

Popular culture is a site of both resistance to and perpetuation of mainstream values.[23] Using ethnographic evidence, I will now discuss the readings of three young Roma members of the dance group Together: Cosmin, Tibi and Giani. Cosmin and Tibi enjoyed the soaps, while Giani dismissed them as appropriating Roma culture. The divergent views of the soaps among these young Roma show that there is no unified 'Roma perspective'; rather, there is an alternative take on dominant narratives that most Roma share through their subject position in Romania – a view from the margins that does not embrace monoethnic national paradigms. While not all Roma shared the views on the soaps discussed here, and some non-Roma may have read the soaps in the same way, the subject positions these views reveal are significant for the delineation of a Roma counterpublic, specifically in this case a young one.

Cosmin was a fan of *Gypsy Heart*. However, he did not agree with one of the main premises of the soap, a heart transplant between a Rom and an ethnic Romanian, 'because a Țigan's heart does not fit a Romanian. A Țigan's heart is different'. He recounted the climactic moment in *Gypsy Heart* when Medalion's brother Giuvaeru died and Medalion transplanted his heart into the body of his lover's father, saving the latter's life:

> Cosmin: They are drug dealers, and he [Giuvaeru] was followed by the police. And he had an accident. And in the film, so they say, he was dead. They took the heart from the Țigan and put it into a Romanian.
>
> Ioana: Hence the title.
>
> Cosmin: Yes, it is called Țigan Heart.

Cosmin insisted that there was a problem there, because 'a Țigan heart is different.' His embrace of essentialism in this case was in the service of romanticizing

Țigan identity, which was always portrayed as lower and lesser than the majority in Romania.

Cosmin signalled to me the instances when he thought Țigani were not accurately represented; for example, 'in the community, the children born Țigani are not baptized by the priest, in reality. They are baptized in the community by the *bulibasha*'. He mentioned that weddings too were not really performed by a priest, but inside the community, near a tree: 'And here [in the soap] they got married by the priest. And they [in real life] do not use wedding rings'. Armando, who was also present during our informal interview, jumped in: 'For Țigani, it's the oath'. Cosmin agreed: 'It's the oath. The woman is sacred, and so is the child'.

I asked Cosmin what he thought about the scenes of domestic violence in *Gypsy Heart*.

Cosmin: State Potcovaru's wife. It's true that there –

Ioana: How is the wife sacred? Do some husbands beat their wives?

Armando: But the wife does not cheat on her husband.

Ioana: Is there a woman cheating on her husband in the film?

Cosmin: There is. In the tradition of the Roma, this does not exist. The wife is the most sacred ... For example, I'm a Țigan from the community. And my community is sacred. If I took a wife, I have to keep her. If my wife cheats on me, I sell the child and she is killed. So the tradition is different. The film was not original.

Cosmin was upholding an 'original' tradition that the soap only partially represented, according to him. Cosmin's images in fact seemed to have stepped out of a wide range of films that romanticized Roma, with passion and murders à la *Carmen* and Kusturica's *Time of the Gypsies*. Cosmin, like many in Pod, liked the fact that Roma were shown as following their own practices of law and order in the soap, whether these were correctly depicted or not. He also enjoyed the images of wealth:

Ioana: But you still liked it. What did you like about it?

Cosmin: All the actors, they were funny ... It was a film like that, a comedy. Let me tell you, there, gold was at the core. In the film. State Potcovaru had the most gold. He was a Mafia guy. And it's true that even in reality he was the richest. And they shot the film on a Țigan's land ... They showed it in an advert on a TV show. They made the film in a *bulibasha*'s house. And that tower was made of gold.

In fact, as mentioned above, the set had been designed and built in a film studio where the community scenes were shot.

Like other Pod residents, Cosmin was fond of depictions of wealth and big clans. Pod residents enjoyed and even identified with American series such as *Dallas*. The fact that Gypsy soaps fixed Gypsy identity in authenticity and tradition, and emulated a wealth that one could not even dream of in Pod, did not bother my interlocutors. Cosmin told me that his 'whole clan' (i.e. his whole family) watched the soap, and they enjoyed it because, according to him, it showed how some Roma lived: 'if they all lived like that they would be the richest in the world'. I told him that I thought the soap only depicted wealth, as all the protagonists were rich. 'It depends', Cosmin replied. 'When they used to be poor, they also wandered abroad'. Cosmin's response suggested a history of deprivation, for the Roma in the soaps and for Roma in general, and a sense of kinship between his family and community and the characters.

I asked Cosmin about the gang of beggars under State's direction, which operated abroad. He said: 'In real life as well, the Kelderara, they used to be like us, those who sell gold, clothes. They used to be poor too. But if they wandered abroad, they went everywhere they could. Now they're rich'. Thus Cosmin identified the characters portrayed in the soap as Kelderara, one of the most visible Roma groups in Romania. He was not bothered by the characters' wealth; on the contrary, he explained it as a result of 'wandering', 'going everywhere they could'. He mentioned them selling gold and clothes, rather than as being part of trafficking networks as the soap represented them. For Cosmin, there was hope for all Roma to escape from poverty, because *they* used to be poor like 'us'. This interpretation was not obvious to me from the soap, where wealth was a result of some characters' illicit activities (State, Giuvaeru and Stiven for example) and a given for others (such as Aurică Fieraru). Cosmin's reading of the soap stemmed from a subaltern position in Romania, and reflected the existence of subject positions that did not endorse hegemonic negative interpretations and stereotypes of Roma wealth.

Cosmin confessed that he had been devastated by the episode with what he called the 'black child': Norocel, the mixed-race child of Roza – Flacăra and State's daughter, played by Nicoleta Luciu – and Thierry, State's Moroccan bodyguard. State ordered Norocel to disappear, because Roza was in an arranged marriage with Medalion, although Medalion did not want her:

> Cosmin: I liked the film, especially that part, with Nicoleta Luciu, with that child, who was black. I was gutted by that part. In fact she had slept with State Potcovaru's man. [Cosmin, Armando and I tried to remember the name of the actor who played Thierry, Cabral Ibracka.] And you can imagine, when State, the grandfather, saw that the child was black, he called someone from Paris and sold the child.

Ioana: Because he was –

Cosmin: A Mafia guy. And he took the child, but she [Roza] was in hospital. That guy took the child abroad, and she could not stop crying. And the black guy asked the doctor, Medalion, to help him find his child. And the doctor helped him a lot, he gave him the keys to his flat.

Ioana: Did they find the child eventually?

Cosmin: Yes, after he [Medalion] married Irina. A Romanian's daughter, Dumbravă's daughter.

Cosmin was most touched by the black child's fate, and the solidarity Medalion showed to Norocel's father. He spoke about the racism the little boy faced from his Roma relatives, rather than about the discrimination Medalion encountered in the world of *gadge*. Cosmin sympathized with the child, who faced discrimination because of the colour of his skin – a parallel with the discrimination Roma faced in the world of *gadge*. As discussed in Chapter 2, the signifier 'black' is used in relation to Roma in Romania to distinguish them as different from the majority, and some Roma use it positively to self-identify.[24]

Tibi enjoyed the humour of the soaps. They portrayed a counterculture that was not necessarily Roma, but which was associated with Roma through State's character. He told me that he enjoyed 'the way they spoke'. When I asked how they spoke, he replied:

Well, I don't know how to explain it. Like that, more like Roma. But not in Romani, in Romanian. [I also liked] the characters, Flăcărica and State. State was a *bulibasha*. Flăcărica was his wife. They argued all the time. I used to laugh at them.

He confessed that he did not like telenovelas and preferred action films, but he enjoyed *Gypsy Heart* because 'it was a comedy and it was in Romanian'. He also affectionately referred to the character Flacăra by her nickname, the diminutive Flăcărica (Little Flame). In a media landscape from which Roma had been absent for over five decades (and for most of Tibi's childhood), the characters in the soaps, performed by famous Romanian actors, were positive, light-hearted, funny representations that contrasted with the negative portrayal of Roma in the news. Roma could enjoy the humour in the soaps without fearing that it would lead to further stereotyping in the media, even if the soaps reinforced those stereotypes for the mainstream public.

Giani had a different take on the soaps, which he only watched because others in Pod watched them. He was critical of these representations and of their parodic aspects, including the accent, which he did not recognize:

Gypsy Heart, I don't really watch it, so I watched it out of obligation …
They speak with an accent, like that, a Ţigan accent. We really don't
speak like that. So we really don't use that strange accent, but they use
it, they make it seem like we do. If they can't speak *ţigăneşte*, at least
they try to use the accent – so that they seem like Ţigani.

He blasted the politics of representation in the soaps, which, according to him,
exploited aspects of Roma culture:

Some people admire us, others don't. If they use us, but don't do it out
of admiration, only for money, why are they using us if we are different from them? And then they avoid us? Why do they use our clothing
style, why do they use us? Why didn't they make a Romanian film?

By 'Romanian film' Giani meant a film about non-Roma. He noted that
Romanian actors took credit for the success of the soaps, while Roma remained
unrecognized. He also criticized the objectification of Roma culture in the
soaps, and the fact that non-Roma performed Roma characters. Asked why he
thought the soaps were popular among many Roma, he explained:

They watch [*Gypsy Heart*] because – because they like that they show
their traditional clothing, or something like that. They think it is something interesting. But I am not curious about their clothing. Because I
know mine.

Giani is a proud young Rom who says he does not need the kind of recognition
of Roma traditions that does not do justice to Roma culture.

Armando also told me that he enjoyed the soaps, confessing that he and
others often got angry about the trouble into which the characters would get
themselves. He enjoyed the costumes, the music and the excellent actors, especially Gheorghe Dinică, who played Aurică Fieraru, State's blood brother. For
Armando, the soaps showed elements of Roma culture, such as the *stabor*, which
he told me were nice to watch in a film; but he never took them seriously, and
did not want any of those traditions to come back again. (Even though they
were not officially recognized, *stabors* were still practised in some Roma communities, such as the Kelderara in the Sibiu region.)

Both the endorsements and the critiques of the soaps from these young
Roma stemmed from a similar desire to be recognized as equals and represented
in a positive way in Romania. Positive and negative stereotypes coexisted as the
two sides of the same ideology that turned Roma into a people without history
(see Trumpener 1992). Armando, Giani, Cosmin and Tibi were identifying
with Roma characters or with a Roma subject position. The endorsements of

'positive' stereotypical images in Pod chimed with a more general thirst among Roma for images that had been suppressed for five decades during socialism. While in themselves they did not change attitudes towards Roma, as their coexistence with anti-Roma racism testifies, it is important to understand that Roma were invested in these positive stereotypes.

Conclusion

Armando remarked that the soaps' actors, including Visu, Tănase and Loredana, had not enjoyed so much media exposure in all their lives, and were doing so now because of Roma culture. The President of the Roma Party criticized the new trend of Gypsy chic in an October 2011 edition of *Roma Caravan*: 'Everyone who puts a scarf on their head thinks they are Țigănci. They don't wash themselves; they go barefoot. Please, try another trick! Our women are the most beautiful and smell the best everywhere, so you don't need to do that!' Some Pod residents, such as Giani, critiqued non-Roma's dressing up as Roma in the soaps; others, including Cosmin and Armando, critiqued the soaps as not authentic enough. This critique, despite the soaps' light and caricatural tone, reveals the stakes Roma had in affirming positive images of their culture in the few instances when they were positively represented in the media. Most Roma in Pod were appreciative of the soaps and engaged with them – even if they critiqued their lack of accuracy in the depiction of Roma tradition – and most were eager to engage in the romanticization of Roma, probably for similar reasons as the guests on the *Roma Caravan* show discussed above.[25]

Many of the fans' comments on the Acasă website congratulated the actors and their acting skills. But there were some comments on the same website – not very many – that were critical of the soaps for focusing on Țigani. Some chat forums and blogs expressed a real dislike of and discontent with the soaps, but these were a minority compared to the soaps' high ratings and the positive endorsements from fans on the soaps' websites.[26] Negative comments (those polite enough not be removed) ranged from 'Why focus on Țigani?' to 'They are already too many, they are going to take us over'. These comments relegated the Roma to the Other and reinforced the citizenship gap. Fans responded to such negative comments by pointing out that the soaps had nothing to do with real Țigani.[27] However, for some non-Roma fans the embrace of positive stereotypes in the soaps did not alter their negative perception of Țigani in real life: such positions equally embrace monoethnic paradigms of citizenship and maintain the citizenship gap, while willingly consuming Gypsy chic as non-threatening to the majority's privilege and subject positions.

Roma appeared on television screens in the soaps as Gypsies and foils for ethnic Romanians, rather than as subjects of self-representation, but Roma spectators' readings of the soaps reflected subject positions that did not endorse mainstream representations and their assumptions. In the instances when

Roma did speak on Romanian television, such as on the talk shows discussed in this chapter, the clashes between Roma activists and non-Roma revealed how non-Roma exercised their power as the majority to impose and maintain the citizenship gap for Roma. Roma activists made public Roma views and citizenship subject positions, from the margins and with an oblique take on majority assumptions. In this way they made a growing Roma counterpublic visible in the Romanian media.

Notes

1. I am calling the television soaps about Roma 'Gypsy soaps' in order to emphasize the Western capital Gypsiness accumulated through the advent of consumerism and commercial television. I call them 'soaps' rather than 'telenovelas', although technically these series followed the telenovela format in both length (they lasted for a season or a little longer) and storyline (rivalry between families or people). The Acasă channel called them 'telenovele', because in Romanian this term is easier to translate than the English 'soap opera'. If we compare them with other soaps, these series are most similar to US primetime soaps. Besides locally produced soaps, the same channel also broadcasts Latin American and Turkish telenovelas.
2. Footage of the gala is available at http://www.youtube.com/watch?v=viTJZeq-1f8 (last accessed 1 March 2012).
3. Roma actor Doiniţa Oancea, who played Minodora, State's adopted daughter, declared in interviews before and after the 2008 gala that she was proud to belong to the 'Ţigan' ethnicity.
4. http://www.inimadetigan.ro/personaj/loredana (last accessed 1 March 2012).
5. There was a non-stop supply of *manele* videos on the private music TV channels Taraf and Mynele, while the Etno channel played Romanian folk music.
6. Romania is an exception among Balkan countries in that most *manele* producers are Roma. Ionita from *Clejanii* is also the producer of his own band. In Chapter 6 I discuss in detail the reality show *Clejanii*.
7. I translate the title *Inimă de Ţigan* as *Gypsy Heart* in order to emphasize that the resurgence of the exotic Gypsy stereotypes was the result of the advent of consumer culture mediated by Western taste. It was also the official translation of the title.
8. http://www.inimadetigan.ro (last accessed 1 March 2012).
9. Some notable exceptions include the British soaps *EastEnders* and *Coronation Street*, and also Egyptian soaps.
10. http://www.inimadetigan.ro/rezumat/5mai-episoduldin5mai (last accessed 22 January 2012).
11. http://www.inimadetigan.ro/pagina/personaje (last accessed 1 March 2012).
12. http://regina.acasatv.ro/ (last accessed 1 March 2012).
13. http://www.inimadetigan.ro/pagina/despre_serial (last accessed 1 March 2012).
14. http://www.inimadetigan.ro/pagina/despre_serial (last accessed 1 March 2012).
15. http://www.acasatv.ro/noutati-acasa/emisiuni/la-povestiri-adevarate-actorii-din-tele-novela-regina-asteapta.html (last accessed 1 March 2012).
16. http://www.inimadetigan.ro/clip/143 (last accessed 29 May 2011).
17. http://www.inimadetigan.ro (last accessed 1 March 2012).

18. http://dantanasescu.ro/2010/04/09/serialul-state-de-romania-promoveaza-rasismul-si-discriminarea-romanilor.html (last accessed 1 March 2012).

19. Euronews channel interview with Connect-R, available at: http://www.youtube.com/watch?v=jXCb4ffXJo8&feature=related (last accessed 1 March 2012).

20. http://www.pudel.ro/2007/10/30/momentul-adevarului-in-inima-de-tigan/(last accessed 1 March 2012).

21. Roma scholar Alexandra Oprea (2005) argues that such discussions obliterate Roma women's voices, and those of women who choose to take a different path.

22. AltFem report, available at: http://www.activewatch.ro/Cercetare-si-Educatie-Media (last accessed 1 March 2012).

23. The study of popular culture from the perspective of readers/spectators includes Janice Radway's (1991) work on women readers of romance novels, gay readings of Broadway musicals (Miller, 1998), and Stacey Wolf's 'A Problem Like Maria' (2009), a lesbian reading of musicals.

24. As I show in Chapter 2, the use of 'black' and 'white' in Romania reflects similarities in the racialization of Roma and people of African descent in Romania and elsewhere, although there are also many differences.

25. As of 2017, a new version of the programme is broadcast weekly on private channel NationalTV as 'I Too Was Born in Romania'; OTV channel no longer exists.

26. For examples of fans' posts on the soaps' websites see http://regina.acasatv.ro/comunitate and http://forum.acasatv.ro/viewforum.php?f=13 (last accessed 1 March 2012).

27. www.inimadetigan.ro (last accessed 10 February 2012).

Chapter 6

The Ambivalence of Success

Roma Musicians and the Citizenship Gap in Romania

In 2010 *manele* singer Florin Salam[1] participated in the competition to be the Romanian entry for that year's Eurovision Song Contest (ESC). His presence in the competition sent shockwaves through a section of the Romanian public and media, who feared the prospect that a *manele* singer, a Țigan, might represent Romania. Despite being one of the most popular singers in Romania, Salam did not make it to the national final; his rejection restored order for those who had feared the worst. The Romanian final was ultimately won by the duo Paula Seling and Ovi with 'Playing with Fire', a song that could be described as 'generic pop'; they came third in that year's contest, held in Oslo.

During 2012 the equally famous Roma musicians Ioniță and Viorica and their two children were the protagonists of the reality TV show *Clejanii*. Viorica and Ioniță were from the countryside and had made a name for themselves in the capital, where they now lived. The show combined a fascination with their stardom and luxurious lifestyle (à la *The Osbournes*) with the assumption that they were uncivilized and lacked taste (à la *The Beverly Hillbillies*). The two artists acted as entertainers for the majority, and in one episode even performed as the Communist presidential couple Nicolae and Elena Ceaușescu.

Focusing on Florin Salam's unsuccessful bid to represent Romania at the ESC and on Viorica and Ioniță's appearances on *Clejanii*, this chapter discusses the limits of success for popular Roma artists and the different strategies that Roma musicians use to carve a space for their music. I argue that these two examples reflect the persistence of the citizenship gap for all Roma, including for popular and prosperous artists, particularly with regard to cultural citizenship and mainstream Romanian media's ambivalence towards successful Roma musicians. Salam's failure to qualify for the Eurovision national final and the media coverage of his participation revealed that he was considered unacceptable to represent Romania at the ESC: the stigmata of being Rom and singing *manele* marked him as an outsider to the nation. Ioniță and Viorica had to pay for their success by playing up to the majority's obsessions with Ţigani on the reality show. The Romanian media, the national Eurovision selection jury and the *Clejanii* reality show producers all framed these examples as failed performances of citizenship and the Roma artists as not 'us', not Romanian.

However, despite *the mise en scène* as failed performances of citizenship, these performers pushed boundaries in their performances; they appealed to a counterpublic that did not embrace the hegemony of monoethnic nationalism, and they challenged Roma's exclusion from citizenship. I will demonstrate that even in the tightly scripted reality show, Viorica was able to subvert some of the roles assigned to her and to offer alternatives to hegemonic representations, including representations of the nation and of women in Romania.

'Gypsy Music', Nationalisms and the ESC

Salam's failure to get into the ESC national final, and the media scandal surrounding his participation, illustrated the identity anxieties that *manele* and *manele* singers prompt in Romania. Often dismissed as light entertainment and kitsch, the ESC represents fertile ground for studying images of Europeanness as well as self-representations and hierarchies among participating nations. In the last few years, Romania's entries have aimed to avoid the stigma of Ţigani and to change the perceived bad reputation of Romania abroad caused by the identification of Romania with Roma, which reached extreme levels in 2010 with the expulsions of migrant Romanian Roma from France.

National juries – in combination with a public vote from 2012 onwards, in the case of Romania – choose the performances that will represent the nation at the ESC. National juries are thus a filter that establishes and maintains acceptable representations of the nation through musical styles and performers. The absence of minorities and ethnic music markers from Romania's ESC entries reflects non-Roma Romanians' reaction to representations of Romania in foreign media, particularly the frequent conflation of Romanians with Roma. Since its first participation in the ESC in 1994, Romania's entries have tended to emulate generic European pop, with several ballad-style performances. Only three entries have emphasized local flavour, folk or 'ethnic' music: 'Liubi, Liubi I Love You' by Todomundo in 2007, 'The Balkan Girls' by Elena Gheorghe in 2009, and 'Zaleilah' by Mandinga in 2012, which I will discuss later in this chapter.

Roma, the largest transnational minority in Europe, have been largely absent from the ESC – and not only from Romania's entries – despite a strong trend in ethnic music at the contest over the last decade and a resurgence of so-called Gypsy music on the international music scene. Nonetheless, despite the absence of Roma from the competition, stereotypes of Gypsies and Țigani have become tropes of romanticization and stigmatization at the ESC in relationships of nesting marginalization, with Romania and Roma occupying marginal positions in Europe and Romania respectively. The absence of Roma and local music from Romania's entries reflects tensions that surface despite their silencing: Roma's lack of actual citizenship in Romania and the EU, the racialized hierarchies of musical genres, and the power differentials between 'Eastern' and 'Western' nations that have persisted despite EU expansion into East Central Europe.

Étienne Balibar (2004, 8) makes a useful distinction between 'demos' (the 'collective subject of representation, decision-making and rights), and 'ethnos' (the historical communities formed on the basis of ethnic belonging). In Romania the collective subject of representation continues to be equated with the ethnos. Starting in the nineteenth century, constructions of the Romanian nation emulated Western European models. Katherine Verdery (1996, 46) discusses the formation of the independent Romanian state as a mobilization of Western allies, where 'those intellectuals who argued about the national essence were constructing the means for ideological subjection of their countrymen, Romanian and non-Romanian, within the new state'. Furthermore, the Romanian nation has always been exposed to and dominated by the larger empires surrounding it, a position that has given rise to what (in a different context) Nelson Maldonado-Torres (2007) calls the 'coloniality of being' – attitudes and mentalities related to colonialism that exist without the institution of colonialism. Scholars of South-East Europe have theorized the region's relationship to the West by reworking Edward Said's *Orientalism* (1978). Maria Todorova's (1997) concept of 'Balkanism' captures the proximity and perceived temporal distance between the West and the Balkan region, while Milica Bakic-Hayden's (1995) notion of 'nesting Orientalisms' reflects the nested hierarchies that such divisions engender, specifically referring to one nationality's projection of Orientalist stereotypes onto other nationalities of the former Yugoslavia.

The expulsions of Romanian EU citizens from Western Europe revealed that power differentials between East and West did not disappear with the extension of EU membership to countries in East Central Europe in 2004 and 2007. Those differentials had been reconfigured, but the lag between West and East persisted, at both rhetorical and political levels. These power differentials become apparent in the rhetorical deployment of Balkanism and nesting Orientalisms, both in the current European configuration and in the conflation between Roma and Romanians, which are visible in the media and at the ESC. The conflation between Roma and Romanians is an example of Balkanism that manifests itself linguistically through popular etymology, where the phonetic similarities between the two words and their appearance together result in their conflation in popular culture. Anthropologist Susan Gal (1991) has analysed the fractal recurrence of the East–West dichotomy within Europe and the role that Europe plays as an ideological concept whose meaning and location shift. In Gal's terms, Romania represents the East in relation or opposition to Europe; whereas within Romania, Țigani stand for the East – the Orient within Romania – while Romania itself stands for Europe. At the ESC, Romania's entries attempted to shed any association with Roma, while on the Western music scene, where 'Gypsy music' is increasingly popular, any music from the Balkans is associated with Gypsies and is coded as exotic through an erasure of ethnic and national differences in the region.

At the same time as Romanian and Bulgarian Roma were being expelled from Western Europe, romantic stereotypes about Roma were playing a central role in the international success of Gypsy music. Apparently positive stereotypes of Roma as talented and natural performers went hand in hand with blatantly negative ones that presented Roma as duplicitous liars and thieves in most countries across Western Europe and some in the former Eastern bloc. This underbelly of romantic stereotypes is always ever-present, as attested by new waves of racism against Roma across Europe in parallel with the growing success of the Gypsy brand of music. The popularity of Gypsy music performances in the West has led to a range of events across continents, from large international festivals featuring Roma bands from the Balkans to 'Gypsy nights' in clubs where audiences sport Gypsy costumes. Western DJs such as Shantel and Gypsy Sound System, and Western bands such as Beirut and Balkan Beat Box, feature or sample music from South-East Europe (Silverman 2007; Szeman 2009). The international festival scene encourages broad distinctions and divisions between Roma and non-Roma, mostly falling along Roma/Balkan and non-Roma/Western lines. This version of Balkanism places all 'native' artists from the Balkans within the same category, disregarding not only the different nationalities in the Balkans but also the differences among Roma from different countries, not to mention differences within the same countries.

However, the ESC provides a very different setting from the commercial music scene in the West, which is orchestrated by Western managers and producers even when the musicians hail from the Balkans. In contrast, the ESC represents an opportunity for the smaller countries of East Central Europe and the Balkans to assert and represent themselves against the more powerful Western nations. While the ESC is not known for being a forum for political statements, the relative absence and invisibility of Roma musicians on its stage are noteworthy, given their popularity across Europe. Roma sometimes serve as tropes in rhetorical and musical battles among participating nations, but their voices remain unheard.

As a transnational ethnic minority, Roma represent a potential ethnicizing element at the ESC, where the resurgence of so-called ethnic music, represented by music with ethnic-sounding elements and/or performers from ethnic minorities, both parallels and differs considerably from the commercial music scene. Alf Björnberg (2007, 20–21) identifies two major representational strategies at the ESC: one in which any local flavour is erased from the nation's entry, and the opposite strategy of emphasizing such ethnic elements. The success of 'ethnic' performances is based on their becoming 'free-floating signifiers representing an unspecified cultural anchorage' (Björnberg 2007, 23). While his focus is on Western European countries, countries from East Central Europe have followed similar trends. The inclusion of ethnic-sounding music and ethnic-minority performers in ESC entries from East Central European countries follows their function as exotic additions that enhance local flavour or transport the audience to a distant exotic space. These performances are open to multiple readings, but they are also heavily grounded in their local contexts, and may offer visibility to minorities in some cases – but not to Roma. Winning songs that fall into this category have included Ruslana's 'Wild Dances', which represented Ukraine in 2002, and Sertab Erener's 'Every Way that I Can' for Turkey in 2003.

'Ethnic' music – the sound of brass instruments and other popular music identified on the commercial scene as Gypsy or Balkan – is redeployed at the ESC as national folklore, without directly referencing Roma, and without Roma artists. In the context of the Western success of Gypsy music, Roma remain hidden in plain sight, and as Gypsies they function as projective mechanisms – a way of reaching the wild, passionate, and unpredictable place that the Balkans are supposed to be (Szeman 2009). For example Moldova, unlike Romania, has mobilized the 'ethnic' element in its entries, using both the 'Balkan' sound and the folk sound in Zdob si Zdub's performance in 2011 and Nelly Ciobanu's in 2009. Ciobanu's song 'Hora din Moldova' ('Line Dancing from Moldova') used a combination of brass and percussion instruments, a sound similar to Zdob si Zdub's 'So Lucky'. However, while for Zdob si Zdub the brass sound and parodic performance evoked 'Gypsy music', Ciobanu and her four accompanying male dancers referenced folk costumes and local line dancing. These performances show that a similar sound can reference national folklore, Balkan music or Gypsy music, depending on its framing.

As I showed in Chapter 1, the national folklores of the Balkan region serve to define nations as ethnically homogenous by denying or instrumentalizing the Roma. Roma musicians have been part of the entertainment scene in Romania for centuries, but they were not credited with music of their own. The post-1989 phenomenon of *manele*, which is seen as the opposite of culture, is now attributed exclusively to Roma. In Romania, music labelled as folklore is seen as Romanian, but contemporary music such as *manele* is not: it is kitsch, and associated with Ţigani. While there are various repertoires that are played exclusively among Roma, popular music in multi-ethnic countries such as Romania reflects multiple cross-influences. Given this complex history, the lack of visibility of Roma at the ESC is reinforced by the competition's nation-based format.

Examples of Roma performers at the ESC international final have included: the Roma rap band Gipsy.cz, who sang for the Czech Republic in 2009; Serbia's entry in the 2007 competition with Marija Šerifović, a singer of Roma descent whose performance was co-opted by a nationalist agenda in Serbia, according to Anikó Imre (2009, 126); and the *chalga* singer Azis, who represented Bulgaria as a backing singer in 2006. The Czech band's name explicitly stated their ethnicity, with the performers claiming both their Roma and their Czech identities. In the other cases, however, the performers' ethnicity may only have been known to spectators already familiar with them; such was the case with bleached-blond, gay *chalga* king Azis, 'the most radical Romani performer in Bulgaria today' (Silverman 2012, 189), whose excess was tempered at the ESC by his position in the background of a slow pop song by non-Roma Bulgarian singer Mariana Popova. TV viewers might even have missed his presence completely, as he only appeared for a few seconds in the televised footage.

Singing in Italian with another pop artist, Roma singer Nico performed in the Romanian ESC entry for 2008; but her presence reinforced the nation as 'ethnos' while erasing Roma, and reflected a process that has been ongoing for centuries in Romania – that is, the appropriation of elements of Roma culture and some Roma performers. Nico's performance is an example of how the citizenship gap is maintained, this time through the appropriation of Roma artists: her performance of citizenship was successful because she sang pop and could be appropriated into the ethnos. In Nico's case, because neither the pop song nor the performer was marked as Țigan(ca), the performance was acceptable as Romanian. Nico's example is similar to Roma singer Caramel, winner of a talent show in Hungary, whose performance was 'whitewashed and nationalized', as Anikó Imre argues (2009, 124). In her analysis of a range of Roma musicians at the Eurovision and in television talent shows or reality shows, Imre demonstrates that Roma musicians have been doubly co-opted by nationalist discourses and commercial media (2009). Indeed, the blending in of Roma performers with the majority in these examples is not a proof of integration and acceptance; on the contrary, it shows that successful individuals can pass as the majority and/or be accepted as exotic without bridging the citizenship gap for Roma. However, in the following section, I show that for the same reasons that his performance failed at the ESC, musicians like Salam appeal to a Roma counterpublic and resist monoethnic nationalism.

Manele, Roma Musicians and Racialized Musical Hierarchies in Romania

Music similar to the very popular *manele* in Romania, bearing influences from an Ottoman form called *mana* and today extending into fusion styles, can be found across the Balkans in other ethnopop incarnations such as turbo-folk and *chalga*.

According to Maria Todorova (1997), the Balkan nations share the legacy of the Ottoman Empire, of which they were all a part, and this music is certainly one of its outcomes.[2] Similarly, Beissinger (2007, 101) provides a history of *manele* and its Ottoman origins, establishing a link between Ottoman domination of the Romanian territories and the spreading of this music via Roma musicians; and Donna Buchanan (2007, 251) argues that the Orientalist vision evident in ethnopop today, which is also present in *manele* with its dominating hypermasculinity and sensuous, accessible femininity, goes back to late-eighteenth- and nineteenth-century Viennese operas with harem settings. Most *manele* singers today are men, often accompanied by scantily dressed belly dancers.

The distinguishing features of *manele*, also known as *muzică orientală*, lie in a series of stylistic effects that relate to rhythm, melody and instrumentation. *Manele* are characterized by 'syncopated Arab rhythms' and 'elaborately ornamented, virtuosic, and often improvisational' melodic passages. The 'Oriental' specificity of *manele* lies in the rhythm, called *kifteteli* or *chifteteli*. The most common instruments employed are the accordion, synthesizer or keyboard, drums, clarinet, electric guitar, saxophone and string bass (Beissinger 2007, 110–15).

Ethnomusicologists attribute the immense success of *manele* and similar music (such as *chalga* and turbo-folk) to the sanitization of folklore during socialism. Marin Marian-Bălaşa (2003, 245), for example, discusses *manele* as a reaction to cultural policies in Romania where 'ethnocentric, purist and dry nationalism has forced the nation to identify with the official, museum-like, outdated folklore': as an antidote to the controlled representation of folklore, *manele* offered unabashed entertainment. Western music, from rock and pop to rap and hip hop, has influenced the evolution of *manele* since 1989, and given

Figure 6.1. Florin Salam performing live on television channel Kanal D; television still.

birth to fusion styles in Romania; and recently Western DJs have mixed *manele* with electronic beats. *Manele*'s favourite topics include money, cars, love and women – all signs of status for those newly rich since the fall of Communism (Beissinger 2007, 117; Marian-Bălașa 2006, 84).

While there are many debates around the origin and ownership of folk music, there is less controversy, in Romania at least, about whom *manele* belongs to: it belongs to the Țigani. This hugely successful and controversial music genre is played almost exclusively by Roma in Romania; unlike in other countries, where genres such as turbo-folk are sung and controlled by non-Roma, in Romania it is Roma who run the *manele* market. Successful music entrepreneurs such as Dan Bursuc, and *manele* singers such as Florin Salam and Nicolae Guță, have gained a privileged position in Romania through music; but they are far from being accepted as full citizens and part of the nation and, in fact, Roma musicians' almost complete control of the *manele* genre in Romania makes the music less acceptable. Tolerated because of their financial success, these musicians are often seen as examples of market corruption, rather than of talent and hard work. Dominant perceptions of and ambivalence towards successful Roma *manele* musicians reflect the segregation at the core of official cultural production in Romania, as well as the limits of cultural production unendorsed by the state or state-supported cultural networks. The stark segregation of musical genres has also prevented engagement with Roma realities and perpetuated abject Țigani stereotypes. The bad reputation of *manele* as music played by Țigani is compounded by the erasure of Roma culture and the equation of Roma with an underclass during socialism.

Manele thus splinters the Romanian public along status and ethnic lines as well as East–West vectors. This places Roma musicians at the crux of debates in Romania about identity, Europe and the 'Orient', modernity and tradition, all of which are epitomized by criticism or praise of *manele*. Certain sections of the Romanian intelligentsia vehemently oppose *manele* and regard pop music and traditional folk music (which is coded as Romanian) as inherently better. *Manele*'s detractors see the musicians who play it as agents of 'Gypsification', with Gypsies embodying the negative pole of the East–West dichotomy.[3] Even though not all Roma take offence at them, the verbs 'to Gypsy' (*a se țigăni)* and 'to Gypsify' (*a se țiganiza*) – similar to 'to jew' (Gilman 1991) – can be offensive, carrying linguistic traces of the racism present in the Romanian language. Moreover, those who play *manele* are perceived in Romania as Țigani, whether they are Roma or not. Salam's failed attempt to qualify for the Romanian Eurovision final illustrated this: he was marked as a *manelist* and Rom/Țigan even when he was performing a pop song.

Romania's Balkan position – as a bridge between East and West, and as equally sensitive to both influences – is thus re-enacted in the ideological battle between *manele*'s supporters and its opponents. Anti-*manelists* are often either highly educated intellectuals or heavy metal and rock fans. Marian-Bălaşa (2006) describes in detail the ideological battle between *manelişti* (*manele* supporters) on the one hand and *rockeri* (rockers) and other *manele* opponents on the other. Anti-*manele* strategies range from online battles, with fake *manele*-making programmes and racist comments, to actual street protests against *manele* concerts.

However, just like the discursive fractal splitting between East and West in relation to identity formations, musical genres only discursively follow ethnic lines: not all and not only Roma enjoy *manele* in Romania. In an article about *chalga* (a sister genre of *manele*) ethnomusicologist Timothy Rice (2002) argues that *chalga* is a form that illustrates Bulgarian culture's multiple influences, emphasizing its Ottoman heritage and Balkan aspects, which are denied by politicians in Bulgaria. Rice suggests that this might contribute to a different form of nationalism that would replace the monoethnic nation and move towards diversity and openness. The same applies to the immense success of *manele*, which as a genre brings together Roma and non-Roma audiences in Romania, and addresses counterpublics that do not share monoethnic paradigms or the racialized hierarchies of musical genres.

From 'Gypsy Frenzy' to *Manele*: What they Talk about when they Talk about Gypsies

Despite their immense popular success, Florin Salam and other *manele* singers are often vilified and ridiculed in Romanian media. In 2008 Salam sang with Paula Seling and a symphony orchestra from Bucharest in order to bridge the ideological divide between pop and *manele* in Romania. He made an appeal for people to stop treating his music as rubbish, and showed that he could sing with a whole symphony orchestra and could match Seling's voice. This performance and its reception provide a telling illustration of the gap between pop and *manele* in Romania.

The presenter at the concert introduced the purpose of the event to the audience:

> ... to show the whole world that for us the word 'discrimination' does not exist, and to prove that there can be a fusion between these two musical genres, which, it's true, clash: *manele* and the extraordinarily beautiful music of Paula Seling, pop ... Listen very carefully to the song that follows, with Paula Seling and Florin Salam, because it is something else. ('Florin Salam and Paula Seling Live' 2008)

The deferential introduction of Seling and her 'extraordinarily beautiful music' contrasts with the dismissive mention of *manele* and the presenter patronizingly asked the audience to listen, as if they might otherwise miss Seling's momentous presence. According to this introduction, the Seling-Salam duo was bringing together two genres that clashed: pop and *manele*, but these only clash ideologically in Romania: just like any form of music, *manele* can mix very well with pop. This national ideology, reflected in the highbrow/lowbrow division between pop and *manele*, diverged from global trends in commercial music.

After performing with Salam, Seling came under fire from her fans for mingling with uncultivated *manele* fans. Asked on the talk show 'Happy Hour' on the ProTV channel why she had participated in a concert for *manelists*, she corrected the moderator, pointing out that they were Roma: 'Don't you want them to listen to something else?' she said. She declared she had taken part so as to cultivate the audience, to offer them something new, and that she had refused payment in order to avoid the accusation that she had done it for the money. Asked how she had helped Roma by singing three songs at Sala Palatului concert venue, she explained: 'By showing the world that it is possible, that if you reach out your hand to people who need culture, and to be cultivated – I gave an example, a very good example. I showed that Roma, if they are exposed to artists who sing something other than just *manele*, they listen and participate'. Seling's attitude reflected how in Romania popular musical genres are ideologically divided and aligned not only with high- and lowbrow but also along West and East vectors, and are valued or devalued accordingly in relationships of nesting Orientalisms exacerbated by the conflation between Roma and Romanians abroad. Note, too, that Seling identified the audience at this concert as Roma, even though *manele* are equally popular with non-Roma in Romania.

Two years later Seling returned from the 2010 ESC final in Oslo, where she had won third place with Ovi for 'Playing with Fire'. Greeted at the airport like an athlete bringing home medals from a sports competition, she declared: 'I wish with all my soul that we could convince the world that Romania is a little different than what Europe has become accustomed to. It is a pity for them to believe we are all the way they think we are' (Arsenie 2010, no page number). If Seling seemed to be speaking in riddles, it was because she had chosen not to explicitly mention certain infamous episodes in relation to Romanian citizens abroad. Roma Romanian citizens had been expelled from France, despite being EU citizens, but Seling was metonymically naming only the effect of those events in terms of Romania's bad reputation abroad. Her statement reproduced, on a smaller scale, general reactions in Romania to those events: what was reported as reprehensible in Romania was not the expulsion of Romanian citizens, but the further deterioration of Romania's reputation. Many non-Roma protested against the mention of Romania in regard to the expulsions, and some politicians even planned to replace the name of the Roma ethnicity with 'Țigani' in order to further distance Roma from ethnic Romanians.

The anxiety among non-Roma about the conflation of Romanians with Roma was also reflected in the choice of performances for the ESC, illustrated by Salam's participation in the national competition in 2010. Even though

Salam participated in the pre-selection campaign with two pop songs, he was unmistakably perceived in Romania as a *manelist*, i.e. Ţigan, and continued to inhabit the ideologically negative Other of Romanian identity. Indeed, he was doubly marked as a Ţigan, first as a Rom and second as a *manelist*.

When Todomundo, Romania's ESC entry in 2007, addressed diversity, it did so by presenting it at a European level: the diversity in question was between nations such as Italy, Spain, France and Russia, and the performers sang in French, Italian, Spanish, Russian and Romanian. Romania was thus placed in a 'family' of Latin nations, rather than in a Balkan context – with Russia as the Other. The 2009 entry 'The Balkan Girls' did index the term 'Balkan', but the music had Latin American overtones rather than characteristics of 'Balkan music' and the non-Roma Romanian singer and dancers performed a short routine that was vaguely reminiscent of line dancing in Romania but also of Riverdance. The song was allegedly inspired by the local legend of *iele* – fairies that lure unassuming men – but these references were almost impossible to read in the ESC performance. The performance also featured scantily dressed women, not unlike *manele* meaning that even though its sound was not similar to *manele*, Romanian audiences had initially accused the song of being one (the final version of the song clearly distanced it musically from the unwanted *manele* genre). Thus associations with Roma or Gypsies surfaced even when they were not present, just as the suspicion that someone is a Ţigan may hang over anyone in Romania.

While avoiding local flavour, Romania's entries occasionally employed a frequent ESC strategy of using outside Others, as in the 2012 entry featuring the Romanian-Cuban group Mandinga. In the case of countries from East Central Europe, the presence of distant Others at the ESC offers a promise of exotic escape and a diversion from the sizeable populations of other ethnic minorities. Ethnic music and performers have also appeared as distant Others in the entries of other 'new' European countries; for example, Estonia's winning entry in 2001 featured the black Dutch singer David Benton. In the 2012 Romanian entry, Cuban musicians and a Latin American sound featured in a song composed by Costi Ioniţă, a non-Roma Romanian musician who at one stage in his career had composed and sung *manele*, but even this was met with criticism. The 2012 ESC song did not resemble *manele*, but some of the brass made it typical of the Balkan sound identified on the music scene with 'Gypsy music', and foreign media identified parts of the song and performance as such. *Associated Press* described the song as: 'a global mishmash: Cuban horns, lashings of salsa, a generous dollop of Gypsy frenzy, and even a smattering of bagpipes' (Bucharest Herald 2012). This description was translated in the Romanian media as *muzica ţigănească*, and some even disparagingly called the song *manele* – a result of the *Associated Press* description combined with the fact that the composer had previously dipped into the *manele* genre. This was taken as an explanation for the relatively poor twelfth place Mandinga gained in the ESC final.

Given the strong reactions that *manele* provokes in Romania, it is not surprising that Florin Salam's participation in the 2010 Romanian competition caused a huge stir in the national media. However, his failure to reach the national final caused a different set of controversies when the composer of the songs he had performed took to the pages of the national newspaper *Libertatea* (2010) to accuse the public television channel that had organized the competition of racism: 'I have a few friends in Romanian television. They told me the Eurovision jury would not let him [Salam] compete because he is a Țigan. They have not even listened to his songs and say that it would be shameful to go to Oslo with a Țigan'. In the same publication, a week later, the competition's main organizer within the television company declared that she would have supported Salam's presence as 'a touch of colour' in the competition, but the jury members had given him very low marks. In contrast, other media outlets rejoiced that he had not made it to the national final: 'Let the whole Eurovision be a huge salami. If until now there have always been scandals when the results were announced, this time there will certainly be "țigănie"... Seriously this time: we need someone serious to represent us in Oslo, Norway. Let Salam take care of weddings and christenings. Let him play at a different table' (Mișcarea de Rezistență 2010, no page number). Carol Silverman reports similar media outrage vis-à-vis the participation of Roma singer Sofi Marinova at the national selection competition for the ESC in Bulgaria: Marinova did not win in the audience voter call-in and there were claims that the vote had been rigged (Silverman 2012, 173).

Figure 6.2. Viorica and Taraful din Clejani performing on national television channel TVR 1; television still.

In several countries in East Central Europe and in Turkey similar incidents with Roma participants in music contests (such as *Pop Idol*) have occurred (Silverman 2012, 173). In a reverse example, Costel Busuioc – a Romanian Roma migrant to Spain who won a talent show on Spanish television by singing opera – was embraced by the Romanian media as Romanian, and his ethnicity was never discussed. In this case the highbrow genre of the music and the performer's success abroad erased any negative connotations associated with him; and he could be appropriated as Romanian, his Roma identity erased in the process.

Salam's failure at the ESC, and the perceived constant danger in Romania of 'Gypsifying' and 'manelizing' Romania's ESC entry, reflected how the citizenship gap was maintained. The success of *manele* in the media and with both Roma and non-Roma audiences represented a threat precisely because it could not be easily appropriated in the way that Roma music had been for centuries. The blandness of most Romanian entries at the ESC in the last decade, or their exoticism, worked to dissociate Romanians from Roma. In eschewing local specificity, Romania's entries – including the few examples that engaged with diversity – reflected a trend at the ESC of projecting a generic diversity through external Others, or promoting a generic pop that attempted to be as unspecific as possible. The Roma haunted Romania's entries, and they resurfaced at the ESC as exotic tropes or negative stereotypes displayed in both foreign and local media, diverting public attention from ongoing and indeed rising racism against Roma at both European and national levels.

The rise of 'Gypsy music' on the dance scene across Europe and beyond has also shone a spotlight on *manele*. Goran Bregovic played with Florin Salam at an event that caused delight among *manele* fans, and shock and utter stupefaction among Bregovic's own fans in Romania. In a video appearance with Bregovic, Salam expressed his hopes of taking this style (i.e. *manele*) further, and confessed that he had suffered for years because of hatred of the style. Beside him, Bregovic declared:

> Since always I have liked *manele*. And if it's *manele*, the best of *manele* is him [i.e. Salam]. Because he is not stuck in the strict form of verse, bridge and refrain. There is always something more than that about him. This is why I like him. It's always an open form … Good *manele* will have strong traces in European music, I'm sure of it, because, first it's based on tradition, it comes out of an old and strong tradition. (Interview with Florin Salam and Goran Bregovic, 2011)

In contrast with the presentation of *manele* in Romania, Bregovic was acknowledging the history of the genre and its links with other types of music in Romania, which I discuss in the next section.

'Ioniță and Viorica Trump the Ceaușescus': Roma Musicians, Dystopia and Counterpublics

Despite the different marketing strategies they use, most Roma musicians – including Ioniță and Viorica, *manele* singers such as Salam, and Roma bands that tour in the West, such as Taraf de Haïdouks – all come from a Lăutari background. However, while the members of Taraf de Haïdouks returned to near-anonymity in Romania after their Western concerts, their former colleague Ioniță cruised television sets and reality TV shows with Viorica, his partner in life and music, and his band Taraful din Clejani (Figure 6.2). Ioniță tapped into the local market and created fusion and old-style songs for parties and weddings, which gradually became huge hits, especially due to Viorica's distinctive voice; and they avoided the double stigma of *manele* and Țigani in order to appeal to certain sections of the Romanian public that were less likely to listen to *manele*. With their repertoire of traditional songs and fusion pieces, they stood out in a market overcrowded with *manele* performers. Their album *From Anton Pann to DJ* featured *muzica lăutărească* and DJ remixes (*muzica lăutărească* is a mix of traditional Romanian music, Ottoman Turkish music and Western European music, played by Roma). While *muzica lăutărească* is advertised as 'Gypsy music' in the West, Viorica and Ioniță marketed the same music as 'authentic Romanian' music within Romania, invoking as their source of inspiration Anton Pann, a legendary Roma Lăutar adopted into Romanian culture.

Many of the *manelists* of today are sons of the old Lăutari, and have focused on *manele* exclusively because of the huge market for this genre. Lăutari were sedentarized Roma musicians, the first performers in the history of Wallachia and Moldavia. Robert Garfias notes that *tarafs* comprised Roma Lăutari (musicians) during the Ottoman domination of Romanian territories. As slaves in the courts of nobles, Roma musicians developed the form known as *muzica lăutărească*; they combined it with Romanian folk music after emancipation in 1856, when they started playing for Romanian villagers (Garfias 1981, 98).

Muzica lăutărească includes a series of dance pieces such as *hora* and *sârba*, whose tempo varies and whose many versions depend on location and musician. The *muzica lăutărească* genre also encompasses: *cântece de pahar* (drinking songs), sometimes called *cântece de petrecere* (songs of pleasure or relaxation); *cântece bătrânești* (epic ballads); and *cântece de dragoste* (songs of love and longing). Many of these songs are shared with the Romanian repertoire; the only 'exclusively Gypsy dance piece' Garfias recorded among the Lăutari was *manele* (Garfias 1981, 99; 1984, 87–88, 91). The sharp divide between traditional folklore and *manele* in Romania in fact hinges upon the idealization of the 'folk': the idea is that the original folklore can be recaptured in an authentic way, unchanged from times immemorial, while *manele* belong to the Roma and represent a low form of entertainment. In defence of *manele*, in a television interview during a celebration of her birthday on the Antena 3 channel in 2011, the famous Roma singer Gabi Luncă explained that *manele* would sit naturally alongside other types of songs and that, like a good meal, a good concert needed to have a little bit of everything.

All of the Lăutari in the Roma bands discussed in this book are men, and the profession has been passed down from father to son, although some of the famous singers of *muzica lăutărească* have been women, including Romica Puceanu and Ileana Ciuculete. Viorica is a female pioneer in a field dominated by male Roma musicians, and her contribution to this music is undisputed. Even though everyone knows they are Roma and descendants of Lăutari families, Viorica and her husband Ioniță do not promote their music as Gypsy music, but rather as authentic Romanian music. None of the family members ever mentioned that they were Roma on *Clejanii*, the reality TV show in which Viorica and Ioniță starred.

Like the talent shows discussed previously, reality TV shows featuring Roma musicians have become popular in other countries of East Central Europe and beyond. In Hungary, a show similar to *Clejanii*, *The Győzike Show*, starred Roma singer Győző Gaspar and his family, and was also modelled on *The Osbournes*. According to Imre (2009, 127), the show was depoliticized, and full of stereotypes, and it poked fun at the Roma entertainers. Imre and Tremlett (2011, 12) argue that the show framed the protagonists' Roma identity and thus provided Gaspar and his partner Bea with a 'license as well as an expectation to perform the Roma stereotype of the out-of-control, irrational, corporeally driven racialised minority'. In contrast, in *Clejanii*, Viorica and Ioniță managed to partially avoid this racialized framing, because they did not play *manele* and did not discuss their Roma identity.

Viorica's challenging of gender roles was a regular feature of *Clejanii*, which was launched in autumn 2011 and featured Ioniță and Viorica's nuclear family. *Clejanii* continued the TV soaps' theme of rich Gypsies, this time focusing on prosperous urban Roma playing themselves: instead of the house with turrets and caravan in the yard, they lived in a villa in Bucharest, and their displays of wealth were contemporary. However, as a middle-aged, slightly overweight Roma singer, Viorica managed to avoid being the matriarch and/or victim of domestic violence familiar from the Gypsy soaps, and was successful despite not conforming either to the models of femininity promoted in the media or to the stereotype of the sexualized, passionate Țiganca. Although it played up to a scenario where silliness and wealth supposedly went together, in the cracks of the obviously staged 'authentically real' scenes, *Clejanii* also offered a view of the two Roma entertainers' performance as labour.

In one episode of *Clejanii*, Viorica and Ioniță crashed a small gathering en route to a wedding. They were recognized and invited to join a birthday party, the host of which started to sing lines from a song that Viorica and her band had made popular in Romania, 'Dragostea de la Clejani' ('Love in Clejani').

She then asked Viorica to sing the song for her guests. The crashing of a fan's birthday party was an illustration of Viorica's immense popularity, and the song was an example of how Viorica's performances overturned the usual objectification of women. The lyrics of the song are meant for a male singer, and the music video for the same song emphasizes in a humorous way its sexual undertones and explicit lyrics. It shows a bored and blasé dinner party of eight, seated at a long table, being slowly revived by Viorica's singing and the song's daring lyrics. An older woman covers her child's ears in disgust when the song starts; a woman slaps her partner, who suddenly seems awakened upon hearing the titillating words; Viorica teases a male guest with explicit sexual moves. Celebrating adultery, the lyrics gain new significance when performed by a woman: while objectifying female body parts such as breasts, they can also be seen as empowering, and the fan who asked her to sing them at the birthday seemed to take them as such. Even if the sexualization of women continues, in Viorica's interpretation women take the initiative:

> Your wife asks you if you've got someone else
> You swear, but not too much, as she knows it is true
> Because you enjoyed love
> With someone else's wife

> Beautiful women
> God bless them
> Where you touch them, they allow you to
> Where you don't know, they teach you how to do it

> You rest your hand on her hips, she shows you further down
> Until you reach soft meat
> Just right for making sarmale.[4]

In the video Viorica – blonde, slightly overweight and in her late thirties – performs as a woman who is playful and confident in her sexuality, without conforming to the image of sexual object. The sexual politics of Viorica's performances are distinct from the usual objectification of women in *manele* and Romanian music videos in general. By the end of the video, some of the guests have joined Viorica in the dance, while other couples have got into fights because of the attention given to the song and singer.

Viorica's slim teenage daughter Margherita played the role of the young, sexy female in *Clejanii*, and would not have looked out of place in a *manele* video (in some of which she had actually featured with *manele* singer Sorinel Copilul de Aur). In one episode, in October 2011, Viorica and Margherita paid a visit to their fashion designer to order new clothes. During this sequence

Viorica openly challenged the idea that looks were the only avenue of success for women. When the designer offered Margherita a modelling job (a way for the designer to gain more publicity through the reality show) and asked her to lose a little weight for the purpose, Viorica told her daughter: 'Yes, make sure you do not end up like me. Once you've gained weight, it's hard to lose it'. Then she turned to the camera: 'Thank God I did not make a living in that way. I suc-ceeded through hard work, through my voice'. Even though she did not attempt to prevent her daughter from conforming to beauty standards, her dismissal of the focus on women's weight and looks in Romania was refreshing, as was her emphasis on performance as hard work.

In another episode Viorica appeared with a swollen upper lip and in pain after having collagen injections. She complained about the numbness and the pain, and when her husband exclaimed that he could not believe she had had it done, she answered that she had been trying to reinvent herself. As Viorica discussed her plastic surgery, her daughter was sitting next to her. Margherita did not say anything, but it was obvious that she too had had the same procedure: her upper lip was healed, but visibly plumped up. Although Viorica had allegedly 'tried to reinvent herself' with collagen to her lips, she remained unapologetic about her body weight, and this was one of the ways in which she did not conform to the stereotypical image of 'attractive' women in the media. One of the first episodes showed her looking at herself in the mirror and pointing, in a tongue-in-cheek way and with no inhibitions, to areas of her body – thus drawing more attention to them – where she would have liked to have plastic surgery in order to look slimmer. Avoiding and playing with the stereotypes of the hillbilly, sexual object and matriarch all at the same time, Viorica was a woman confident of her sexual-ity, full of life, who did not take herself too seriously.

Similarly to *The Osbournes*, the children in *Clejanii* were constructed as the spoiled offspring of celebrities. This is illustrated by the celebration of Viorica and Ioniță's son Fulgy's fourteenth birthday, at an expensive club. The family all arrived dressed up as fairy-tale royals, with the exception of Fulgy, who was dressed as a pirate. The guests were offered colourful mocktails, a magician performed several numbers, and a languorous half-naked singer danced with Fulgy and sang happy birthday to him. A journalist reported on this episode in a national newspaper, noting the gasps of some of Fulgy's classmates' parents in reaction to the luxury displayed at the party. 'We hardly make ends meet and they bathe in luxury,' exclaimed the mother of one of the students at the Bucharest music school where Fulgy studied. Despite the ostentatious wealth, and the many reminders from Viorica and Margherita in their one-to-ones with the camera about how spoiled Fulgy was, his father proudly announced that the party was a reward for the top mark he had received in his piano exam.

The subversive aspects of this reality show were mostly due to Viorica's per-sona and her ease in front of the camera. When she faded into the background the show became clichéd, reproducing all the ingredients ubiquitous in similar Romanian shows: during Ioniţă's birthday celebrations, for example, there were striptease artists and a belly dancer, and the guests included a *manele* singer and *muzica lăutărească* singers. Moreover, Viorica made the staged aspects of the show less onerous. In one such staged incident, Viorica left her daughter and a friend cooking a family meal while she went out to buy another piece of meat for one of the dishes, because she was unhappy with the piece being used. Her daughter wanted to get back at her for her nagging, and used a smoke machine magically supplied by a 'friend', whom she thanked on camera. As Viorica returned to find her state-of-the-art kitchen filled with smoke, she melo-dramatically dropped her bag and seemed very upset. She told her daughter that everything they had was achieved through hard work: 'It is not easy, you know. If it were easy, everyone would have kitchens like this and houses like this'. She went on to describe the countless days and sleepless nights spent on tour and performing, and the bad food. Here again Viorica was undercutting the premise of spoiled celebrities by emphasising the long hours of labour that went into each performance and tour. In the process she also subverted stereotypes about wealthy Roma who used illegal means or stole, a common way to stigmatize and discredit Roma success. Even though the show followed *The Beverly Hillbillies* formula to some extent, making the Clejanis look like coarse fools unashamedly basking in consumption and luxury – an urban version of the Ţigănci in the Gypsy soaps and also similar to the protagonists of *The Gyözike Show* – Viorica managed to circumvent these stereotypes. She spoke common sense and was not ashamed to be from Clejani.

In another incident a passer-by shouted at Viorica in the street as she got out of a cab that was parked illegally: 'Bucharest is full of hillbillies'. She responded: 'Didn't you know that all the peasants had moved to Bucharest?' This exchange focused on city versus countryside, with Viorica identifying with the country-side. When she and her husband went shopping at a local farmers' market for 'organic produce', as Ioniţă put it, everyone recognized her and praised her beauty. She talked to everyone who greeted her, and sang a segment of her famous song 'Love in Clejani', to unanimous applause. These instances placed Viorica and Ioniţă as representatives of the countryside – peasants – a claim they made when they called their music 'authentic Romanian music'. This continued the historical trajectory of Roma Lăutari, seen for centuries as vehicles for the expression of Romanian folklore.

Through its 'hillbilly' premise the show implied that peasants could not become urbanites, and that their lack of taste and refinement would show. But there is another way of seeing Viorica's appeal to rural and newly urban populations, Roma and non-Roma alike: by claiming her identity as a working woman – further evidenced by footage in the music studio, where she spent hours on end rehearsing and recording during one episode – Viorica reached out to audiences irrespective of ethnicity, gender or class. Offering an alternative to images of women as sex objects, and playing a popular music repertoire, she subverted the rural–urban divide that associated the former with bad taste and *manele*, and she appealed to a counterpublic that did not share dominant divides and gender stereotypes.

However, beyond the hillbilly premise, which Viorica managed to subvert, this reality show had racist undertones that framed some of the episodes as failed performances of citizenship. Despite Viorica's successful debunking of some of the stereotypes she was supposed to embody, there were moments when the scenario written for the two musicians was difficult to disrupt. In one cringe-worthy episode, Viorica and Ioniță performed as the former presidential couple Nicolae and Elena Ceaușescu on one of their notorious visits to the countryside. Performing as the Ceaușescus, the two Clejanis visited a village not far from Bucharest, where they were treated and entertained by the whole community, starting with the village mayor. This was a dystopian moment similar to State becoming mayor of Cloncatele in the television soap *State of Romania*, discussed in Chapter 5. Ceaușescu's assimilation policies aimed to erase Roma identities and culture, and to turn Roma, who were seen as *Lumpenproletariat*, into Romanians. However, despite these policies, Ceaușescu was often called a Țigan in popular culture, a way to distance him from the 'people' and to blame another ethnicity for his dictatorship. To have the two Roma perform as the Ceaușescus in 2011 was to put down and ridicule Viorica and Ioniță, abjecting them as the Ceaușescus in the same way that the Ceaușescus were abjected during their rule by those who called them Țigani. The fun to be had at the protagonists' expense departed here from *The Beverly Hillbillies* recipe and became racist. Although they had obviously cast the couple in the show in the first place because of their success, it was almost as if the show's producers felt a need to tell audiences, in a thoroughly chilling way, that the Clejanis were just as alien and 'foreign' as the Ceaușescus. Viorica and Ioniță's success – evidenced elsewhere in the show by their hard work, their long hours in the studio, on the road and onstage, and their consequent physical exhaustion – was made less legitimate by association with the 'horrid dictator couple'.

Conclusion

Roma artists' performances in music and on reality shows had the potential to appeal to and build counterpublics that went beyond ethnic and gender divides, and to bring different people together in the idea of a shared musical and cultural repertoire. However, the state-run and commercial institutions that framed and controlled these performances applied their own scenarios, drawing 'official' lines between who is 'us' and who is 'them'; Salam and the Clejanis were relegated to the latter category. As Imre and Tremlett (2011, 20) argue 'Győzike causes heightened anxiety because the show dares to represent the nuclear Roma family as the national middle-class family'; similarly, as much as the Clejanis and Salam challenged stereotypes and the framing of their show and music, respectively, the larger structures in place limited the radical potential of their performances and framed them as failed performances of citizenship.

While I have shown the potential of a counter-reading and counterpublic appeal for the examples discussed in this chapter, I agree with Imre and Silverman, respectively, that the double co-optation of Roma music and artists leaves them 'suspended between global media and nation-state' (Imre 2009, 121) and their political potential is minimal or sometimes non-existent (Silverman 2012, 173), due to the generally accepted stereotypes about Roma as natural musicians. The suspension of Roma cultural production between states and markets – its lack of an institutionalized place, in de Certeau's sense – is one of the reasons for both the lack of legitimacy of Roma culture and its limited outreach.

Roma activists' unequivocal and radical performances of citizenship on the Roma-produced programme *Roma Caravan*, discussed in Chapter 5, were not subject to the racialized framing, driven by commercial or nationalist agendas, which was imposed on the performances discussed in this chapter. Silverman (2012, 291–92) argues that, increasingly, Roma artists use international festivals to express Roma identity through music and in relation to 'Romani communities' that are 'open-ended, transnational and diasporic'. However, as long as non-Roma control the cultural means of production and script Roma into failed performances of citizenship, and as long as Roma need to rely exclusively on NGO or international support for politically invested cultural production, the power of growing Roma counterpublics will be limited and the citizenship gap will persist. In the Conclusion I point to possible ways in which performance and cultural production can contribute to bridging the citizenship gap for Roma.

Notes

1. His real name is Florin Stoian; his nickname 'Sala(a)m' comes from the Arabic word for peace. In Romanian, 'salam' means 'salami', and this coincidence has been the pretext for numerous jokes and jibes about the singer.

2. A note should be made here about different ways of framing the same geopolitical realities, i.e. nations or countries in the Balkans. Although geographically in Europe, Romania belongs to at least two other geopolitical categories that supersede it. During the Cold War and as a post-war legacy, it was part of Eastern Europe or the Eastern bloc, a term recently replaced with 'East Central Europe'. On the other hand, it also belongs to the Balkans, the territory of South-East Europe that Todorova (1997) discusses.

3. Marin Marian-Bălaşa (2006) reports anti-*manele* websites, and even an anti-*manele* protest in Romania.

4. My translation. Video available at https://www.youtube.com/watch?v=bSLJJ1iiHnk (last accessed 30 June 2016). 'Sarmale' means 'stuffed cabbage leaves' in Romanian.

Conclusion

Unlearning the Forgetting

To experience *Rain of Tears*, you entered a tall white box, two metres high and one metre square. The door closed behind you. Inside, a bare bulb hung from the ceiling, and the four walls, ceiling and floor were all papered with coverage of the Roma Holocaust, including newspaper clippings about Nazi concentration camps, commemorations of the Holocaust and documents about current Roma life. Upon entering, each visitor received a test tube in which to collect their tears, which they could return through a window on one side of the booth. A performative installation displayed in the 'Hidden Holocaust' exhibition at the Mücsarnok in Budapest in 2004, *Rain of Tears* was the work of Hungarian Roma artist Tibor Balogh. The test tubes gathered during this installation in turn became a new installation at the Roma Pavilion in Venice in 2007. They were hung from the ceiling of the Palazzo Pisani, the site of the exhibition, which presented works by Roma artists from across Europe during the 2007 Venice Biennale. Timea Junghaus, curator of the Roma Pavilion, reported that a Roma wake took place at the Budapest exhibition, where hundreds of participants gathered to commemorate the Roma Holocaust victims (Junghaus 2007, 62–63).

Rain of Tears challenged the timelessness of performance paradigms about Roma and their typical role as Gypsies, strategically maintaining Roma history in plain sight and connecting it to the present. The 2004 installation was an example of performative strategies that attempt to destabilize the hegemony of monoethnic nationalism and its adjacent normative monoethnic performativity. It is also a great metaphor for unlearning the forgetting of the Roma presence in history, and for the process through which European states and individuals alike need to go to renounce hegemonic paradigms and the privilege of the majority in order to close the citizenship gap for Roma.

The tightness of the space inside Balogh's booth for *Rain of Tears* in Budapest ensured that each visitor had to face the documents on display. Whether or not it lit up what Baz Kershaw calls 'the slow burning fuse' (1992, 28) of a change in perspective for visitors, the slight discomfort audience members may have felt while temporarily trapped inside the booth reflected the shift in viewpoint necessary to listen to and hear the perspectives of Roma and disidentify with monoethnic nationalism. The installation's tactics reflected the 'shock to the system' that willing ignorance needs to undergo in order to shake off hegemonic assumptions and the acceptance of compulsory monoethnic performativity. Balogh's installation worked as a guerrilla performance, forcing its audiences to bear witness to the documents displayed in the booth, and prescribing mourning – with the test tubes provided for their tears – as a result of that witnessing. While they might be read as ironic, the prescriptive guidelines about the test tubes ensured a trace of each visit. The distribution of the test tubes also implied a manipulation of the visitors in the sense that their presence would be archived as witnesses and mourners, irrespective of their actual reactions. Through their presence and their test tubes, participants in the 2004 installation became scripted into the 2007 installation.

As an example of NGO historiography, the performative aspects of *Rain of Tears* forced audiences to remember the Roma Holocaust, and dislodged the centrality of the monoethnic nation (Hungarian, in this case) from the writing of history. The installation presented the Roma Holocaust as minor history, one that is about both Roma and non-Roma, with many documents in Hungarian, thus challenging the hegemonic history of the Hungarian nation. Visitors were forced to witness, in the sense of looking into absences for that which 'is clearly there but not allowed to be seen' (Taylor 1997, 27), i.e. the Roma Holocaust. The newspaper clippings about the deportations and killings of Roma made the realities of the Holocaust present in the very places in Hungary where the newspapers had been issued. Just as in Romania, the history of Roma deportations and mass killings in Hungary makes it difficult to shift the blame for these events onto a foreign perpetrator, as has often been the case with the history of the Roma Holocaust in East Central Europe. Newspapers – which Benedict Anderson (1983) credits with building national communities – here established that everyone able to read Hungarian (or not) became a witness to the Holocaust and its commemoration. They made each witness aware that they had already been part of this history, knowingly or otherwise, and established the accountability of everyone who visited the booth, thus creating a community that shared a minor history.

The installation's guerrilla tactics, the makeshift booth and the bare bulb were reminiscent of conditions in the concentration camps, and also served as reminders of the poverty and marginalization many Roma across Europe face today. The precarity and fragility of the booth were also reminders of the need for financial support for NGO historiography and performance. A permanent Holocaust Museum opened in Hungary in 2004, and it includes references to the Roma Holocaust. However, oral histories and testimonies recorded by Bársonyi and Daróczi (2008) and Katalin Katz (2006) in Hungary reveal the continued marginalization that survivors experienced when returning home from concentration camps and other places of deportation. Similarly to the survivors in Romania, many were even reluctant to claim their suffering as part of the Holocaust, because they were not recognized as Holocaust survivors, and continued to struggle. Furthermore, in villages where mass killings of Roma took place, there were often no witnesses, or the surviving community members refused to face their past and its implications for the present.

The history of *Rain of Tears* as an artwork illustrates the tension and resistance met when Roma are included in events commemorating the Holocaust. Ian Hancock (2006) reports a long history of neglect, partial endorsement and then neglect again by the US Holocaust Memorial Council. Critic Alan Siegel notes that at both the Holocaust Memorial in Washington DC and the Budapest Holocaust Memorial there was great reluctance to include Roma in the exhibitions. He writes of 'the legitimacy (or illegitimacy) of the voices and representations that shape Holocaust narratives and … a double form of invisibility apropos past and present social prejudices toward Roma' (Siegel 2004, no page number). As a guerrilla performance, *Rain of Tears* snatched at the proof of the Roma Holocaust's existence, despite resistance to the dissemination of knowledge about it.

Through the documents that lined the inside of the booth, *Rain of Tears* linked past and present, showing that the ongoing marginalization of the Roma is both evidence of and a partial reason for the absence of Roma from national histories. The documents in the installation pointed to a continuous timeline between the horrors of the Holocaust and the current marginalization of the Roma; the Holocaust and its connection to 'racial science' and the attempt to annihilate the Roma during Nazism appeared as the most extreme moment in a long history of marginalization. *Rain of Tears* thus positioned minor history as a necessary tool for understanding the present. In this spirit, NGO historiography places the poverty, exclusion and complete citizenship gap that some Roma experience today, including in places like Pod, on a continuum of the history of marginalization of the Roma. Pod represents subaltern, unrecognized modes of survival, part of the history and present condition of the Roma. Roma in Pod and other such settlements need to be included in the discussion of Roma culture and citizenship in order to disrupt the erasure of all Roma from citizenship in the crucible of neoliberalism and ethnic nationalism.

In order to close the citizenship gap for Roma, European states need to provide legitimizing strategies that include Roma in the symbolic 'us' of cultural citizenship. This would mean redefining who the 'us' is by understanding the intersections between official national history and Roma history; it would also mean providing the same cultural and political institutions and institutional access to Roma as are granted to other minorities. Roma institutions need to be placed on an equal footing with those of other minorities. It is therefore urgent that the Romanian state and other states in Europe step up their cultural policies for Roma to the level of those for other minorities, from schools to theatres to cultural centres; it is no less urgent that they take seriously the discrimination and abuse young and old Roma endure on a daily basis. At the same time, the compulsory monoethnic performativity that sees the majority and minorities coexist but never intersect needs to be dismantled through a rejection of monoethnic nationalism and the binary division of 'us' and 'them'. Here NGO historiography can make a great contribution: if it cannot dismantle monoethnic nationalism altogether, it can at least offer the perspective of a Roma counterpublic from the inside, as *Rain of Tears* did.

Some exercises in NGO historiography, such as the Roma Fair at the Museum of the Romanian Peasant, risk being incorporated into commercial neoliberalism, and their radical potential becomes muted because they cannot compete with the hegemony of monoethnic nationalism. For other institutions, such as the recently opened Museum of Roma Culture in Romania, the risk of ghettoization looms large, as the experience of similar institutions in countries such as the Czech Republic and Russia has shown. The work of these institutions needs to go hand in hand with the reappraisal of the collective 'we' and the transgression of normative monoethnic performativity in favour of a pluralistic approach to identification across all cultural institutions.

Cultural performances, media shows featuring Roma and successful musical performances often reproduce lucrative stereotypes. Mainstream appropriations of Roma music, dance and cultural performances coexist with a growing Roma counterpublic where Roma express alternative views of citizenship and intersectional identities, and where Roma can be Romanian and European at the same time. This book has analysed a wide range of Roma voices and contributions to current discussions and debates, and has shed light on how these voices remain marginal to national culture or are appropriated into stereotypical versions because the Romanian state has not fully embraced Roma as citizens and has maintained the citizenship gap, both culturally and structurally. Although current political-economic structures and official state recognition have granted new visibility to some Roma, and have also given rise to new counterpublics that have the power to transform the status quo, most of the television shows, music and dance performances discussed in this book were produced by non-Roma. Roma rarely have access to the means of cultural production, whether in state or commercial media, despite being featured onstage and on the screen. The power of these counterpublics therefore needs to be coupled with serious commitment in these institutions to equal opportunities for Roma to represent themselves in these media, and not always with a concern for commercial success.

The two exhibitions where *Rain of Tears* was included (one national and the other transnational) correspond to two necessary frames for understanding Roma activists' and artists' negotiations at the European and national levels. These multiple positions denaturalize the nation-state and its hegemonic power, and show how European institutions support Roma artists and sometimes substitute for the absence of national institutions. As citizens in European countries revert to essentialist understanding of identity and exclusionary endorsements of nationalism, Roma counterpublics offer a model for non-essentialist understandings of identity, as this book has shown. Despite racism and a lack of actual citizenship, Roma do belong, and show that they belong, to their country. Their own statements about citizenship and nation sound a discordant note against the hegemony of ethnonationalism in the region. However, as this book has shown, there is a long way to go from the EU's abstract endorsements of intersections with Roma visions to the actual and substantive inclusion of Roma as citizens in Europe.

I conclude this book by pointing to a necessary two-way process. Roma cultural institutions and social policies need to be supported by states and the EU – with definitions of culture that take political economy and history into account; and, at the same time, monoethnic national histories and cultures need to be revised to include Roma. In the process, ethnic purities need to be deconstructed, and definitions of national cultures need to be enlarged to include oral, embodied and improvised performances and repertoires of minorities and the majority alike.

Note

Parts of the conclusion have been previously published as Ioana Szeman, 'Collecting Tears: Remembering the Romani Holocaust' in *Performance Research* 15(2), pp. 54–59, by Taylor and Francis, http://www.tandfonline.com. Reprinted by permission of the publisher.

Bibliography

Achim, Viorel. 1998. *Țiganii în istoria României*. Bucharest: Ed. Enciclopedică.

Abu-Lughod, Lila. 2005. *Dramas of Nationhood: The Politics of Television in Egypt*. Chicago, IL: University of Chicago Press.

ActiveWatch. 2011. 'Imaginea Femeii in Societatea Romaneasca. Raport de Analiza Media', Altfem. O Campanie pentru Schimbarea Imaginii Femeii in Societate. Bucuresti.

Acton, Thomas. 1974. *Gypsy Politics and Social Change: The Development of Ethnic Ideology and Pressure Politics among British Gypsies from Victorian Reformism to Romany Nationalism*. London: Routledge and Kegan Paul.

———. 1994. 'Categorizing Irish Travellers', in May McCann et al. (eds), *Irish Travellers: Culture and Ethnicity*. Belfast: Queen's University Press.

Agamben, Giorgio. 1998. *Homo Sacer: Sovereign Power and Bare Life*. Stanford, CA: Stanford University Press.

———. 2000. *Remnants of Auschwitz: The Witness and the Archive*, trans. D. Heller-Roazen. Cambridge, MA: MIT Press.

Ahmed, Sara. 2000. *Strange Encounters: Embodied Others in Post-Coloniality*. London: Routledge.

———. 2007 'The Language of Diversity', *Ethnic and Racial Studies* 30: 235–56.

Aluas, Ioan and Liviu Matei. 1998. 'Discrimination and Prejudice: Minorities in Romania', in Daniele Joly (ed.), *Scapegoats and Social Actors: The Exclusion and Integration of Minorities in Western and Eastern Europe*. New York: St. Martin's, pp. 101–12.

Anderson, Benedict. 1983. *Imagined Communities: Reflections on the Origin and Spread of Nationalism*. London: Verso.

Andrijasevic, Rutvica. 2013. 'Acts of Citizenship as Methodology', in Engin I. Fisin and Michael Saward (eds), *Enacting European Citizenship*. Cambridge: Cambridge University Press, pp. 47–65.

Anthias, Floya. 1998. 'Evaluating Diaspora: Beyond Ethnicity?' *Sociology* 32: 557–80.

———. 1999. 'Institutional Racism, Power and Accountability', *Sociological Research Online* 4(1). http://www.socresonline.org.uk/4/lawrence//anthias.html (last accessed 23 July 2010).

———. 2001. 'New Hybridities, Old Concepts: The limits of Culture', *Ethnic and Racial Studies* 24: 619–41.

———. 2009. 'Translocational Belonging, Identity and Generation: Questions and Problems in Migration and Ethnic Studies', *Finnish Journal of Ethnicity and Migration* 4: 6–16.

Anonymous. *Jurnalul Naţional*, 2002, 1.

Appadurai, Arjun. 1996. *Modernity at Large: Cultural Dimensions of Globalization*. Minneapolis, MN: University of Minneapolis Press.

Aradau, Claudia et al. 'Mobility Interrogating Free Movement: Roma Acts of European Citizenship', in Engin I. Fisin and Michael Saward (eds), *Enacting European Citizenship*. Cambridge: Cambridge University Press, pp. 132–154.

Arsenie, Dan. 2010. 'Paula Seling despre rezultatul la Eurovision 2010: 'Mai bine de atât nu se putea!'" *Evenimentul Zilei*, 30 May. http://www.evz.ro/detalii/stiri/eurovision-2010-romania-bronz-germania-locul-intai-896221.html#ixzz1ky86Irw4.

Bakić-Hayden, Milica. 1995. 'Nesting Orientalisms: The Case of Former Yugoslavia', *Slavic Review* 54: 917–31.

Balibar, Etienne. 2004. *We, the People of Europe? Reflections on Transnational Citizenship*. Princeton, NJ: Princeton University Press.

Balibar, Etienne, and Immanuel Wallerstein. 1991. *Race, Nation, Class: Ambiguous Identities*. London and New York: Verso.

Ballinger, Pamela. 2003. *History in Exile: Memory and Identity at the Borders of the Balkans*. Princeton, NJ: Princeton University Press.

⸻. 2004. '"Authentic Hybrids" in the Balkan Borderlands', *Current Anthropology* 45: 31–60.

Bársony, János, and Daróczi Ágnes. 2008. *Pharrajimos: The Fate of the Roma during the Holocaust*, trans. G. Komaromy. New York: International Debate Education Association.

Barth, Frederik (ed.). 1969. *Ethnic Groups and Boundaries: The Social Organization of Cultural Difference*. Boston, MA: Brown and Company.

Bartók, Béla. 1947. 'Gypsy Music or Hungarian Music?' *The Musical Quarterly* 33: 240–57.

Bauman, Richard, and Patricia Sawin. 1991. 'The Politics of Participation in Folklife Festivals', in Ivan Karp and Steven D. Lavine (eds), *Exhibiting Cultures: The Poetics and Politics of Museum Display*. Washington, DC: Smithsonian Institution Press, pp. 288–314.

Beck, Ulrich. 2004. 'The Truth of Others: A Cosmopolitan Approach', trans. P. Camiller. *Common Knowledge* 10: 430–49.

Beissinger, Margaret H. 2001. 'Occupation and Ethnicity: Constructing Identity among Professional Romani (Gypsy) Musicians in Romania', *Slavic Review* 60: 24–49.

⸻. 2007. '*Muzica Orientala*: Identity and Popular Culture in Postcommunist Romania', in Donna A. Buchanan (ed.), *Balkan Popular Culture and the Ottoman Ecumene: Music, Image and Regional Political Discourse*. Lanham, MD: Scarecrow Press, pp. 95–141.

Beissinger, Margaret et al, eds. 2016. *Manele in Romania: Cultural Expression and Social Meaning in Balkan Popular Music*. Lanham, MD and London: Rowman and Littlefield.

Bendix, Regina. 1997. *In Search of Authenticity: The Formation of Folklore Studies*. Madison, WI: University of Wisconsin Press.

Benjamin, Walter. 1968. *Illuminations*. New York: Schocken Books.

Bennett, Tony. 2006. 'Exhibition, Difference and the Logic of Culture', in Ivan Karp et al. (eds), *Museum Frictions: Public Cultures/ Global Transformations*. Durham, NC: Duke University Press, pp. 46–69.

Benson, Susan. 1996. 'Asians Have Culture, West Indians Have Problems: Discourses of Race and Ethnicity in and out of Anthropology', in Terence Ranger, Yunas Samad, and Ossie Stuart (eds), *Culture, Identity and Politics: Ethnic Minorities in Britain*. Aldershot: Avebury, pp. 47–57.

Berdahl, Daphne, Matti Bunzl and Martha Lampland (eds). 2000. *Altering States: Ethnographies of Transition in Eastern Europe and the Former Soviet Union*. Ann Arbor, MI: University of Michigan Press.

Bhabha, Homi K. 1990. 'DissemiNation: Time, Narrative, and the Margins of the Modern Nation', Homi K. Bhabha (ed.), *Nation and Narration*. London and New York: Routledge, pp. 291–322.

———. 1994. *The Location of Culture*. London: Routledge.

Björnberg, Alf. 2007. 'Return to Ethnicity: The Cultural Significance of Musical Change in the Eurovision Song Contest', in Ivan Raykoff and Robert Deam Tobin (eds), *A Song for Europe: Popular Music and Politics in the Eurovision Song Contest*. Aldershot, England; Burlington, VT: Ashgate, pp. 13–23.

Blaga, Iulia. 2007. 'Taraful Haiducilor: Noi putem să cântăm și manele, dar nu ne plac', *România Liberă* July 2007. Retrieved 8 October 2007 from http://agenda.liternet.ro/articol/5273/Iulia-Blaga/Taraful-Haiducilor-Noi-putem-sa-cantam-si-manele-dar-nu-ne-plac.html.

Botea, Bianca. 2006. 'La construction symbolique de la Transylvanie: une approche des pratiques muséales à Cluj-Napoca', *Martor* 11. Retrieved 19 January 2010 from http://martor.memoria.ro/?location=view_article&id=197&page=0.

Bourdieu, Pierre, and Loïc Wacquant. 1999. 'On the Cunning of Imperialist Reason', *Theory, Culture, and Society* 16: 41–58.

Bradeanu, Adina, and Rosie Thomas. 2006. 'Indian Summer, Romanian Winter: A "Procession of Memories" in Post-communist Romania', *South Asian Popular Culture* 4: 141–46.

Braidotti, Rosi. 2004. 'Gender and Power in Post-Nationalist European Union', *Nora* 3: 130–42.

Brown, Marilyn R. 1985. *Gypsies and Other Bohemians: The Myth of the Artist in Nineteenth-Century France*. Ann Arbor, MI: UMI Research Press.

Brown, Wendy. 2006. *Regulating Aversion: Tolerance in the Age of Identity and Empire*. Princeton, NJ: Princeton University Press.

Brubaker, Rogers. 1999. 'The Manichean Myth: Rethinking the Distinction Between "Civic" and "Ethnic" Nationalism', in Hanspeter Kriesi et al, (eds), *Nation and National Identity: The European Experience in Perspective*. Zurich: Ruegger, pp. 55–71.

———. 2005. 'The "Diaspora" Diaspora', *Ethnic and Racial Studies* 28: 1–19.

———. 2009. 'Ethnicity, Race and Nationalism', *Annual Review of Sociology* 35: 21–42.

Brubaker, Rogers, et al. 2006. *Nationalist Politics and Everyday Ethnicity in a Transylvanian Town*. Princeton, NJ: Princeton University Press.

Brubaker, Rogers, and Margit Feischmidt. 2002. '1848 in 1998: The Politics of Commemoration in Hungary, Romania, and Slovakia', *Comparative Studies in Society and History* 44: 700–44.

Buchanan, Donna. 2007. 'Bulgarian Ethnopop along the Old Via Militaris: Ottomanism, Orientalism, or Balkan Cosmopolitanism?' in Donna A. Buchanan (ed.), *Balkan Popular Culture and the Ottoman Ecumene: Music, Image and Regional Political Discourse*. Lanham, MD: Scarecrow Press, pp. 225–67.

Bucharest Herald. 2012. 'Associated Press: Mandinga's Zalelilah, a Global Mishmash.' 31 May. Available at http://www.bucharestherald.ro/dailyevents/41-dailyevents/33593-associated-press-mandingas-zaleilah-a-global-mishmash.

Burawoy, Michael, and Katherine Verdery (eds). 1999. *Uncertain Transition: Ethnographies of Change in the Postsocialist World*. London: Rowman and Littlefield Publishers.

Butler, Judith. 1990. *Gender Trouble: Tenth Anniversary Edition*. New York: Routledge.

———. 1993. *Bodies That Matter: On the Discursive Limits of 'Sex'*. New York: Routledge.

———. 1997. *Excitable Speech: A Politics of the Performative*. New York: Routledge.

———. 2004. *Undoing Gender*. New York and London: Routledge.

Cace, Sorin, et al. 1999. *Copiii romi din România/Roma Children in Romania: Research Report*. Bucharest: Organizaţia 'Salvaţi Copiii România', with the support of the Foundation for an Open Society, Bucharest.

Calhoun, Craig. 2003. 'The Class Consciousness of Frequent Travellers: Towards a Critique of Actually Existing Cosmopolitanism', in Daniele Archibugi (ed.), *Debating Cosmopolitics*. London: Verso, pp. 86–116.

Carby, Hazel. 1999. *Cultures in Babylon: Black Britain and African America*. London: Verso.

Carrier, Peter. 2005. *Holocaust Monuments and National Memory Cultures in France and Germany since 1989*. New York: Berghahn Books.

Cartwright, Garth. 2005. *Princes Amongst Men: Journeys with Gypsy Musicians*. London: Serpent's Tail.

Castle-Kanerová, Mít'a. 2001. 'Romani Refugees: The EU Dimension', in Will Guy (ed.), *Between Past and Future: The Roma of Central and Eastern Europe*. Hertfordshire: University of Hertfordshire Press, pp. 117–33.

Chakrabarty, Dipesh. 2000. *Provincializing Europe: Postcolonial Thought and Historical Difference*. Princeton, NJ: Princeton University Press.

———. 2002. *Habitations of Modernity*. Chicago: University of Chicago Press.

Chari, Sharad, and Katherine Verdery. 2009. 'Thinking between the Posts: Postcolonialism, Postsocialism, and Ethnography after the Cold War', *Comparative Studies in Society and History* 51: 6–34.

Cheah, Pheng. 1998. 'Given Culture: Rethinking Cosmopolitical Freedom in Transnationalism', in Pheng Cheah and Bruce Robbins (ed.), *Cosmopolitics: Thinking and Feeling Beyond the Nation*. Minneapolis, MN: University of Minnesota Press, pp. 290–328.

Chiriac, Marian, and Alina Constantinescu. 2007. 'Se poate ieşi din impas? Inventar de probleme şi soluţii privind situaţia romilor din România', Bucharest: Centrul de Resurse Pentru Diversitate Etnoculturală.

Chirot, Daniel. 1978. *Social Change in a Peripheral Society: The Creation of a Balkan Colony*. New York: Academic Press.

Chow, Rey. 1991. *Woman and Chinese Modernity: The Politics of Reading between West and East*. Minnesota and Oxford: University of Minnesota Press.

———. 1993. *Writing Diaspora: Tactics of Intervention in Contemporary Cultural Studies*. Bloomington, IN: Indiana University Press.

———. 1995. *Primitive Passions: Visuality, Sexuality, Ethnography, and Contemporary Chinese Cinema*. New York: Columbia University Press.

———. 2002. *The Protestant Ethnic and the Logic of Capitalism*. New York: Columbia University Press.

Cioabă, Luminiţa Mihai. 2006. *Romane Asva. Lacrimi Rome.* Bucharest: Ro Media/UNICEF.

Claude, Patrice. 2000. 'Sus aux mendiants et aux gitans au Royaume-Uni', *Le Monde* 21 March 2000.

Clifford, James. 1992. 'Traveling Cultures', in Larry Grossberg, Cary Nelson and Paula A. Treichler (eds), *Cultural Studies: Now and in the Future.* New York: Routledge, pp. 96–112.

———. 1997. *Routes: Travel and Translation in the Late Twentieth Century.* Cambridge, MA and London, England: Harvard University Press.

Comaroff Jean, and John Comaroff (eds). 2001. *Millennial Capitalism and the Culture of Neoliberalism.* Durham, NC: Duke University Press.

Comaroff John L., and Jean Comaroff. 2009. *Ethnicity, Inc.* Chicago, IL: University of Chicago Press.

Connolly, Kate. 2002. 'New World, Old Struggle', *Guardian* 7 June 2000. Retrieved 11 June 2002 from http://www.guardian.co.uk/Archive/Article/0,4273,4026159,00.htm.

Conquergood, Dwight. 1991. 'Rethinking Ethnography: Towards a Critical Cultural Politics', *Communication Monographs* 58: 179–94.

———. 1995. 'Of Caravans and Carnivals: Performance Studies in Motion', *TDR: The Drama Review* 39: 137–41.

———. 1997. 'Street Literacy', in James Flood, Shirley Brice Heath and Diane Lapp (eds), *Handbook of Research on Teaching Literacy through the Communicative and Visual Arts.* New York: Macmillan, pp. 354–75.

———. 2001. 'Field Methods in Performance Studies'. Course at Northwestern University.

———. 2002. 'Performance Studies: Interventions and Radical Research', *TDR: The Drama Review* 46: 145–56.

Cosma, Viorel. 1996. *Lăutarii de ieri şi de azi.* Bucharest: DU Style.

Cowan, Jane K., et al. (eds). 2001. *Culture and Rights: Anthropological Perspectives.* Cambridge: Cambridge University Press.

Croegaert, Ana. 2011. 'Who Has Time for Ćejf? Postsocialist Migration and Slow Coffee in Neoliberal Chicago.' *American Anthropologist* 113(3): pp. 463–477.

Crowe, David. 1995. *A History of the Gypsies in Eastern Europe and Russia.* New York: St. Martin's.

Crowe, David, and John Kolsti (eds). 1991. *The Gypsies of Eastern Europe.* Armonk and London: M.E. Sharpe.

Dávila, Arlene. 2001. *Latinos, Inc.: The Marketing and Making of a People.* Berkeley, CA: University of California Press.

Dediu, Marcel. 2008. 'Romania de dincolo de paradis', *Romaworld* 18 March 2008. Retrieved 21 June 2008 from http://www.romaworld.ro/editoriale/romania-de-dincolo-de-paradis.html.

de Certeau, Michel. 1984. *The Practice of Everyday Life*, trans. S.F. Rendall. Berkeley, CA: University of California Press.

———. 2002. *The Writing of History*, trans. Tom Conley. New York: Columbia University Press.

De Genova, Nicholas. 2002. 'Migrant "Illegality" and Deportability in Everyday Life', *Annual Review of Anthropology* 31: 419–47.

De Kock, Rachelle. 1986. *Garbage Picking as a Strategy for Survival.* Durban: Development Studies Unit, University of Natal.

Delanty, Gerard. 1997. 'Models of Citizenship: Defining European Identity and Citizenship', *Citizenship Studies* 1(3): 285–303.

Deleuze, Gilles, and Felix Guattari. 1986. *Kafka: Toward a Minor Literature*. Minneapolis, MN: University of Minnesota Press.

Deloria, Philip. 1998. *Playing Indian*. New Haven, CT: Yale University Press.

Di Leonardo, Micaela. 1991. 'Introduction: Gender, Culture, and Political Economy. Feminist Anthropology in Historical Perspective', in Micaela Di Leonardo (ed.), *Gender at the Crossroads of Knowledge: Feminist Anthropology in the Postmodern Era*. Berkeley, CA: University of California Press, pp. 1–48.

———. 1998. *Exotics at Home: Anthropologies, Others, American Modernity*. Chicago, IL: University of Chicago Press.

———. 2008. 'Introduction: New Global and American Landscapes of Inequality', in Jane Collins et al. (eds), *New Landscapes of Inequality: Neoliberalism and the Erosion of Democracy in America*. Santa Fe, NM: School of Advanced Research Press, pp. 3–19.

———. 2012. 'Grown Folks Radio: US Election Politics and a "Hidden" Black Counterpublic', *American Ethnologist* 39(4): 661–72.

Dodd, Vikram. 2002. 'East Europeans Lead Growing Army of Beggars', *Guardian* 10 March 2000. Retrieved 23 May 2017 from https://www.theguardian.com/uk/2000/mar/10/immigration.immigrationandpublicservices2.

Drewal, Margaret Thompson. 1992. *Yoruba Ritual: Players, Play, Agency*. Bloomington, IN: Indiana University Pres.

Durst, Judit. 2010. '"What Makes Us Gypsies Who Knows…!?" Ethnicity and Reproduction', in Michael Stewart and Marton Rovid (eds), *Multidisciplinary Approaches to Romany Studies*. Budapest: Central European University, pp. 13–34.

Edwards, Brent-Hayes. 2001. 'The Uses of *Diaspora*', *Social Text* 66: 45–73.

Elam, Harry J., and Kennell Jackson (eds). 2005. *Black Cultural Traffic: Crossroads in Global Performance and Popular Culture*. Ann Arbor, MI: University of Michigan Press.

Elyachar, Julia. 2005. *Markets of Dispossession: NGOs, Economic Development, and the State in Cairo*. Durham, NC: Duke University Press.

Emigh, J.R. and I. Szelényi (eds). 2002. *Poverty, Ethnicity, and Gender in Eastern Europe During the Market Transition*. Westport, CT and London: Praeger.

Emerson, Michael (ed.). 2011. *Interculturalism: Europe and Its Muslims. In Search of Sound Societal Models*. Brussels: Center of European Policy Studies.

Engebrigtsen, Ada. 2007. *Exploring Gypsiness: Power, Change and Interdependence in a Transylvanian Village*. New York: Berghahn Books.

Englund, Harri. 2006. *Prisoners of Freedom: Human Rights and the African Poor*. New York: Columbia University Press.

European Roma Rights Center. 2004. *Stigmata: Segregated Schooling of Roma in Eastern and Central Europe*. Budapest. Retrieved 6 September 2010 from http://www.errc.org/cikk.php?cikk=1892

European Roma Rights Center. 2007. 'Europe's Highest Court Finds Racial Discrimination in Czech Schools.' Budapest. Available at http://www.errc.org/cikk.php?cikk=2866.

Fabian, Johannes. 1983. *Time and the Other: How Anthropology Makes Its Object*. New York: Columbia University Press.

Fings, Karola, et al. 1997 *From 'Race Science' to the Camps: The Gypsies during the Second World War*, trans. Donald Kenrick. Gypsy Research Centre: University of Hertfordshire Press.

Fleming, K.E. 2000. '*Orientalism*, the Balkans, and Balkan Historiography', *American Historical Review* 105: 1218–33.

Flores, William V., and Rita Benmayor (eds). 1997. *Latino Cultural Citizenship: Claiming Identity, Space and Rights*. Boston, MA: Beacon Press.

Flores, William V. 1997. 'Mujeres en Huelga: Cultural Citizenship and Gender Empowerment in a Cannery Strike', in William Flores and Rita Benmayor (eds), *Latino Cultural Citizenship: Claiming Identity, Space and Rights*. Boston, MA: Beacon Press.

'Florin Salam and Paula Seling Live.' 2008. 'Tu nu vezi.' Retrieved on 27 November 2011 from: http://www.youtube.com/watch?v=yVOnP250pI0&feature=related.

Fosztó, László, and Marian-Viorel Anăstăsoaie. 2001. 'Romania: Representations, Public Policies and Political Projects,' in Will Guy (ed.), *Between Past and Future: The Roma of Central and Eastern Europe*. Hatfield: University of Hertfordshire Press, pp. 351–69.

Foucault, Michel. 1977. *Discipline and Punish: The Birth of the Prison*, trans. A. Sheridan. New York: Pantheon Books.

———. 1978. *The History of Sexuality*, Vol. 1, trans. R. Hurley. New York: Random House.

Fraser, Nancy. 1992. 'Rethinking the Public Sphere: A Contribution to the Critique of Actually Existing Democracy', in Craig Calhoun (ed.), *Habermas and the Public Sphere*. Cambridge, MA: MIT Press.

———. 1997. *Justice Interruptus: Critical Reflexions on the 'Postsocialist' Condition*. New York: Routledge.

———. 1998. 'From Redistribution to Recognition? Dilemmas of Justice in a 'Post-Socialist' Age', in Cynthia Willet (ed.), *Theorizing Multiculturalism: A Guide to the Current Debate*. Oxford: Blackwell, pp. 19–49.

Fricker, Karen, and Milija Gluhovic (eds). 2013. *Performing the 'New Europe': Identities, Feelings and Politics in the Eurovision Song Contest*. London and New York: Palgrave Macmillan.

Gal, Susan. 1991. 'Bartók's Funeral: Representations of Europe in Hungarian Political Rhetoric', *American Ethnologist* 18: 440–58.

———. 1995. 'Language and the "Arts of Resistance"', review of *Domination and the Arts of Resistance: Hidden Transcripts*, by James C. Scott, *Cultural Anthropology* 10: 407–24.

Gal, Susan, and Gail Kligman (eds). 2000a. *Reproducing Gender: Politics, Publics and Everyday Life after Socialism*. Princeton: Princeton University Press.

———. 2000b. *The Politics of Gender after Socialism*. Princeton, NJ: Princeton University Press.

Garfias, Robert. 1981. 'Survivals of Turkish Characteristics in Romanian Musica Lautareasca', *Yearbook of Traditional Music* 13: 97–107.

———. 1984. 'Dance among the Urban Gypsies of Romania', *Yearbook of Traditional Music* 16: 84–96.

Gates, Henry Louis. 1986. 'Introduction', in Henry Louis Gates (ed.), *'Race', Writing and Difference*. Chicago, IL: Chicago University Press.

Gedalof, Irene. 2013. 'Sameness and Difference in Government Equality Talk', *Ethnic and Racial Studies*, 36 (1): 117–135.

Gay y Blasco, Paloma. 1999. *Gypsies in Madrid: Sex, Gender and the Performance of Identity*. Oxford: Berg.

Geertz, Clifford. 1973. *The Interpretation of Culture*. New York: Basic Books.

Gheorghe, Nicolae. 1983. 'Origins of Roma Slavery in the Romanian Principalities', *Roma* 7: 12–27.
_____. 1991. 'Roma-Gypsy Ethnicity in Eastern Europe', *Social Research* 58: 829–45.
Gheorghe, Nicolae, and Thomas Acton. 2001. 'Citizens of the World and Nowhere: Minority, Ethnic and Human Rights for Roma', in Will Guy (ed.), *Between Past and Future: The Roma of Central and Eastern Europe*. Hertfordshire: University of Hertfordshire Press, pp. 54–71.
Gilbert, Helen. 1998. *Sightlines: Race, Gender and Nation in Contemporary Australian Theatre*. Ann Arbor, MI: Michigan University Press.
Gilman, Sander. 1986. *Jewish Self-Hatred: Anti-Semitism and the Hidden Language of the Jews*. Baltimore, MD: Johns Hopkins University Press.
_____. 1991. *The Jew's Body*. New York: Routledge.
Gilroy, Paul. 2000. *Between Camps: Nations, Cultures and the Allure of Race*. London: Penguin Books.
_____. 1993. *The Black Atlantic: Modernity and Double Consciousness*. Cambridge: Harvard University Press.
_____. 1992 [1982]. 'Steppin' out of Babylon: Race, Class and Autonomy', in Centre for Contemporary Cultural Studies (ed.), *The Empire Strikes Back: Race and Racism in 70s Britain*. Abingdon and New York: Routledge, pp. 276–314.
Gluhovic, Milija. 2013. *Performing European Memories: Trauma, Ethics and Politics*. Basingstoke: Palgrave Macmillan.
Godwin, Peter. 2001. 'Gypsies the Outsiders', *National Geographic* 199: 72–101.
Goldberg, David Theo (ed.). 1994. *Multiculturalism: A Critical Reader*. Oxford: Blackwell.
_____. 2006. 'Racial Europeanization', *Ethnic and Racial Studies* 29: 331–64.
Goode, Judith, and Jeff Maskovsky (eds). 2001. *New Poverty Studies: The Ethnography of Power, Politics and Impoverished People in the United States*. New York: New York University Press.
Grigoraş, N. 2000. 'Robia în Moldova', in Vasile Ionescu (ed.), *Robia ţiganilor în Ţările Române: Moldova*. Bucharest: Ed. Aven Amentza, pp. 75–172.
Grobbel, Michaela. 2003. 'Contemporary Romany Autobiography as Performance', *The German Quarterly* 72: 140–54.
Guterman, Gad. 2014. *Performance, Identity and Immigration Law: A Theatre of Undocumentedness*. New York: Palgrave Macmillan.
Gutman, Amy (ed.). 1994. *Multiculturalism: Examining the Politics of Recognition*. Princeton, NJ: Princeton University Press.
Guy, Will. 2001. 'Romani Identity and Post-Communist Policy', in Will Guy (ed.), *Between Past and Future: The Roma of Central and Eastern Europe*. Hertfordshire: University of Hertfordshire Press, pp. 3–33.
Hall, Stuart. 1980. 'Race Articulation and Societies Structured in Dominance', *Sociological Theories: Race and Colonialism*. Paris: UNESCO.
_____. 1996. 'Politics of Identity', in Terence Ranger, Yunas Samad, and Ossie Stuart (eds), *Culture, Identity and Politics: Ethnic Minorities in Britain*. Aldershot: Avebury, pp. 129–49.
Hanchard, Michael. 2003. 'Acts of Misrecognition: Transnational Black Politics, Anti-imperialism and the Ethno-centrisms of Pierre Bourdieu and Loïc Wacquant.' *Theory, Culture and Society* 20 (4): 5–29.

Hancock, Ian. 1987. *The Pariah Syndrome: An Account of Gypsy Slavery and Persecution*. Ann Arbor: Karoma Publishers.

———. 1997. 'Dom Za Vesanje, O Vaxt a Rromengo: Time of the Gypsies', film review, *The Journal of Mediterranean Studies* 7: 52–57.

———. 2006. 'On the Interpretation of a Word: Porrajmos as Holocaust'. Retrieved 15 March 2010 from http://www.radoc.net/radoc.php?doc=art_e_holocaust_interpreta tion&lang=en&articles=true.

———. 2002. *We Are the Romani People. Ame Sam e Romane Džene*. Heartfield: University of Hertfordshire Press.

Hanson, Karl, and Olga Nieuwenhuys. 2013. 'Living Rights, Social Justice, Translations', in Karl Hanson and Olga Nieuwenhuys (eds), *Reconceptualizing Children's Rights in International Development: Living Rights, Social Justice, Translations*. Cambridge: Cambridge University Press, pp. 3–26.

Happy Hour Interview with Paula Seling, ProTV channel. 2008. Retrieved on 27 November 2011 from http://www.youtube.com/watch?v=_VA6vvErvYQ&feature=related.

Harvey, Jen. 2005. *Staging the UK*. Manchester: University of Manchester Press.

Hasdeu, Iulia. 2008. 'Imagining the Gypsy Woman', *Third Text* 22: 347–57.

Hayes, Michael, and Thomas Acton (eds). 2006. *Counter-Hegemony and the Postcolonial 'Other'*. Newcastle: Cambridge Scholars Press.

Hemment, Julie. 2007. *Empowering Women in Russia: Activism, Aid and NGOs*. Bloomington, IN: Indiana University Press.

Hepworth, Kate. 2015. *At the Edges of Citizenship*. Farnham: Ashgate.

Hitchcock, Peter. 2001. 'Slumming', in María Carla Sánchez and Linda Schlossberg (eds), *Passing: Identity and Interpretation in Sexuality, Race, and Religion*. New York: New York University Press, pp. 160–86.

hooks, bell. 1992. *Black Looks: Race and Representation*. London: Turnaround.

Humphrey, Caroline. 1994. 'Remembering an "Enemy": The Bogd Khaan in Twentieth-Century Mongolia', in Rubie S. Watson (ed.), *Memory, History and Opposition under State Socialism*. Santa Fe, NM: School of American Research Press, pp. 21–44.

Ignatiev, Noel. 1995. *How the Irish Became White*. London and New York: Routledge.

Imre, Anikó. 2005. 'Whiteness in Post-socialist Eastern Europe: The Time of the Gypsies, the End of Race', in A.J. Lopez (ed.), *Postcolonial Whiteness: A Critical Reader on Race and Empire*. New York: SUNY Press, pp. 79–102.

———. 2009. *Identity Games: Globalization and the Transformation of Media Cultures in the New Europe*. Cambridge, MA: MIT Press.

Imre, Anikó, and Annabel Tremlett. 2011. 'Reality TV Without Class: The Postsocialist Anti-Celebrity Docusoap', in H. Wood and B. Skeggs (eds), *Reality Television and Class*. London: BFI/Palgrave.

Imre, Anikó, et al. (eds). 2013. *Popular Television in Eastern Europe during and since Socialism* London: Routledge.

Interview with Florin Salam and Goran Bregovic. 2011. 'Another Step Towards Europe'. Retrieved on 27 November 2011 from http://www.youtube.com/ watch?v=RLTDyyiYFoo.

Ion, Raluca. 2007. 'Istoria descoperirii unui holocaust. Al romilor', *Cotidianul*. Retrieved 2 June 2010 from http://www.9am.ro/stiri-revista-presei/2007-10-27/istoria-descoper-irii-unui-holocaust-al-romilor.html.

Ioanid, Radu. 2000. *The Holocaust in Romania: The Destruction of Jews and Gypsies under the Antonescu Regime, 1940–1944*. Chicago, IL: Ivan R. Dee Publishers.

Iordanova, Dina. 2001. *Cinema of Flames*. London: BFI Publishing.

Iordanova, Dina, et al. 2006. 'Indian Cinema's Global Reach: Historiography through Testimonies', *South Asian Popular Culture* 4: 113–40.

Irvine, Judith T., and Susan Gal. 2000. 'Language Ideology and Linguistic Differentiation' in Paul V. Kroskrity, *Regimes of Language*. Santa Fe, NM: SAR Press, pp. 35–83.

Jackson, John L. 2005. *Real Black: Adventures in Racial Sincerity*. Chicago, IL: Chicago University Press.

Jacobs, Fabian and Johannes Ries (eds). 2008. *Roma/Gypsy Cultures in New Perspectives*. Leipzig: Universitätsverlag.

Jestrovic, Silvija. 2012. *Performance, Space, Utopia: Cities of War, Cities of Exile*. Basingstoke: Palgrave Macmillan.

Johnson, E. Patrick. 2003. *Appropriating Blackness: Performance and the Politics of Authenticity*. Durham, NC: Duke University Press.

Joseph, May. 1999. *Nomadic Identities: The Performance of Citizenship*. Minneapolis, MN: University of Minnesota Press.

Jowitt, Kenneth (ed.). 1978. *Social Change in Romania, 1860–1940: A Debate on Development in a European Nation*. Berkeley, CA: Institute of International Studies, University of California.

Junghaus, Timea, and Székely, Katalin (eds). 2007. *Paradise Lost: The First Roma Pavilion*, La Biennale di Venezia, Open Society Institute, pp. 62–63.

Kallai, Laszlo. 2002. 'Romii și-au promovat imaginea cu lăutari, mici și vinul lu' Dinescu', *Ziua*, 28 October 2002. Retrieved 10 February 2010 from http://www.ziua.ro/display.php?data=2002-10-28&id=103346.

Karp, Ivan. 1991. 'Festivals', in Ivan Karp and Steven D. Lavine (eds), *Exhibiting Cultures: The Poetics and Politics of Museum Display*. Washington, DC: Smithsonian Institution Press, pp. 279–87.

Katz, Michael B. (ed.). 1993. *The 'Underclass' Debate: Views from History*. Princeton, NJ: Princeton University Press.

Katz, Katalin. 2006. 'The Roma of Hungary in the Second World War', in Donald Kenrick (ed.), *The Gypsies Duringthe Second World War: The final chapter*, vol. 3. Hatfield, UK: University of Hertfordshire Press, pp. 47–87.

Keck, Margaret E., and Kathryn Sikkink. 1998. *Activists beyond Borders: Advocacy Networks in International Politics*. Ithaca, NY and London: Cornell University Press.

Kelley, Robin D.G. 1992. 'Notes on Deconstructing "The Folk"', *American Historical Review* 97: 1400–8.

Kelsall, Tim. 2003. 'Rituals of Verification: Indigenous and Imported Accountability in Northern Tanzania', *Africa* 73: 174–201.

Kelso, Michelle. 2007. 'Hidden History: Perceptions of the Romani Holocaust in Romania Viewed through Contemporary Race Relations.' *Anthropology of East Europe Review* 25 (2): 44–61.

Kenrick, Donald (ed.). 2006. *The Gypsies during the Second World War: The Final Chapter*, vol. 3. Hatfield: University of Hertfordshire Press.

Kenrick, Donald, and Grattan Puxon. 1972. *The Destiny of Europe's Gypsies*. London: Chatto Heinemann in association with Sussex University Press.

Kershaw, Baz. 1992. *The Politics of Performance: Radical Theatre as Cultural Intervention*. London and New York: Routledge.

Kideckel, David. 2008. *Getting by in Postsocialist Romania: Labor, the Body and Working Class Culture*. Bloomington and Indianapolis, IN: Indiana University Press.

Kim, Suk-Young. 2014. *DMZ Crossing: Performing Emotional Citizenship Across the Korean Border*. New York: Columbia University Press.

Kirshenblatt-Gimblett, Barbara.1991. 'Objects of Ethnography', in Ivan Karp and Steven D. Lavine (eds), *Exhibiting Cultures: The Poetics and Politics of Museum Display*. Washington, DC: Smithsonian Institution Press, pp. 386–443.

———. 1995. 'Confusing Pleasures', in George E. Marcus and Fred R. Myers (eds), *The Traffic in Culture: Refiguring Art and Anthropology*. Berkeley, CA: University of California Press, pp. 224–55.

———. 1998. *Destination Culture: Tourism, Museums and Heritage*. Berkeley, CA: University of California Press.

———. 2006. 'World Heritage and Cultural Economics', in Ivan Karp et al. (eds), *Museum Frictions: Public Cultures/Global Transformations*. Durham: Duke University Press, pp. 161–202.

Kligman, Gail. 1998. *The Politics of Duplicity: Controlling Reproduction in Ceausescu's Romania*. Berkeley, CA: University of California Press.

Kogălniceanu, Mihail. [1837] 2000. 'Schiţă asupra maorvurilor şi limbii ţiganilor', in Vasile Ionescu (ed.), *Robia ţiganilor în Ţările Române: Moldova*, trans. V. Ionescu and D. Palade. Bucharest: Ed. Aven Amentza, pp. 233–52.

Koonz, Claudia. 1994. 'Between Memory and Oblivion: Concentration Camps in German Memory', in John R. Gillis (ed.), *Commemorations: The Politics of National Identity*. Princeton, NJ: Princeton University Press.

Kovalcsik, Katalin. 2010. 'The Romani Musicians on the Stage of Pluri-culturalism: The Case of Kalyi Jag Group in Hungary', in Michael Stewart and Marton Rovi, (eds), *Multidisciplinary Approaches to Romany Studies*. Budapest: Central European University, pp. 55–70.

Kristeva, Julia. 1982. *Powers of Horror: An Essay on Abjection*, trans. L.S. Roudiez. New York: Columbia University Press.

Kymlicka,Will. 2000. 'Nation-building and Minority Rights: Comparing West and East', *Journal of Ethnic and Migration Studies* 26: 183–212.

———. 2010. 'The Rise and Fall of Multiculturalism? New Debates on Inclusion and Accommodation in Diverse Societies'. *International Social Science Journal* 61 (199): pp. 97–112.

LaCapra, Dominick. 1998. *History and Memory after Auschwitz*. Ithaca, NY: Cornell University Press.

Ladányi, János and Iván Szelényi. 2006. *Patterns of Exclusion: Constructing Gypsy Ethnicity and the Making of an Underclass in Transitional Societies of Europe*. New York: Columbia University Press.

Lancaster, Roger N., and Micaela Di Leonardo (eds). 1997. *The Gender/Sexuality Reader*. London: Routledge.

Lee, Ronald. 2005. *Learn Romani: Das-dúma Rromanes*. Hatfield: University of Hertfordshire Press.

Lemon, Alaina. 2000a. *Between Two Fires: Gypsy Performance and Romani Memory from Pushkin to Post-Socialism*. Durham, NC: Duke University Press.

———. 2000b. 'Talking Transit and Spectating Transition: The Moscow Metro' in Daphne Berdahl et al. (eds), *Altering States: Ethnographies of Transition in Eastern Europe and the Former Soviet Union*. Ann Arbor, MI: University of Michigan Press.

———. 2001. 'Russia: Politics of Performance', in Will Guy (ed.), *Between Past and Future: The Roma of Central and Eastern Europe*. Hertfordshire: University of Hertfordshire Press, pp. 227–41.

———. 2002a. 'Without a "Concept?" Race as Discursive Practice', *Slavic Review* 61: 54–61.

———. 2002b. '"Form" and "Function" in Soviet Stage Romani: Modeling Metapragmatics through Performance Institutions', *Language in Society* 31: 29–64.

Lentin, Ronit. 2007. 'Racial State and Crisis Racism', *Ethnic and Racial Studies* 30: 610–27.

Libertatea. 2010. 'Il vor descalifica pentru că e țigan.' 25 January 2010. Retrieved 27 November 2011 from: http://www.libertatea.ro/detalii/articol/il-vor-descalifica-pentru-ca-este-tigan-273398.html.

Lionnet, Françoise, and Shu-mei Shih. 2005. 'Introduction: Thinking through the Minor, Transnationally', in Françoise Lionnet and Shu-mei Shih (eds), *Minor Transnationalism*. Durham, NC and London: Duke University Press, pp. 1–23.

Livezeanu, Irina. 1995. *Cultural Politics in Greater Romania: Regionalism, Nation Building, and Ethnic Struggle, 1918–1930*. Ithaca, NY: Cornell University Press.

Loveman, Mara. 1999. 'Is "Race" Essential?' *Annual Review of Sociology* 64: 891–98.

Lowe, Lisa, and David Lloyd (eds). 1997. *The Politics of Culture in the Shadow of Capital*. Durham, NC: Duke University Press.

Madison, Soyini D. 2005. *Critical Ethnography: Methods, Ethics, and Performance*. London: Sage Publications.

———. 2011. *Acts of Activism: Human Rights as Radical Performance*. Cambridge: Cambridge University Press.

Magyari-Vincze, Enikő. 2007. 'Reproducing Inequalities through Reproductive Control: The Case of Romani Women from Romania', *The Anthropology of East Europe Review*. 25: 108–21.

Maldonado-Torres, Nelson. 2007. 'On the Coloniality of Being: Contributions to the Development of a Concept.' *Cultural Studies* 21 (2-3), pp. 240–270.

Malvinni, David. 2004. *The Gypsy Caravan: From Real Roma to Imaginary Gypsies in Western Music and Film*. New York and London: Routledge.

Mandel, Ruth. 2008. *Cosmopolitan Anxieties: Turkish Challenges to Citizenship and Belonging in Germany*. Durham, NC and London: Duke University Press.

Manolescu, Anca. 2006. 'Un musée contre la muséification', *Martor* 11. Retrieved 19 January 2010 from http://martor.memoria.ro/?location=view_article&id=200.

Marchant, Elizabeth A. 2005. 'National Space as Minor Space: Afro-Brazilian Culture and the Pelourinho', in Françoise Lionnet and Shu-mei Shih (eds), *Minor Transnationalism*. Durham, NC and London: Duke University Press, pp. 301–15.

Marian-Bălașa, Marin. 2003. 'Maneaua –o creație a politicilor culturale românești' in *Studii și materiale de antropologie muzicală*. București: Editura Muzicală, pp. 221–254.

———. 2006. 'Virusul "antimanele" sau Despre muzică și segregare în cultura și societatea românească', *Anuarul Institutului de Etnografie și Folclor 'Constantin Brăiloiu'* Serie Nouă, Tomul 17: 77–87.

Maroushiakova, Elena, and Vesselin Popov. 2001a. 'Bulgaria: Ethnic Diversity – A Common Struggle for Equality', in Will Guy (ed.), *Between Past and Future: The Roma of Central and Eastern Europe*. Hertfordshire: University of Hertfordshire Press, pp. 370–88.

_____. 2001b. *Gypsies in the Ottoman Empire*. Hatfield: University of Hertfordshire Press.

_____. 2016. *Gypsies in Central Asia and Caucasus*. London: Palgrave Macmillan.

Matras, Yaron. 2000. 'Romani Migrations in the Post-communist Era: Their Historical and Political Significance.' *Cambridge Review of International Affairs* 13(2): 32–50.

_____. 2002. *Romani: A Linguistic Introduction*. Cambridge: Cambridge University Press.

_____. 2015. *The Romani Gypsies*. Cambridge, MA: Harvard University Press.

Mărginean, Ioan (ed.). 2001. *Research on the Roma*. Bucharest: CEID and Expert. Retrieved 15 November 2002 from http://www.rroma.ro.

McClintock, Anne. 1997. '"No Longer in a Future Heaven": Gender, Race and Nationalism', in Anne McClintock, Aamir Mufti and Ella Shohat (eds), *Dangerous Liaisons: Gender, Nation & Postcolonial Perspectives*. Minneapolis, MN: University of Minnesota Press, pp. 89–112.

McKenzie, Jon. 2001. *Perform or Else: From Discipline to Performance*. London: Routledge.

_____. 2003. 'Performance and Globalization', Paper presented at the Performance Studies International Conference, 2003.

Meerzon, Yana. 2012. *Performing Exile, Performing Self: Drama, Theatre and Film*. London and New York: Palgrave Macmillan.

Mesnil, Marianne. 2006. 'Histoire tourmentée d'un «lieu de mémoire»: le Musée du Paysan Roumain avant, pendant, après le communisme', *Martor* 11. Retrieved 19 January 2010 from http://martor.memoria.ro/?location=view_article&id=201.

Mihai Cioabă, Luminiţa. 2006. *Lacrimi Rome: Romane asva*. Bucharest: Ro Media.

Mihăilescu, Vintilă. 1991. 'Nationalité et nationalisme en Roumanie,' *Terrain* 17. Retrieved 19 January 2010 from http://terrain.revues.org/index3015.html.

_____. 2006. 'The Romanian Peasant's Museum and the Authentic Man', *Martor* 11. Retrieved 19 January 2010 from http://martor.memoria.ro/?location=view_article&id=202.

Miller, D.A. 1998. *Place for Us*. [Essay on the Broadway Musical]. Cambridge: Harvard University Press.

Mills, Amy. 2004. 'Dancing Yourself, Dancing for Others: Performing Identity in a Transylvanian-Romanian Dance Ensemble', *The Anthropology of East Europe Review* 22(1): 37–49.

Ministerul Economiei şi Finanţelor. 2006. 'Accelerarea Implementării Strategiei Naţionale de Îmbunătăţire a Situaţiei Romilor în domeniile: Pregătire Vocaţională şi ActivităţiGeneratoare de Venit', Proiecte de finanţare Program Phare, Schema de Grant. Retrieved from http://www.prefecturavaslui.ro/ae-romi.html (last accessed 12 November 2012).

Mircea, Ion Radu. 2000. 'Termenii rob, serb şi holop în documentele slave şi române', in Vasile Ionescu (ed.), *Robia ţiganilor în Ţările Române: Moldova*. Bucharest: Ed. Aven Amentza, pp. 61–74.

Mişcarea de Rezistenţă. 2010. "Eurovision de tot salamu'." *Jurnalul Naţional*, 22 January 2010. Retrieved 11 December 2013 from: http://www.jurnalul.ro/miscarea-de-rezis-tenta/eurovision-de-tot-salamu-533359.htm.

Miskovic, Maja. 2009. 'Roma education in Europe: in support of the discourse of race', *Pedagogy, Culture and Society* 17: 201–20.

Morley, David, and Kuan-Hsing Chen (eds). 1996. *Stuart Hall: Critical Dialogues in Cultural Studies*. London: Routledge.

Nicolae, Valeriu. 2003a. 'No Tambourines, Dancing Bears or Golden Earrings: A Snapshot of Romani Life in Today's Romania', in *Ronald Lee et al. (eds), The Romani Diaspora in Canada: History, Culture & Equity Issues*. Toronto: Canadian Scholars Institute Press. Retrieved 22 November 2009 from http://kopachi.com/articles/no-tambourines-dancing-bears-or-golden-earrings-by-valeriu-nicolae/#more-132.

———. 2003b. 'Roma in Romania', in *Ronald Lee et al. (eds), The Romani Diaspora in Canada: History, Culture & Equity Issues*. Toronto: Canadian Scholars Institute Press. Retrieved 22 November 2009 from http://kopachi.com/articles/roma-in-romania-by-valeriu-nicolae/#more-211.

———. 2008. 'Multiculturalismul eşuat: discriminarea romilor în mass-media', *Observatorul cultural* 434(31 July 2008). Retrieved 22 May 2017 from http://www.observatorcultural.ro/Multiculturalismul-esuat-discriminarea-romilor-in-mass-media*articleID_20212-articles_details.html.

Nield, Sophie. 2006. 'On the Border as Theatrical Space: Appearance, Dis-location and the Production of the Refugee', in Joe Kelleher and Nick Ridout (eds), *Contemporary Theatres in Europe: A Critical Companion*. London: Routledge, pp. 61–72.

Nielsen, Lara, and Patricia Ybarra (eds). 2015. *Neoliberalism and Global Theatres: Performance Permutations*. London and New York: Palgrave Macmillan.

Nora, Pierre. 1989. 'Between Memory and History: *Les Lieux de Mémoire*', *Representations* 26: 7–25.

Okely, Judith. 1983. *The Traveller-Gypsies*. Cambridge: Cambridge University Press.

———. 1996. *Own or Other Culture*. London: Routledge.

———. 2015. 'Constructing Culture through Shared Location, *Bricolage* and Exchange: The Case of Gypsies and Roma', in Thomas Fillitz and Jamie Saris (eds), *Debating Authenticity: Concepts of Modernity in an Anthropological Perspective*. New York: Berghahn Books.

Omi, Michael, and Howard Winant. 2014. *Racial Formation in the United States*, 3rd edn. New York: Routledge.

Ong, Aihwa (ed.). 1996. *Ungrounded Empires: The Cultural Politics of Modern Chinese Transnationalism*. Florence, KY: Routledge.

———. 2003. *Buddha Is Hiding: Refugees, Citizenship, and the New America*. Ewing, NJ: University of California Press.

———. 2006. *Neoliberalism as Exception: Mutations in Citizenship and Sovereignty*. Durham: Duke University Press.

Oprea, Alexandra. 2005. 'The Arranged Marriage of Ana Maria Cioaba, Intra-Community Oppression and Romani Feminist Ideals: Transcending the 'Primitive Culture' Argument', *European Journal of Women Studies* 12: 133–48.

Orta, Lucy (ed.). 2010. *Mapping the Invisible: EU-Roma Gypsies*. London: Black Dog Publishing.

Palade, Rodica. 2005. 'Imbunatatirea situatiei romilor (Mariea Ionescu, Presedinta Agentiei Nationale Pentru Romi)', 22(XIV):817. Retrieved 21 June 2008 from http://revista22online.ro/2171/.html.

Paredez, Deborah. 2009. *Selenidad: Selena, Latinos, and the Performance of Memory*. Durham, NC and London: Duke University Press.

Patraka, Vivian M. 1999. *Spectacular Suffering: Theatre, Fascism, and the Holocaust.* Bloomington, IN: Indiana University Press.

Patrasconiu, Cristian. 2009. 'Exterminarea Țiganilor: Mărturii și Documente', *Cotidianul* 5 March 2009. Retrieved 16 April 2010 from http://www.cotidianul.ro/extermin-area_tiganilor__marturii_si_documente-75649.html.

Phillips, Sarah D. 2008. *Women's Social Activism in the New Ukraine: Development and the Politics of Differentiation.* Bloomington, IN: Indiana University Press.

Pilkington, Hilary, and Anton Popov. 2008. 'Cultural Production and Transmission of Ethnic Tolerance and Prejudice: Introduction', *Anthropology of East Europe Review* 26: 7–21.

Pons, Emmanuelle. 1999. *Țiganii din România: o minoritate în tranziție*, trans. G. Ciubuc. Bucharest: Compania.

Potra, George. 1939. *Contribuțiuni la istoricul țiganilor din România.* Bucharest.

Povinelli, Elizabeth A. 1998. 'The State of Shame: Australian Multiculturalism and the Crisis of Indigenous Citizenship', *Critical Inquiry* 24: 575–610.

———. 2003. *The Cunning of Recognition: Indigenous Alterity and the Making of Australian Multiculturalism.* Durham, NC: Duke University Press.

Preoteasa, Ana Maria et al., coordinators. 2009. 'Strategia Națională de Îmbunătățire a Situației Romilor: Vocea Comunității.' Bucharest: Editura Expert. Retrieved 22 March 2010 from www.publicinfo.gov.ro/library/10_raport_tipar_p_ro.pdf.

'Protests against Roma expulsions held in France', http://www.bbc.co.uk/news/world-europe-11186592, 4 September 2010.

Radway, Janice. 1991. *Reading the Romance: Women, Patriarchy and Popular Literature.* Chapel Hill, NC and London: University of North Carolina Press.

Rădulescu, Speranța. 2004. *Taifasuri despre muzica țigănească. Chats about Gypsy Music*, trans. A. Solomon. Bucharest: Paideia.

Reyniers, Alain. 2000. 'Les Tsiganes entre ostracisme et pauvreté', *Courrier de l'Unesco* June: 38–40.

Rice, Timothy. 2002. 'Bulgaria or Chalgaria: The Attenuation of Bulgarian Nationalism in a Mass-Mediated Popular Music', *Yearbook for Traditional Music* 34: 25–46.

Rivkin-Fish, Michele. 2005. *Women's Health in Post-Soviet Russia: The Politics of Intervention.* Bloomington, IN: Indiana University Press.

Roma Fair Guide. 2002. 'Târgul de toamnă al romilor "Mahala și Țigănie"', Programul de revalorizare a mestesugurilor traditionale rome'. Printed brochure.

Roman, Denise. 2003. *Fragmented Identities: Popular Culture, Sex, and Everyday Life in Postcommunist Romania.* Lanham, MD: Lexington Books.

Rosaldo, Renato. 1993. *Culture and Truth: The Remaking of Social Analysis.* Boston, MA: Beacon Press.

———. 1994. 'Cultural Citizenship and Educational Democracy', *Cultural Anthropology* 9(3): 402–11.

Rossen, Rebecca. 2014. *Dancing Jewish: Jewish Identity in American Modern and Postmodern Dance.* Oxford: Oxford University Press.

Roxworthy, Emily. 2008. *The Spectacle of Japanese American Trauma: Racial Performativity and World War II.* Honolulu, HI: University of Hawaii Press.

Said, Edward W. [1978] 1994. *Orientalism.* New York: Vintage Books.

———. 1993. *Culture and Imperialism.* New York: Knopf.

Sampson, Anthony. 2002. 'Final Frontier', *Guardian* 1 April 2000. Retrieved 11 June 2002 from https://www.theguardian.com/uk/2000/apr/01/immigration. immigrationandpublicservices1.

Sampson, Steven. 1996. 'The Social Life of Projects: Importing Civil Society to Albania', in Chris Hann and Elizabeth Dunn (eds), *Civil Society: Challenging Western Models*. London: Routledge.

Sassen, Saskia. 1998. *Globalization and Its Discontents*. New York: New Press.

Schechner, Richard. 2013. *Performance Studies: An Introduction*. 3rd edn. New York: Routledge.

Schein, Louisa. 'Importing Miao Brethren to Hmong America: A Not-So-Stateless Transnationalism', in Pheng Cheah and Bruce Robbins (eds), *Cosmopolitics: Thinking and Feeling Beyond the Nation*. Minneapolis, MN: University of Minnesota Press, pp. 163–91.

———. 2000. *Minority Rules: The Miao and the Feminine in China's Cultural Politics*. Durham, NC: Duke University Press.

Scheper-Hughes, Nancy. 1992. *Death without Weeping: The Violence of Everyday Life in Brazil*. Berkeley, CA: University of California Press.

Scheper-Hughes, Nancy, and Daniel Hoffman. 1998. 'Brazilian Apartheid: Street Kids and the Struggle for Urban Space', in Nancy Scheper-Hughes and Carolyn Sargent (eds), *Small Wars: The Cultural Politics of Childhood*. Berkeley, CA: University of California Press, pp. 352–88.

Scheper-Hughes, Nancy, and Carolyn Sargent. 1998. 'The Cultural Politics of Childhood. Introduction', in Nancy Scheper-Hughes and Carolyn Sargent(eds), *Small Wars: The Cultural Politics of Childhood*. Berkeley, CA: University of California Press, pp. 1–33.

Schlossberg, Linda. 2001. 'Rites of Passing', Introduction in María Carla Sánchez and Linda Schlossberg (eds), *Passing: Identity and Interpretation in Sexuality, Race, and Religion*. New York: New York University Press, pp. 1–12.

Scott, James C. 1990. *Domination and the Arts of Resistance: Hidden Transcripts*. New Haven, CT: Yale University Press.

Seeman, Sonia Tamar. Forthcoming. *Sounding Roman: Performing Social Identity in Western Turkey*. Oxford: Oxford University Press.

Sell, Mike. 2007. 'Bohemianism, the Cultural Turn of the Avantgarde, and Forgetting the Roma', *TDR: The Drama Review* 51: 41–59.

Seminar Organizat de ONU si guvernul României, privind îmbunătățirea situației rromilor din România. Bucharest, 2–3 November 2001. Bucharest: Romanian Senate.

Shimakawa, Karen. 2002. *National Abjection: The Asian American Body Onstage*. Durham, NC and London: Duke University Press.

Shohat, Ella, and Robert Stam (eds). 1994. *Unthinking Eurocentrism: Multiculturalism and the Media*. London and New York: Routledge.

Sieg, Katrin. 2002. *Ethnic Drag: Performing Race, Nation and Sexuality in West Germany*. Ann Arbor, MI: University of Michigan Press.

Siegel, Alan. 2004. 'Hidden Holocaust. Exhibition Review'. Retrieved 12 February 2009 from http://www.artmargins.com/index.php?option=com_content&view=article&id=218%3Ahidden-holocaust&Itemid=133.

Sigona, Nando. 2015. 'Campenization: Reimagining the camp as a social and political space', *Citizenship Studies* 19(1): 1–15.

_____. 2016. 'Everyday Statelessness: Status, Rights and Camps', *Ethnic and Racial Studies*, 39(2): 263–79.

Sigona, Nando, and Nidhi Trehan (eds). 2009. *Romani Politics in Contemporary Europe: Poverty, Ethnic Mobilization and the Neoliberal Order*. Basingstoke and New York: Palgrave Macmillan.

Sigona, Nando, and P. Vermeersch (eds). 2012. 'The Roma in the new EU: polices, frames and everyday experiences', *Journal of Ethnic and Migration Studies* (special issue) 38(8).

Silverman, Carol. 1996. 'Music and Marginality: Roma (Gypsies) of Bulgaria and Macedonia', in Mark Slobin.Durham (ed.), *Retuning Culture: Musical Changes in Central and Eastern Europe*. Durham, NC: Duke University Press, pp. 231–53.

_____. 2000. 'Rom (Gypsy) Music', in Timothy Rice, James Porter and Chris Goertzen (eds), *The Garland Encyclopedia of World Music*, vol. 8. New York and London: Garland Publishing, pp. 270–91.

_____. 2003. 'The Gender of the Profession: Music, Dance, and Reputation among Balkan Muslim Rom Women', in Tullia Magrini (ed.), *Music and Gender: Perspectives from the Mediterranean*. Chicago, IL: University of Chicago Press, pp. 119–45.

_____. 2007. 'Trafficking in the Exotic with "Gypsy" Music: Balkan Roma, Cosmopolitanism and "WorldMusic" Festivals', in Donna A. Buchanan (ed.), *Balkan Popular Culture and the Ottoman Ecumene: Music, Image and Regional Political Discourse*. Lanham, MD: Scarecrow Press, pp. 335–61.

_____. 2012. *Romani Routes: Cultural Politics and Balkan Music in the Diaspora*. Oxford: Oxford University Press.

Spivak, Gayatri. 1996. 'Diasporas Old and New: Women in the Transnational World', *Textual Practice* 10: 245–69.

Steele, Jonathan. 2000. 'Gypsies Feel Lash of Europe's Hatred', *Guardian* 13 April 2000. Retrieved 11 June 2002 from https://www.theguardian.com/world/2000/apr/08/immigration.uk1.

Stewart, Michael. 1997. *The Time of the Gypsies*. London: Westview Press.

_____. 2002. 'Deprivation, the Roma and "the Underclass"', in Chris Hann (ed.), *Postsocialism: Ideals, Ideologies and Practices in Eurasia*. London: Routledge, pp. 133–55.

_____. 2004. 'Remembering without Commemoration: The Mnemonics and the Politics of Holocaust Memories among European Roma', *Journal of the Royal Anthropological Institute* 10: 561–82.

_____. 2007. 'How Does Genocide Happen?' in Stafford Charles (ed.), *Questions of Anthropology*, Questions of Anthropology series. London: London School of Economics.

_____. 2010. 'Introduction', in Michael Stewart and Marton Rovid (eds), *Multidisciplinary Approaches to Romany Studies*. Budapest: Central European University, pp. 1–12.

Stoler, Ann Laura. 1997. 'Carnal Knowledge and Imperial Power: Gender, Race, and Morality in Colonial Asia', in Roger N. Lancaster and Micaela di Leonardo (eds), *Gender/ Sexuality Reader*. New York: Routledge, pp. 13–36.

_____. 2009. *Along the Archival Grain: Epistemic Anxieties and Colonial Common Sense*. Princeton, NJ and Oxford: Princeton University Press.

Szalai, Julia. 2011. 'Ethnic Differences in Education and Diverging Prospects for Urban Youth in an Enlarged Europe', EDUMIGROM Summary Findings, Budapest.

Szeman, Ioana. 2003. 'Finding a "Home" on Stage: A Place for Romania in Europe?' *Theatre Research International* 28: 193–210.

———. 2005.'Lessons for Theatre of the Oppressed from a Romanian Orphanage', *New Theatre Quarterly* 21: 340–72.

———. 2009. '"Gypsy Music" and Deejays: Orientalism, Balkanism and Romani Musicians', *TDR: The Drama Review* 53: 98–116.

———. 2010. 'Collecting Tears: Remembering the Romani Holocaust', *Performance Research* 15: 54–9.

———. 2013. '"Playing with Fire" and Playing it Safe: With(out) Roma at the Eurovision Song Contest," in Karen Fricker and Milija Gluhovic, (eds), *Performing the 'New' Europe: Identities, Feelings, and Politics in the Eurovision Song Contest*. London: Palgrave Macmillan, pp. 125–141.

———. 2017, forthcoming '"Black and White Are One": Anti-Amalgamation Laws, Roma Slaves and the Romanian Nation on the Mid-nineteenth Century Moldavian Stage', in Tracy C. Davis and Stefka Mihaylova (eds), *The Transnational Histories of Uncle Tom's Cabin*. Ann Arbor, MI: University of Michigan Press.

Szwed, John F. 1975. 'Race and the Embodiment of Culture', *Ethnicity* 2: 19–33.

Taussig, Mick. 1989. 'Terror as Usual: Walter Benjamin's Theory of History as a State of Siege', *Social Text* 23: 3–20.

Taylor, Diana. 1997. *Disappearing Acts: Spectacles of Gender and Nationalism in Argentina's 'Dirty War'*. Durham, NC and London: Duke University Press.

———. 2003. *The Archive and the Repertoire: Performing Cultural Memory in the Americas*. Durham, NC: Duke University Press.

Todorova, Maria. 1997. *Imagining the Balkans*. New York: Oxford University Press.

Toninato, Paola. 2014. *Romani Writing: Literacy, Literature, and Identity Politics*. Abingdon and New York: Routledge.

Traynor, Ian. 2010. 'French Anti-Gypsy Policy Denounced by European Parliament', *Guardian*. Retrieved 9 September 2010. from http://www.guardian.co.uk/world/2010/sep/09/french-anti-gypsy-european-parliament.

Trehan, Nidhi. 2009. 'The Romani Subaltern within Neoliberal European Civil Society: NGOization of Human Rights and Silent Voices', in *Romani Politics in Contemporary Europe: Poverty, Ethnic Mobilization, and the Neoliberal Order*. Basingstoke and New York: Palgrave Macmillan, pp. 51–71.

Tremlett, Annabel. 2009. 'Bringing Hybridity to Heterogeneity in Romani Studies', *Romani Studies* 19: 147–68.

———. 2013. 'Why Must Roma Minorities be Always Seen on the Stage and Never in the Audience? Children's Opinions of Reality Roma TV', in Anikó Imre, Timothy Havens and Katalin Lustyik (eds), *Popular Television in Eastern Europe during and since Socialism*. London: Routledge, pp. 241–58.

Trumpener, Katie. 1992. 'The Time of the Gypsies: A "People without History"', in the Narratives of the West', *Critical Inquiry* 18: 843–84.

Turner, Victor. 1969. *The Ritual Process: Structure and Anti-Structure*. Chicago, IL: Aldine.

———. 1982. *From Ritual to Theatre*. New York: PAJ Publications.

van Baar, Huub. 2008. 'The Way Out of Amnesia?' *Third Text* 22: 373–85.

———. 2011. 'The European Roma', Ph.D. dissertation. Amsterdam: University of Amsterdam.

_____. 2017. 'Evictability and the Biopolitical Bordering of Europe', *Antipode* 49: 212–30.

van de Port, Mattijs. 1998. *Gypsies, Wars and Other Instances of the Wild: Civilisation and Its Discontent in a Serbian Town.* Amsterdam: Amsterdam University Press.

Vaughan, Megan. 1991. *Curing Their Ills: African Illness and Colonial Power.* Stanford, CA: Stanford University Press.

Verdery, Katherine. 1983. *Transylvanian Villagers: Three Centuries of Political, Economic, and Ethnic Change.* Berkeley, CA: University of California Press.

_____. 1991. *National Ideology under Socialism: Identity and Cultural Politics in Ceausescu's Romania.* Berkeley, CA: University of California Press.

_____. 1994. 'Beyond the Nation in Eastern Europe', *Social Text* 38: 1–19.

_____. 1996. *What Was Socialism, and What Comes Next?* Princeton, NJ: Princeton University Press.

_____. 1999. *The Political Lives of Dead Bodies: Reburial and Postsocialist Change.* New York: Columbia University Press.

_____. 2003. *The Vanishing Hectare: Property and Value in Postsocialist Transylvania.* Ithaca, NY: Cornell University Press.

Vergès, Françoise. n.d. 'A Museum Without a Collection: Musée des Civilisations et de l'Unité Réunionnaise' Retrieved 14 February 2010 from http://translate.eipcp.net/Actions/discursive/lines/verges/verges_en.pdf.

Vermeersch, Peter. 2006. *The Romani Movement: Minority Politics and Ethnic Mobilization in Contemporary Central Europe.* New York: Berghahn Books.

_____. 2008. 'Exhibiting Multiculturalism', *Third Text* 22: 359–71.

Vidmar-Horvat, Ksenija. 2013. 'Racing for the Audience: National Identity, Public TV and the Roma in Post-Socialist Slovenia', in Anikó Imre et al. (eds), *Popular Television in Eastern Europe during and since Socialism.* London: Routledge, pp. 259–74.

Vincze, Enikő. 2010. 'Ethnic Differences in Education in Romania: Community Study', EDUMIGROM Community Studies, Budapest.

_____. 2011. 'Social Inclusion through Education in Romania: Policy Recommendation.' EDUMIGROM Policy Recommendations, Budapest.

Wallace Michele. 1994. 'The Search for the "Good Enough" Mammy: Multiculturalism, Popular Culture, and Psychoanalysis', in David Theo Goldberg (ed.), *Multiculturalism: A Critical Reader.* Oxford: Blackwell.

Warner, Michael. 2002. 'Publics and Counterpublics', *Public Culture* 14(1): 49–90.

Warren, Kay B., and Susan C. Bourque. 1991. 'Women, Technology and International Development Ideologies: Analyzing Feminist Voices', in Micaela Di Leonardo (ed.), *Gender at the Crossroads of Knowledge: Feminist Anthropology in the Postmodern Era.* Berkeley, CA: University of California.

Wedel, Janine. 2001. *Collision and Collusion: The Strange Case of Western Aid to Eastern Europe.* New York: Palgrave Macmillan.

Wickstrom, Maurya. 2006. *Performing Consumers: Global Capital and Its Theatrical Seductions.* London: Routledge.

_____. 2012. *Performance in the Blockades of Neoliberalism: Thinking the Political Anew.* Basingstoke: Palgrave Macmillan.

Williams, Patrick. 1991. 'Le Miracle et la necessité: à propos du developpement du pentecôtisme chez les Tsiganes', *Archives de Sciences Sociales des Religions* 73: 81–98.

———. 2003. *Gypsy World: The Silence of the Living and the Voices of the Dead*, trans. Catherine Tihanyi. Chicago, IL: University of Chicago Press.

Williams, Susan. 2007. 'The 'Civilized Trap of Modernity and Romanian Roma, 1918–1934', *The Anthropology of East Europe Review* 26: 18–27.

Wolf, Eric. 1982. *Europe and the People without History*. Berkeley, IL: University of California Press.

Wolff, Larry. 1994. *Inventing Eastern Europe: The Map of Civilization on the Mind of the Enlightenment*. Stanford, CA: Stanford University Press.

Wolf, Stacy. 2002. *A Problem like Maria: Gender and Sexuality in the American Musical*. Ann Arbor, MI: University of Michigan Press.

Woodcock, Shannon. 2007. 'Romani Romanian Resistance to Genocide in the Matrix of the *Țigan* Other'. *Anthropology of East Europe Review* 25(2): 28–43.

Young, Harvey. 2010. *Embodying Black Experience: Stillness, Critical Memory and the Black Body*. Ann Arbor, MI: University of Michigan Press.

Yudice, George. 2003. *The Expediency of Culture: Uses of Culture in the Global Era*. Durham, NC: Duke University Press.

Yuval-Davis, Nira. 1997a. *Gender & Nation*. London: Sage.

———. 1997b. 'Women, Citizenship and Difference.' *Feminist Review* 57: 4–27.

Yuval-Davis, Nira, and Floya Anthias (eds). 1989. *Woman, Nation, State*. London: Macmillan.

Yuval-Davis, Nira, Floya Anthias and Eleonore Kofman. 2005. 'Secure borders and safe haven and the gendered politics of belonging: Beyond social cohesion', *Ethnic and Racial Studies* 28: 513–35.

Zamfir, Elena and Cătălin Zamfir (eds). 1993. *Țiganii: între ignorare si îngrijorare*. Bucharest: Alternative.

Zoon, Ina. 2001. *La periferia societății: Rromii și serviciile publice în România*. Open Society Institute.

Index

www.ingramcontent.com/pod-product-compliance
Lightning Source LLC
Chambersburg PA
CBHW070929030426
42336CB00014BA/2591